FULVIA

Also by Jane Draycott:
Cleopatra's Daughter: Egyptian Princess, Roman Prisoner,
African Queen

Jane Draycott is a historian and archaeologist, and the author of *Cleopatra's Daughter: Egyptian Princess, Roman Prisoner, African Queen*. She is currently Lecturer in Ancient History at the University of Glasgow and co-director of the University of Glasgow's Games and Gaming Lab.

FULVIA

THE WOMAN WHO BROKE ALL
THE RULES IN ANCIENT ROME

JANE DRAYCOTT

Atlantic Books
London

First published in Great Britain in 2025 by Atlantic Books,
an imprint of Atlantic Books Ltd

A CIP catalogue record for this book is available
from the British Library.

Hardback ISBN 978 1 80546 193 7
Export trade paperback ISBN 978 1 80546 365 8
E-book ISBN 978 1 80546 194 4

Printed by CPI Group (UK) Ltd, Croydon CR0 4YY

10 9 8 7 6 5 4 3 2 1

Atlantic Books
An imprint of Atlantic Books Ltd
Ormond House
26–27 Boswell Street
London WC1N 3JZ

MIX
Paper | Supporting
responsible forestry
FSC® C171272

For Evelyn Maeve Boyce, whether she becomes
the heroine or villain of her own story.

CONTENTS

ILLUSTRATIONS

BLACK & WHITE ILLUSTRATIONS

COLOUR SECTION

MAPS

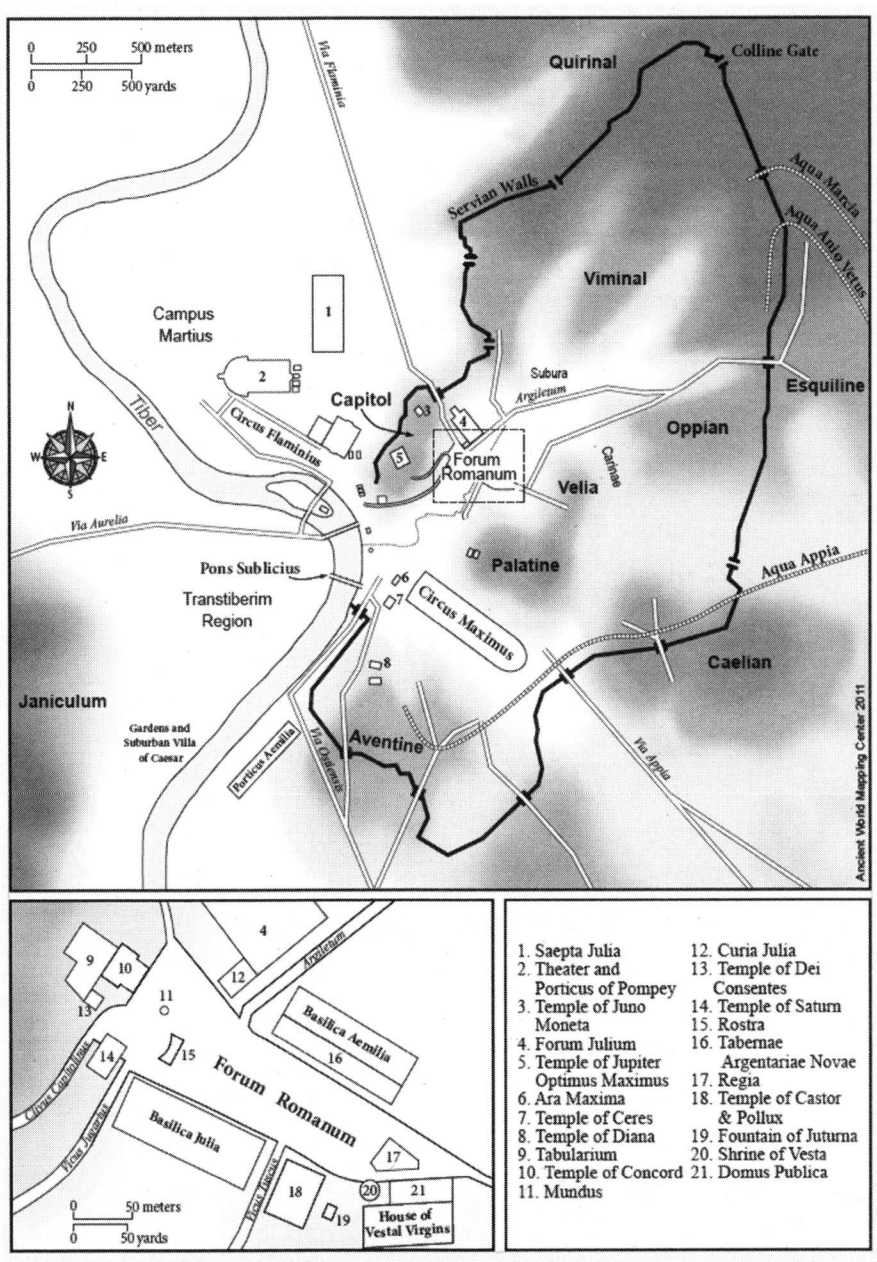

1. Saepta Julia
2. Theater and Porticus of Pompey
3. Temple of Juno Moneta
4. Forum Julium
5. Temple of Jupiter Optimus Maximus
6. Ara Maxima
7. Temple of Ceres
8. Temple of Diana
9. Tabularium
10. Temple of Concord
11. Mundus
12. Curia Julia
13. Temple of Dei Consentes
14. Temple of Saturn
15. Rostra
16. Tabernae Argentariae Novae
17. Regia
18. Temple of Castor & Pollux
19. Fountain of Juturna
20. Shrine of Vesta
21. Domus Publica

Map 1: Rome during the mid-first century BCE.

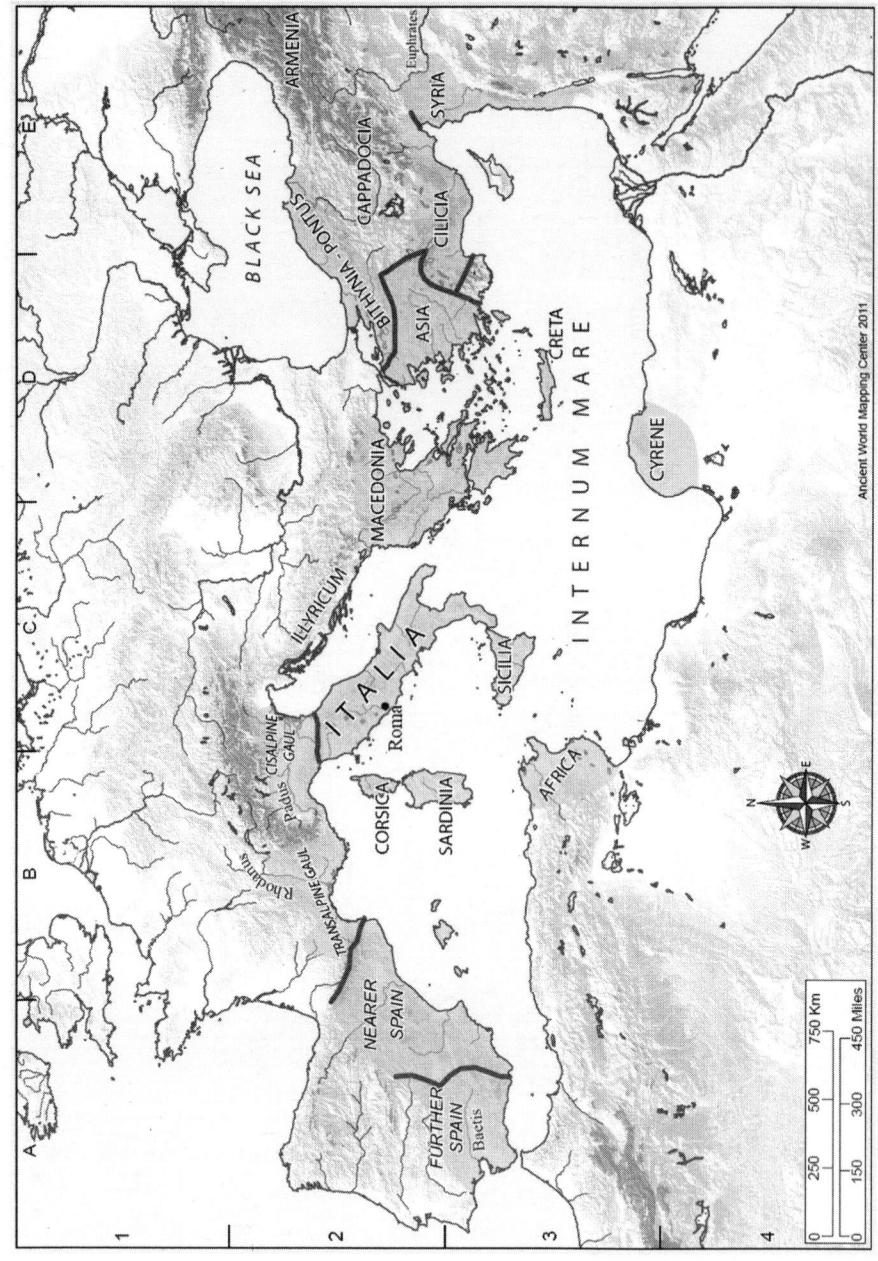

Map 2: The Roman Empire during the mid-first century BCE

FULVIA – FAMILY TREE

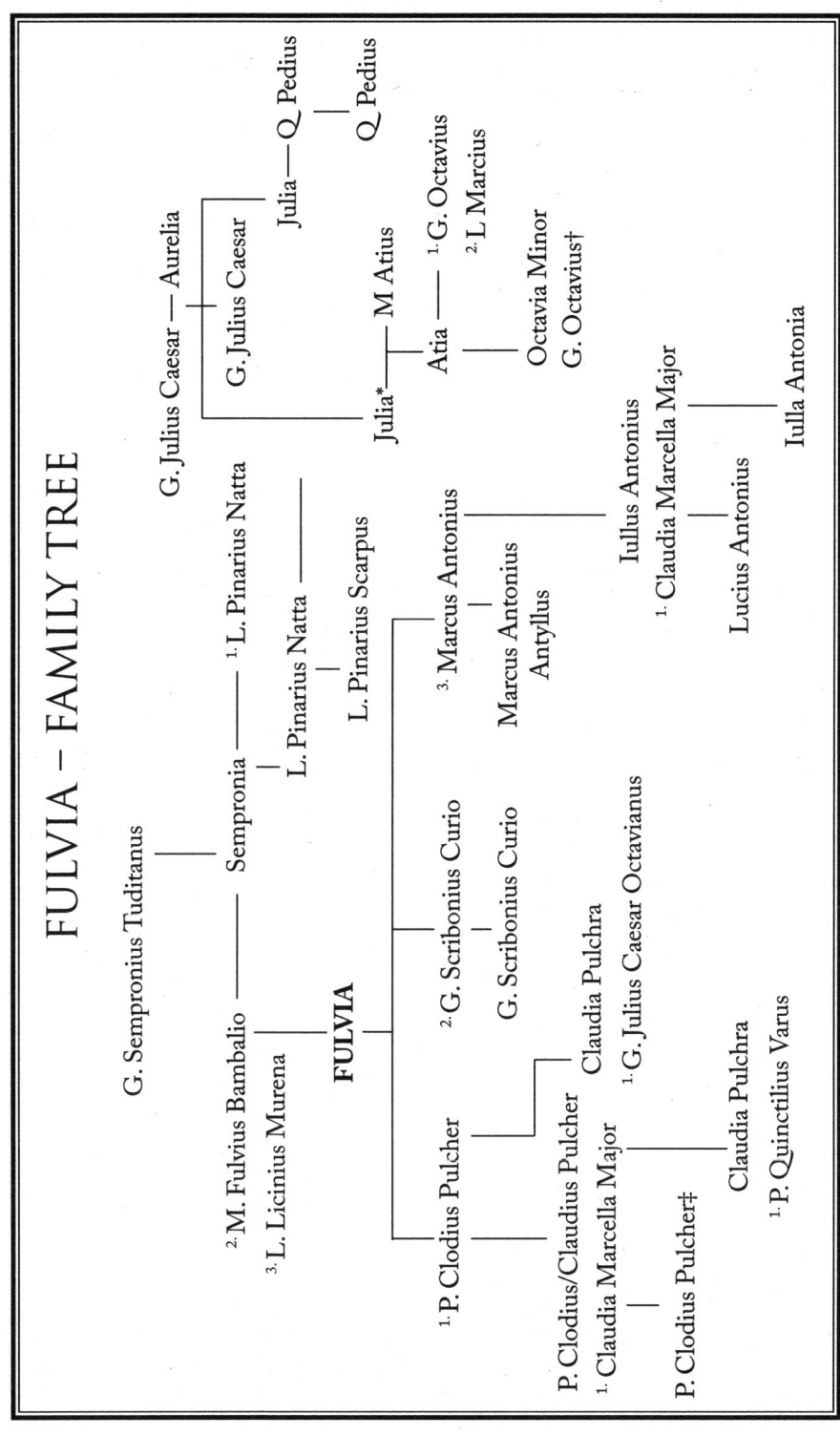

For notes see next page.

NOTES TO FAMILY TREE

* Three siblings, two girls called Julia and a boy called G. Julius Caesar (i.e. THE Caesar).

† This is the same person as G. Julius Caesar Octavianus to the left. He was born G. Octavius, he became G. Julius Caesar Octavianus in 44 BCE.

‡ From a second marriage, not a first marriage to Claudia Marcella Major.

TIMELINE

c. 80 BCE – Birth of Fulvia

63 BCE – Marcus Tullius Cicero is elected consul

    The Catilinarian Conspiracy

62 BCE – Lucius Licinius Murena elected consul

61 BCE – The Bona Dea Scandal

60 BCE – Establishment of the First Triumvirate

60 BCE (?) – Marriage of Fulvia and Publius Clodius Pulcher

59 BCE (?) – Birth of Publius Claudius Pulcher ('Young Publius')

58 BCE – Publius Clodius Pulcher is elected tribune

    Marcus Tullius Cicero is exiled

57 BCE (?) – Birth of Claudia Pulchra

57 BCE – Marcus Tullius Cicero returns from exile

August/September 53 BCE – Marcus Antonius allegedly attempts to

    murder Publius Clodius Pulcher

18 January 52 BCE – Murder of Publius Clodius Pulcher by Titus

    Annius Milo

April 52 BCE – Trial of Titus Annius Milo

50 BCE (?) – Marriage of Fulvia and Gaius Scribonius Curio

49 BCE (?) – Birth of Gaius Scribonius Curio ('Young Gaius')

49 BCE – Gaius Julius Caesar crosses the Rubicon

    Civil war between Gaius Julius Caesar and Gnaeus Pompeius

    Magnus (Pompey) breaks out

49 BCE – Death of Gaius Scribonius Curio in Africa

48 BCE – Gaius Julius Caesar defeats Gnaeus Pompey at the Battle of

    Pharsalus

    Murder of Gnaeus Pompey in Egypt

48 BCE (?) – Marriage of Fulvia and Marcus Antonius

48–47 BCE – Marcus Antonius in charge of Rome and Italy in Gaius
   Julius Caesar's absence
   Statue of Publius Clodius Pulcher set up in Rome

46 BCE – Birth of Marcus Antonius Antyllus

15 March 44 BCE – Assassination of Gaius Julius Caesar

2 September 44 BCE – *First Philippic* delivered to the Senate

October 44 BCE – Marcus Antonius and Fulvia go to Brundisium to
   inspect the legions

October/November 44 BCE – *Second Philippic* composed and disseminated amongst a select group of Marcus Tullius Cicero's friends

20 December 44 BCE – *Third Philippic* and *Fourth Philippic* delivered
   to the Senate

43 BCE – Marcus Antonius declared a public enemy. Fulvia and Julia
   intercede with senators on his behalf

21 April 43 BCE – Battle of Mutina

43 BCE – Establishment of the Second Triumvirate
   Marriage of Gaius Octavius and Claudia Pulchra
   Expulsion of Volumnia Cytheris from Marcus Antonius' house

November 43 BCE – Proscriptions list drawn up

7 December 43 BCE – Murder of Marcus Tullius Cicero

42 BCE (?) – Birth of Iullus Antonius

42 BCE – Hortensia leads a delegation of women to the Forum

3 and 23 October 42 BCE – Battle of Philippi

41 BCE – Divorce of Gaius Octavius and Claudia Pulchra
   Perusine War breaks out between Fulvia and Lucius Antonius
   and Gaius Octavius
   Marcus Antonius meets Cleopatra VII, Queen of Egypt, at
   Tarsus and begins their relationship

40 BCE – Defeat of Lucius Antonius

40 BCE – Death of Fulvia
   Birth of Marcus Antonius and Cleopatra's twins
   Marriage of Marcus Antonius and Octavia

1 August 30 BCE – Suicide of Marcus Antonius

August 30 BCE – Murder of Marcus Antonius Antyllus and Gaius Scribonius Curio

2 BCE – Execution of Iullus Antonius

A NOTE ON ROMAN NAMES

DURING THE LATE REPUBLIC (*circa* 133–31 BCE), Roman naming conventions were fairly static. Male Roman citizens either had three names – a *praenomen*, a *nomen* and a *cognomen* – one example being Gaius Julius Caesar, or two names – a *praenomen* and a *nomen* – such as Marcus Antonius. Depending on the circumstances of their political or military career, or life circumstances, they might add one or more names to their original nomenclature. If a Roman commander was successful in waging warfare, he might be awarded an additional *cognomen* to reflect this. Most of these were geographical, in reference to the peoples subjugated, so Publius Cornelius Scipio became Publius Cornelius Scipio Africanus after his victory over Hannibal Barca at the Battle of Zama in 202 BCE during the Second Punic War. However, Gnaeus Pompeius became Gnaeus Pompeius Magnus ('the Great') in imitation of Alexander the Great, to reflect his unprecedented military prowess at a relatively early age. Alternatively, a Roman might change his name of his own volition, such as Publius Claudius Pulcher adjusting his *nomen* from Claudius to Clodius (this may have reflected an alternative Latin pronunciation that was considered more fashionable by his sophisticated circle – at least one of his sisters likewise changed her name, going from Claudia to Clodia). If a Roman was adopted into another family (something that could happen in childhood but, unlike today's adoptions, tended to happen in adulthood, once a man had survived childhood and then proved himself a worthy addition to a family), he would change his name entirely. Caesar posthumously adopted his great-nephew Gaius Octavius Thurinus and made him his primary heir in his will, prompting the boy to change his name to Gaius Julius Caesar Octavianus. However, he subsequently preferred not to use the Octavianus, wanting to associate himself as closely with Caesar as possible in order to bolster his own personal reputation and authority.

The firstborn son was usually given the same name as his father, so Marcus Antonius Creticus (his personal *cognomen* referenced his undertakings on Crete, and was not used by his descendants) named his eldest son Marcus Antonius, while his subsequent sons were named Lucius Antonius and Gaius Antonius. Daughters were likewise given a version of their father's name, albeit the *nomen*. This meant that a family that had multiple daughters needed some way to differentiate them. So we see Servilia's daughters with Decimus Junius Silanus being named Junia Prima ('First'), Junia Secunda ('Second'), and Junia Tertia ('Third'), while Octavia's daughters with Gaius Claudius Marcellus were named Claudia Marcella Major ('Elder') and Claudia Marcella Minor ('Younger'). Another way of differentiating sisters once they were grown women was to refer to them according to the man they married, or at least the family that they married into. So Clodia, the oldest of three sisters, became Clodia Metelli ('Metellus' Clodia') upon her marriage to Quintus Caecilius Metellus Celer, whereas her younger sister Claudia became Claudia Luculli ('Lucullus' Claudia') upon her marriage to Lucius Licinius Lucullus.

When it comes to modern authors writing about the Roman period, the situation becomes rather more complicated. The Anglicization (in modern authors writing in English, at least; modern authors writing in other languages have their own practices and preferences) of Greek and Latin names is to be expected and is applied in a fairly consistent manner – for example, Kleopatra is usually (although not always) referred to as Cleopatra. Yet the modernization of Greek and Latin names is rather more varied – for example, Marcus Antonius can be referred to in that way, or as Antonius, or as Marc or Mark Antony, or even just Antony depending upon the writer's preference. Other Romans might be referred to using their *nomen*, thus Publius Clodius

Pulcher becomes Clodius and Gaius Cassius Longinus becomes Cassius, or their *cognomen*, thus Marcus Junius Brutus becomes Brutus and Marcus Aemilius Lepidus becomes Lepidus. Additionally, for various reasons of their own, some modern authors choose to refer to Romans using names by which they were never actually known in antiquity. This can be historically problematic, such as referring to Fulvia as Fulvia Flacca Bambula in an attempt to link her to earlier known Republican historical figures, despite there being no evidence that she was actually related to them, but it can also be an attempt to be helpful, e.g. referring to Gaius Octavius Thurinus/Gaius Julius Caesar Octavianus as Octavian, to distinguish him from his birth father Gaius Octavius as well as his adoptive father Caesar – up to the point in his life where he took on the name Augustus ('Revered One').

In what follows, I have tended to refer to the Romans I discuss using their full names at their first appearance, and their most common (and thus hopefully familiar to the reader) modernization on all subsequent occasions, for brevity as much as anything else. There are, however, a few exceptions to this. The first instance is in my discussion of Fulvia's children. Her first and second sons were named after their fathers (Publius Claudius/Clodius Pulcher and Gaius Scribonius Curio), but I refer to them as young Publius and young Gaius while they are children, both to distinguish them from their fathers and to emphasize their extreme youth. I refer to her third son by his *cognomen*, Antyllus, while I call her fourth Iullus, his *praenomen*. Her daughter I refer to as Claudia rather than Clodia, to distinguish her from her infamous aunt. The second is in my treatment of the Roman born Gaius Octavius Thurinus – I refer to him as Octavian throughout, even in my discussion of his life after he took the name Augustus upon becoming emperor in 27 BCE, since I do jump backwards and forwards in time throughout this book in order to make connections and highlight resonances between people, events and occurrences.

I hope you bear with me.

INTRODUCTION

O F ALL THE BAD years (and there were many) in the lead-up to the final fall of the Roman Republic, the year 52 BCE got off to an especially bad start. Since the Romans sincerely believed that certain days were unlucky, it followed that if the first day of the year happened to fall on one of these unlucky days, the whole year would be marked by misfortune.[1] Sure enough, ominous portents began to appear, indicating that things were about to go from bad to worse.[2] First, an owl was seen and captured in the city of Rome. While to us this might seem fairly innocuous, albeit a little spooky, to the Romans the owl was associated with blood-drinking and cannibalistic child-killing witches known as *striges*, and its hoot was thought to signal impending death.[3] Second, a cult statue of the god Mars started to sweat, and its perspiration continued unabated for three days.[4] This undeniable sign of divine displeasure could only have been worse if the statue had been sweating blood. Third, a meteor streaked across the sky. Like the hoot of an owl, this was often considered a sign of impending death or other sort of doom. Finally, thunderbolts sounded while clods of earth, stones, shards of pot, and blood flew through the air, all obvious signs of the gods in the heavens attempting to communicate with the mortals down below. But what, exactly, were they saying? And was anyone listening, in any case? In such ill-starred circumstances, it was perhaps unwise for the Senate to vote to tear down the city of Rome's temples of the Egyptian gods Serapis and Isis, which only increased the sense of unease.

This febrile climate of superstition and fear was further exacerbated by the fact that, due to electoral malfeasance, bribery and corruption,

no consuls had been installed in office on 1 January, as would have been
the usual practice. The positions, Rome's supreme magistracies, would
remain vacant until July, by which time the elections for the following
year's consulships were imminent. Everyone agreed: something terrible
was about to happen.

On 18 January, a senator named Publius Clodius Pulcher was travelling north up the Appian Way to Rome, returning from an overnight
trip to Aricia (modern Ariccia), an ancient town up in the Alban Hills,
south-east of the city. He was accompanied by three friends – and, he
thought, amply protected by a bodyguard comprising around thirty
enslaved men armed with swords.[5] Late in the afternoon, the group
reached the ancient town of Bovillae (modern Frattocchie), where they
passed a shrine to the goddess Bona Dea, the 'Good Goddess'. She was
a deity with whom Clodius had history, having been accused of impiety
towards her back in 62 BCE after interrupting an evening of sacred
women-only rites. This resulted in him being put on trial for sacrilege,
though he was ultimately acquitted of the charge. It was near this shrine
that he and his entourage suddenly encountered a man named Titus
Annius Milo, Clodius' fellow senator, political rival and one of his many
enemies. Milo was on his way south to his villa at Lanuvium (modern
Lanuvio), accompanied by his wife Fausta Cornelia, several friends, and
his own substantial bodyguard comprising perhaps as many as three
hundred enslaved people, as well as his wife's entourage of singers, maids
and pages.[6] Numbered amongst Milo's bodyguard were several fearsome
gladiators – first and foremost Eudamus and Birria, a pair sufficiently
deadly in the arena that they had achieved celebrity status.[7]

As the two groups filed past each other, male members of each
entourage began heckling their rivals. Roman toxic masculinity having
much in common with its counterpart today, from there, things swiftly
escalated into what would later be referred to as the 'Battle of Bovillae'.
Cicero covered the fracas extensively in perhaps his most famous
speech, the *Pro Milone*, 'In Defence of Milo', composed and delivered
a few months after the event. One hundred years later, the historian
Asconius wrote a detailed commentary on that speech, providing

crucial information that Cicero neglected to include, focused as he was on implicating his enemy Clodius and exonerating his friend Milo for the massacre. Caught up in the violent and bloody chaos, the gladiator Birria hurled a *rhomphaia* – a Thracian bladed weapon resembling a spear or javelin – into the fray, and it caught Clodius in the shoulder. Clodius and his friends fled to a nearby inn in pursuit of sanctuary and medical treatment, leaving his hapless slaves to cover their retreat. Unfortunately for Clodius, Milo's forces quickly managed to overpower the servile rearguard. At this point, Milo seems to have decided that he might as well go big or go home, since a dead Clodius was obviously preferable to a surviving and vengeful one.[8]

So Milo ordered Clodius' death and his crony Marcus Saufeius was happy to oblige, hauling Clodius out of the inn, wrenching his gold senatorial ring from his finger, and leaving him bleeding in the middle of the road that his ancestor Appius Claudius Caecus had built three centuries before, surrounded by the family's tombs.[9] Then Milo's party continued on its journey to Lanuvium as if nothing had happened, trampling Clodius into the cobbles under the wheels of their carriage and the hooves of their horses for good measure. A short while later, Sextus Teidius, a fellow senator who happened to be passing that way, found the body and ordered his servants to transport it on a litter back to Clodius' famously well-appointed house on the Clivus Victoriae, on the north-west side of the Palatine Hill, a prime location in the centre of Rome. Here Clodius' wife Fulvia was waiting, eagerly anticipating his return from his business trip.

Had Fulvia adhered to social convention, as his closest female relation and someone roughly equivalent to the modern next of kin, she would have had Clodius' body brought inside and then overseen the process of preparing it for cremation as he was washed in warm water, anointed with scented oils, dressed in his finest pure white woollen toga, and garlanded with flowers to symbolize the fragility of life, with a coin to pay the ferryman Charon for the journey across the River Styx to the Underworld placed in his mouth. Then, she would have super-vised the body's arrangement on a bier in the centre of the atrium with his insignia of office, surrounded by portrait busts of eminent ancestors – of which he had many – ready to be viewed by family members, friends, acquaintances, and Clodius' many loyal supporters amongst the urban *plebs*, the common people. Finally, she would have had a plaster cast mould of his face made, to facilitate the production of a death mask and portraits in the future.

Yet what Fulvia actually did was quite different, and entirely unexpected: she immediately sought to unleash terrible vengeance on her husband's murderers.[10] She proceeded to incite the curious crowd of plebeians and enslaved people who had gathered outside, by throwing open the doors and inviting them in – perhaps the first time people such as this would have been inside such a fine Roman home.[11] And then she stripped Clodius' body naked and displayed the extent of his gory wounds. Enraged and egged on by several of Clodius' friends, who loathed Milo as much as he had, the crowd seized his body, paraded it down from the slope of the Palatine Hill, along the Sacred Way, and through the Forum. This was a complete subversion of the traditional Roman funerary procession, which under normal circumstances was highly regulated and ritualized; we can see just such a procession depicted in a relief dating from the mid to the late first century BCE, from Amiternum (modern Abruzzo) in Italy.[12] Usually, the differences between the aristocrats holding the funeral – giving the honorific speeches, wearing the ancestor masks, and sitting on the ivory chairs – and the common or garden onlookers were starkly demarcated; here, they were non-existent. Indeed, Cicero would later blame Clodius' associate Sextus Cloelius specifically for depriving him of a proper aristocratic funeral, and leaving the smouldering remnants of his corpse to be mauled by stray dogs.[13] There were some historical precedents for this, on previous occasions when popular (and populist) heroes had died under mysterious circumstances: for example, in 133 BCE, an unnamed friend of Tiberius Gracchus was thought to have been poisoned by the Senate, and his body, covered with boils, was likewise snatched up by a crowd and taken down to the Forum in a politically charged gesture.[14]

A relief depicting a Roman funerary procession, circa late first century BCE–early first century CE

The ringleaders displayed Clodius' battered body to yet more crowds on the Rostra, the public speaker's platform, in sight of the stone lion that was thought to mark the grave of Faustulus, the foster father of Rome's founder and first king Romulus and his twin brother Remus, and statues of individuals who had either met their deaths in the service of Rome or performed exemplary deeds of valour.[15] No doubt they considered it appropriate, although Clodius' many enemies thought differently. Finally, they deposited the corpse in the Curia Hostilia, the Senate House, and there, in a frenzy, they built a makeshift funerary pyre from benches, tables and public records. Once lit, it not only succeeded in cremating Clodius' body – illegally and sacrilegiously, since bodies were supposed to be disposed of far away, outside the *pomerium*, the sacred boundary of the city – but also in burning down the Senate House and part of the Basilica Porcia, a building used for legal and financial business, next door. It was not just buildings that were affected: Rome's earliest example of public painting, a depiction of Marcus Valerius Maximus Messala defeating Hiero and his Carthaginian army in Sicily in 264 BCE, painted the following year on the exterior west wall of the Senate House, was utterly destroyed, and the ancient statue of Attus Navius, the famous augur of King Tarquinius Priscus, which stood outside the Senate House, was scorched.[16] This left a smoking crater in the very heart of the ancient city that would not be filled in for months.[17] It would

appear that the portents had been right, and an extremely dark future
had come to pass.

⁂

Fulvia was born into wealth, privilege and prestige sometime around
the year 80 BCE, but there was nothing inherently special about her –
she was not a goddess, a saint, an empress, a queen or even a princess.
Rather, she differentiated herself from her peers by her actions. What
fascinates me about her is that she clearly wanted more than the
normal lot of an elite Roman woman – which, our predominantly male
sources tell us, was to be a shy and retiring wife and mother, and a silent
helpmeet to her husband and sons. We so rarely hear about women like
this in ancient Roman sources.

At almost every stage of her life, Fulvia faced both extraordinary
challenges and devastating setbacks, so the temptation to quietly give
up and accept what everyone told her was her fate must have been
extreme. But even more fascinating is the fact that, for a time at least,
she remained undaunted and succeeded in her endeavours despite all
that Rome's patriarchal and chauvinistic society could throw at her.
Securely positioning herself at the centre of ancient Roman society via
strategic marital alliances for two decades over the course of the fall of
the Republic, by the time of her death in 40 BCE Fulvia had amassed a
degree of political and military power unprecedented for a woman. Her
profile was such that – like Cher, Madonna or Zendaya today – she was
and remains known by a single name: Fulvia. Once I learned of her, I
was determined to find out how, in a patriarchal society where even the
highest-status women were kept far from the reins of power simply by
virtue of their sex and gender, she achieved this.

Fulvia's success came at considerable cost, not only to her but also
to her family. While she made three advantageous marriages to men
at the peak of their political and military careers, neither the unions
nor the men lasted. As we have just seen, her first husband, Publius
Clodius Pulcher, was brutally murdered in the street. Her second,
Gaius Scribonius Curio, was killed in battle far from home in North

Africa, his body desecrated by the opposing general. Her third, Marcus Antonius (more commonly known today as Marc Antony), was openly and unashamedly unfaithful to her with numerous women, finally and most famously Cleopatra, Queen of Egypt. His final act in their marriage was to abandon her on her deathbed in the name of self-preservation and diplomacy, despite the fact that she had gone to war with his rival in Italy in order to protect his interests while he was dallying in Egypt on an extended dirty weekend. And although Fulvia bore five children, three of them came to violent ends, with one executed, one murdered and one forced to commit suicide.

She was repeatedly publicly pilloried in front of the entire Roman Senate and wider Roman society for daring to step outside the confines of the domestic sphere, and this deliberate and systematic destruction of her reputation ensured that the allegations made against her have survived for two millennia, while most attempts at defence have faded from view. I suspect most women living in the supposedly enlightened twenty-first century can relate only too well to this situation.[18] I am no stranger to the ways in which prominent women, from politicians to activists to royals to academics to celebrities, are excoriated in public discourse for daring to break with convention, and have to fight tooth and nail for even the smallest amount of bodily autonomy.

We have more literary, documentary and archaeological evidence for Fulvia than we have for almost any other Roman woman during the Late Republic, so we should be able to reconstruct something of her life, should we not? Unfortunately, the problem is that much of this evidence is negative in the extreme. Nearly all of the authors writing during her life or immediately after her death were enormously hostile towards her. The foremost orator of the age, Cicero, called her 'a thoroughly rapacious female' and 'a woman as cruel as she is greedy'.[19] Later authors took these portrayals and doubled down on them, adding spicy details that may be true or may simply be exaggerated falsehoods designed to infuriate as well as titillate. Seven decades after her death, the historian Velleius Paterculus described her as having 'nothing of the woman in her except her sex', while several decades after that, Antony's biographer Plutarch elaborated, claiming that she was 'a woman who took no thought for spinning or housekeeping', but who 'wished to rule a ruler and command a commander'.[20] Fulvia was described as greedy for coveting the wealth and possessions of others, cruel for overseeing the corporal punishment of soldiers, murderous for ordering the executions of her enemies, and bloodthirsty for mistreating a corpse. She was accused of using her children as props to curry favour with the *plebs*. Even the details of her sex life were raked over in public, with allegations of adultery and prostitution made against her, homosexual activity made against each of her three husbands, and what amounts to wife-swapping made against all four of them.

In an attempt to get to some semblance of the truth, I have had to reverse-engineer a portrait of Fulvia, casting a critical eye over the ancient evidence, reading between the lines, and proposing an alternative interpretation, rather than simply assuming the worst in the manner of an ancient Roman man. The criticisms levelled at Fulvia are standard ones that appear throughout Roman invective directed at transgressive women, one contemporaneous and highly pertinent example being aimed at her sister-in-law Clodia Metelli by Cicero in his speech the *Pro Caelio*, 'In Defence of Caelius', on 4 April 56 BCE.[21] Since that speech was given in an attempt to convince a jury to acquit Cicero's protégé Marcus Caelius Rufus of the charge of *vis* (political violence, in this instance encompassing a range of unsavoury activities including civil disturbance, assault, property damage, the attempted murder of Clodia herself, and assassination), it is actually an early example of the DARVO (deny, attack, reverse victim and offender) response, in which 'a certain kind of indignant self-righteous, and overly stated, denial may in fact relate to guilt'.[22] The criticisms will no doubt also prove familiar to contemporary readers, as women in public life today are still being subjected to variations on these themes – consider the myriad conspiracy theories that continue to circulate about Hillary Rodham Clinton, many of which are highly sexualized in nature. What is unusual, however, is the sheer *amount* of vitriol directed at Fulvia. What was so special about her that she enraged not only her peers but also their descendants to such a degree?

The misogyny directed at Fulvia is flexible, selective and convenient, and part of a larger tactic of character assassination that Romans frequently used against their political opponents: if you wanted to gain the upper hand in either verbal or written communication with a rival, the fastest way to do so was to humiliate them, usually by casting aspersions on their masculinity in some way. Anything they could think of was brought into play to score points, so she served as collateral damage in the propaganda war between Antony and Octavian that raged across the ancient Mediterranean throughout the late 40s and into the early 30s BCE as they each attempted to assassinate each other's character and undermine each other's position in their fight to replace Gaius Julius Caesar as the sole master of the Roman world. Then, after her death, she was replaced – in all senses – by Cleopatra and reduced to a footnote in her third husband's story, with Plutarch going so far as to say that 'Cleopatra was indebted to Fulvia for teaching Antony to endure a woman's sway, since she took him over quite tamed, and schooled at the outset to obey women'.[23]

Of course, it is entirely possible that Fulvia was guilty of everything her ancient Roman critics accused her of – that she was calculating and manipulative, cruel and violent, covetous and acquisitive. But even if this is the case, her motivations for her actions were likely to have been rather more complex and nuanced, even perhaps justified, than she is given credit for, and in what follows I have worked hard to try to recover or reconstruct them in a plausible manner.

Unlike other historical figures, we do not have an exact date of birth or date of death for her, and although we know she married three times and bore five children – generally the most important and impactful things a Roman woman *could* do – we do not know precisely when she did those things, either. Despite the fact that many members of the Roman elite wrote (or at least attempted to write) poetry, we do not have autobiographical or even semi-autobiographical poems by Fulvia, such as those written by her contemporary Sulpicia about her love for her beau Cerinthus.[24] We do not have an account of her life in her own words, with her own explanations and justifications for her actions. As far as we know, only one such account was written by a woman in antiquity, and this was a memoir written by Agrippina the Younger, the great-granddaughter of the emperor Augustus, the wife of the emperor Claudius and the mother of the emperor Nero.[25]

While that must have made fascinating reading, and was used as a source by numerous ancient authors, to date only two fragments of it have been identified in extant ancient literature. The first is in Tacitus' *Annals* (he records Agrippina's mother begging the emperor Tiberius to allow her to marry again after the premature death of her husband, Agrippina's father), and the second is in Pliny the Elder's *Natural History* (he records Nero's breech birth), but for some reason it has not survived to the present day, more's the pity.[26] But no ancient author mentions Fulvia writing any such thing; she is as silent as the proverbial grave, and this has allowed others to put words in her mouth.

What we do have are detailed and vivid accounts of several episodes from Fulvia's life.[27] When ancient authors wrote about her, even those who were her contemporaries and wrote about her during her lifetime as she was doing the very things they were writing about, they seem to have had wildly diverging opinions about her. Even one author could change their perspective considerably from work to work, and genre to genre: for example, Cicero, writing about Fulvia over a period of some ten years, from 53 BCE to 43 BCE, starts out fairly neutral and becomes progressively more negative, in both his public speeches and his private letters (these were collected, curated and disseminated by his secretary Tiro after his death). And ancient authors built on the works of their predecessors: by the time we get to the historian Cassius Dio, writing in the third century CE and drawing on more than two centuries of negative accounts of her doings, we have the most lurid portrayals of her. Fulvia is a palimpsest, comprising layer upon layer of ancient literary, documentary and numismatic evidence. But she is also a Rorschach test. Scholarly treatments by classicists and ancient historians, which were relatively rare until about twenty years ago, seem to vary in their interpretations almost as much as those written two millennia ago, with scholars manufacturing their own portrayals.[28] These swing between seeing Fulvia as the prime mover and shaker in her circle, 'the first princess of Rome' and 'the missing empress', the precursor to the empresses of the imperial period, and dismissing her as entirely irrelevant, almost a fictitious recreation, with optimistic historians assigning her far more influence than she actually possessed.[29] Might we have similar contradictory views of other ancient women if so many sources discussing them had survived?

Turning to material evidence for our enigmatic subject and her peers, we do not have a securely identified marble portrait bust of any of the elite women from the Late Republic comparable to those that survive of their menfolk Caesar, Pompey, Cicero, Antony and Octavian (we do, however, have portraits from the imperial period of Octavian's sister and his wife, Octavia and Livia, who were Fulvia's younger contemporaries, due to his position as the first Roman emperor, Augustus, and their own importance in ensuring a line of succession through the creation of the Julio-Claudian dynasty). While one marble head reportedly recovered from a villa in the Alban Hills in the late nineteenth century has been proposed as a portrait of Fulvia, this identification is tenuous indeed, based solely on its resemblance to a series of coin portraits that may or may not represent Fulvia too.[30] Due to a quirk of the Roman epigraphic habit – that tendency to record both public and personal information on stone and other durable materials – we do, however, have some written descriptions of women lower down the social hierarchy.

One example of this practice can be found in the actions of the husband of a woman who is known to modern scholars as 'Turia': he commemorated his wife and enumerated her virtues in the lengthy inscription known as the *Laudatio Turiae* ('In Praise of Turia'), set up in the latter part of the first century BCE and currently the longest-surviving personal inscription from ancient Rome.[31] Unfortunately, neither the husband's nor the wife's name has been preserved in the

The funerary inscription known as the Laudatio Turiae *('In Praise of Turia'), circa late first century* CE

fragments of the inscription that have been identified as having survived from antiquity and reunited in the Museo Nazionale Romano at the Terme di Diocleziano (Baths of Diocletian) in Rome.[32] But despite that omission, we are given a considerable amount of insight into the intricacies and intimacies of their four-decade-long marriage:

> Why should I mention the virtues of your private life: your sexual morality, your obedience, your considerateness, your reasonableness; your attentive weaving, your religious devotion free of superstition, your unassuming appearance and sober attire? Why should I talk about your love and devotion to family? … You have countless other things in common with all married women who keep up a good reputation. The qualities that I assert you have belong to you alone.[33]

Unfortunately for Fulvia, she outlived two husbands (it is worth noting that we have no portraits or epitaphs of Clodius or Curio either) and was abjured by a third immediately prior to her death, so she was left without a bereft and loving spouse to commemorate her, giving us no insight into what her nearest and dearest might have thought of her to set alongside the impressions of her enemies.

The lives of elite women in this period were surprisingly culturally, socially and even politically rich, yet they have been consistently overlooked in favour of their fathers, brothers, husbands and sons. Using Fulvia as our guide, we can visit an unfamiliar Rome – one in which women played a crucial, albeit less high-profile, role in many of the events leading up to the fall of the Roman Republic. This is not the Rome we often get to visit in history books, but it is a Rome that I want to spend time in, and I hope you will join me.

CHAPTER 1

FULVIA'S WORLD

F ULVIA WAS BORN AT the close of one outbreak of civil war (Sulla versus Marius, 83–81 BCE), lived through two more (Caesar versus Pompey, 49–45 BCE; Second Triumvirate versus the Liberators, 44–42 BCE), and her actions caused a fourth (Octavian versus Lucius Antonius, 41–40 BCE) and contributed directly to a fifth (Octavian versus Antony, 32–30 BCE), although this last one would not break out fully until after her death. What was the political situation in Rome like during her lifetime? What follows is not intended to be a blow-by-blow account of the fall of the Republic, nor a comprehensive account of all the political and military events that took place in the period 80–40 BCE. Rather, it is intended as an attempt to reconstruct, as far as possible, Fulvia as a living, breathing, flesh-and-blood Roman woman, someone who loved her husbands, bore their children, loved those children, and worked her fingers to the bone – rightly or wrongly – in the service of her family. But here at the outset, some scene-setting is necessary.

By the time of Fulvia's birth, it is reasonable to describe Roman politics as comprising two factions, the *optimates* and the *populares*. The *optimates* considered themselves *boni*, 'the best men', and saw themselves as conservative and traditional, the guardians of the status quo (for example, Cicero, despite the fact that he was a *novus homo*, a 'new man', without any consular ancestors). The *populares*, on the other hand, saw themselves as representing the Roman people, and sought to increase the power of the Roman people and thereby the elected officials of the tribunate (for example, Clodius, Curio, Antony), at the expense of the Senate as a body, although they were of course members of it. It would be too rigid to describe these as political parties or even ideologies, as individuals crossed between the factions depending on where they believed their best interests to lie on any given day. Likewise, it would be too reductive to say that the *optimates* represented the wealthy senatorial and equestrian elite and the *populares* the common people and the poor.[1] All three of Fulvia's husbands can be described as *populares*, and all three of them held the position of tribune of the *plebs*, inciting the people to further their own political agendas.

Patricians and plebeians were two categories of Roman citizen, a division that went all the way back to the city's very beginnings. When Romulus founded Rome in 753 BCE, the Senate's first one hundred members were the *patres* ('fathers'), and they and their descendants through the male line comprised the patrician order. Everyone else comprised the plebeian order. At the beginning of the Republic in 509 BCE, the patricians enjoyed a monopoly on political power since only they could be members of the Senate, elected consuls, and hold the priesthoods. In response, the so-called Struggle of the Orders lasted until the start of the Middle Republic (264 BCE), with plebeians attempting to extract concessions from the patricians in order to achieve some semblance of political equality. Thus, for example, eventually, each year one consul would be a patrician and the other plebeian, while the tribunes would always be plebeians.

The consuls held a type of power known as *imperium*, which entitled them to convene and preside over the Senate and other popular assemblies, execute the decrees that these assemblies settled on, command armies, and undertake foreign affairs on behalf of the

Roman state. Yet they did not have absolute power, as one consul could veto the other if they disagreed, and the tribunes of the *plebs* could veto them both. Similarly, the tribunes of the *plebs* presided over the plebeian assembly, passed legislation that affected the *plebs* alone, and could also call the Senate and present proposals to it, as well as vetoing senatorial decisions. In theory, tribunes were sacrosanct, and interfering with them was punishable by death, which was meant to protect them from obstruction in the execution of their duties, but in reality, by the time of the Late Republic, a number of tribunes had been physically accosted, assaulted and even murdered while in office. Thus the checks and balances that were intended to safeguard the Roman political system were becoming progressively more unchecked and unbalanced.

The *cursus honorum*, 'ladder of offices', was the hierarchy of magistracies, starting with aedile, then quaestor, then proconsul, and finally consul. In exceptional circumstances, one person could be appointed dictator for a limited period of time in order to address a specific issue (for example, Sulla was appointed dictator in order to restore order after the first outbreak of civil war). Additionally, there were two tribunes of the *plebs*, elected as officers of the assembly of the *plebs*. They had the power to prevent the Senate from convening, and to veto senatorial decrees.

Due to the limited number of positions available, there was a huge amount of competition for each one. Consequently, ancient Rome was an agonistic society, and people had exceedingly long memories when it came to their own personal *dignitas*, 'dignity', and *auctoritas*, 'personal prestige' or 'authority' – the ability to exert influence over those around them – and the extent to which they felt like they had been either supported or slighted by their peers in their pursuit of individual achievement. This means that not only was ancient Rome a quid pro quo society, with agreements and alliances contracted between individuals and their families that could extend across different generations, it was also a tit-for-tat society where defending oneself did not just involve the repelling of an attack, but also reprisal. Thus rivalries and

feuds could easily be acquired and, as we shall soon see, the consequences could be severe.

What was life like for an elite Roman woman like Fulvia in the middle
of the first century BCE? Born to parents who were Roman citizens,
she was a Roman citizen too, albeit one with fewer rights than a male
one. She could not vote in the annual elections, nor have any say in the
government of what was fast becoming a vast empire with territories
located all around the Mediterranean. Only under exceptional circumstances would a woman's input into state business be sought – one rare
case was when Sempronia, sister of Tiberius and Gaius Gracchus and
wife of Scipio Aemilianus, was brought in front of a public assembly
by the tribune of the *plebs* to validate the claims of an imposter who
sought recognition and reputation as her nephew, but she stood her
ground and refused to acknowledge him.[2]

A woman could not hold any sort of political or military office herself.
Yet she might exert influence upon those who could – perhaps in the
manner of Praecia, a courtesan famous for her beauty and wit who used
her powers of persuasion to advance the policies of her friends and
'added to her other charms the reputation of being a true comrade, and
one who could bring things to pass'; for this reason, she was courted
by the general Lucius Licinius Lucullus for her power to convince her
lover, the political powerhouse Publius Cornelius Cethegus, to grant
him the command he sought in the Mithridatic War, since Lucullus
despised Cethegus and did not wish to deal with him himself.[3]

A Roman woman could, however, hold a *very* few select religious
offices. She could be a priestess of Vesta, the Roman goddess of the
hearth (assuming she was fortunate enough to be selected for one of the
six positions while still a child, with both parents living), with responsibility for tending the sacred flame and protecting the Palladium (a
wooden statue of the goddess Athena, an heirloom supposedly salvaged
by Aeneas from the legendary city of Troy after the Greeks sacked
it at the close of the Trojan War) and the *fascinum* (an erect phallus

that averted evil) in the Temple of Vesta. Additionally, on the earthly plane, the Temple of Vesta was something akin to a safe-deposit-box facility, used to store important documents including copies of wills and treaties and valuable possessions, which gave Vestals immense power over certain individuals and their affairs. That is not to say that their lives were entirely taken up with sacred or even administrative drudgery: an account of a luxurious banquet celebrating the inauguration of the new priest of Mars, Lucius Cornelius Lentulus Niger, in 69 BCE has survived, and the feast was attended by four of the six Vestal Virgins serving at that time (the remaining two had presumably drawn the short straws and been left back at the temple tending the sacred flame). Popillia, Perpennia, Licinia and Arruntia, along with the new priest's wife and mother-in-law, enjoyed the perks of a private dining room. The lavish spread set out before them comprised starters including sea urchins, raw oysters, cockles and mussels, thrush over asparagus, fattened hen, baked oysters and cockles, white and black acorn-molluscs, clams, jellyfish, fig-peckers, loin of roe deer, loin of boar, and fattened fowl wrapped in dough, murex and purple-shell; and main courses of sow's udders, boar's cheek, baked fish, baked sow's udder, ducks, boiled waterfowl, hares, roasted fattened fowl, and gruel with bread from Picenum on the side.[4]

If her husband held one of the three major priesthoods, serving as the priest of Jupiter, Mars or Quirinus, she would serve as the priestess by virtue of being his wife – he would be the *flamen Dialis* (or *Martialis*, or *Quirinalis*), she would be the *flaminica* (for the duration of her husband's lifetime, at least) – and since her person was intrinsically holy, she was bound by a lifetime of arcane rules and religious obligations, which dictated such things as her hairstyle (she was not allowed to comb or dress her hair, and had to wear a headdress with a twig from a fruitful tree in it) and clothing (she had to wear dyed robes), and forbade her from mounting a staircase of more than three steps.[5] She could be a priestess of Ceres in her own right, expected to perform the religious rites in Greek since the goddess and her worship had originated there, and so women from Roman locales with a strong

Greek heritage like Neapolis (modern Naples) and Velia (modern Ascea) were often selected.[6] This role, like that of the priesthood of Vesta, seems to have required celibacy from the start of the individual's tenure, although since it would be taken on much later in life (Vestals were recruited around the age of six years old) it might require setting aside a husband.[7] She could also bear temporary responsibility for certain female-centric rites and rituals celebrated annually, one famous example being the Bona Dea festival, held in celebration of the Italic deity known simply as the 'Good Goddess' because her actual name is unknown, so secret were the rites surrounding her, which were hosted by the wife of a magistrate in the privacy of her home.[8]

A Roman woman with some kind of religious power and influence could parlay that into other types of power and influence. A Vestal Virgin did not necessarily set aside her family ties and familial obligations for the three decades of her tenure, and there are numerous examples of Vestals using their clout to further the interests of their male relatives, safe in the knowledge that, due to their sacrosanctity, they were safe from reprisal. For example, in 143 BCE one named Claudia shielded her father Appius Claudius Pulcher from physical violence by riding with him in his chariot during his illegal triumphal parade celebrating his victory over the Salassi tribe from Cisalpine Gaul.[9] During Fulvia's formative years, she would have witnessed several examples of similar behaviour. In 69 BCE one named Fonteia embraced her brother Marcus Fonteius during his trial for corruption while serving as provincial governor in Gaul, in an attempt to influence the judges, arguing that she had the goddess Vesta on her side and there would be severe consequences if her intercession were ignored and her brother found guilty; while a few years later, in 63 BCE, a Vestal named Licinia granted her prominent seat at a gladiatorial bout to her relative Lucius Licinius Murena in order to boost his public profile as he campaigned for the position of consul in the following year's elections.[10]

Yet becoming involved with the politics and political figures of the day was not without a degree of personal risk, even for a Vestal Virgin: the same Licinia who attended gladiatorial games (and the aforementioned banquet) was accused of breaking her vows of chastity with Marcus Licinius Crassus, one third of the First Triumvirate alongside Caesar and Pompey (this was an unofficial political alliance in which all three magnates sought to use their respective influence to support each other, thereby bypassing normal senatorial procedures). If she had been found guilty of the offence, she would have been buried alive. Luckily, she was able to explain that the reason that Crassus had been hanging around and paying attention to her was that he wished to purchase her suburban villa, and she was acquitted.[11]

In some respects, the Vestal Virgins were subjected to more stringent policing of their behaviour than were other Roman women: one priestess named Postumia was accused of unchastity and put on trial because of the way that she dressed and her scurrilous wit.[12] Although she was acquitted, she was ordered to dress more sedately and refrain from joking in the future. Subsequently, the prosecution and defence of a Vestal Virgin became a popular rhetorical exercise.[13]

A Roman woman did not even need an official religious position to use some aspect of religion to further her own agenda. She might suddenly have a dream fraught with foresight, such as Caecilia Metella's during the Marsian War (91–89 BCE) in 90 BCE, in which she saw the goddess Juno fleeing from the city because she was aghast at the filth in the Temple of Juno Sospita, a place of worship that had fallen into such disrepair that a bitch had commandeered it as her lair and borne a litter of puppies inside, which was subsequently restored; or Calpurnia's in 44 BCE, which foretold the assassination of her husband Caesar on the Ides of March.[14] She might witness an omen and seek to interpret it, like Terentia's construing of the reignition of the ashes and bark on the sacrificial altar during the Bona Dea rites in 63 BCE as support for her husband Cicero's actions in putting down the Catilinarian Conspiracy (a disgruntled aristocrat's efforts to kill key political figures such as the consuls and seize power for himself).[15] Or she might use a religious benefaction to draw attention to herself even while ostensibly highlighting her male relatives, in the manner of Publicia's restoration of the Temple of Hercules sometime in the first half of the first century BCE, which she marked with the following inscription: 'Publicia, daughter of Lucius Publicius, wife of Gnaeus Cornelius, son of Aulus Cornelius, built this temple of Hercules and the doors, and she adorned it. And she restored the altar sacred to Hercules. All these things she did with her own and with her husband's money. She oversaw that it was done.'[16] This same emphasis on money as a means of agency is also found in Ansia Rufa's inscription commemorating her restoration of the sacred grove at Padula (near modern Salerno): 'Ansia Rufa, daughter of Ansius Tarvus, by order of the decurions (local officials), ensured that a brick wall and (another) wall and a gate were built around the grove. She paid for it with her own money.'[17] Finally, Octavia's inscription detailing her own activities at the sanctuary of the Bona Dea in Ostia in the period 70–60 BCE is even more specific: 'Octavia, daughter of Marcus Octavius, wife of Gamala, saw to it that the Bona Dea's portico was adorned, benches were set up, and the kitchen was given a roof.'[18]

A woman would bear a version of her father's name, so that her paternity and paternal line would be instantly perceivable – and, depending upon her behaviour, she would be viewed as either an ornament to or a stain upon that line. Some of the highest praise she could expect to receive would be comments on how similar to her father she was, either in appearance or in spirit. She was expected to embody the virtue of *pietas*, a sort of moral righteousness not too dissimilar to our modern concept of piety, towards her family, her fatherland and the gods. We find this illustrated in several curious mythological episodes where lactating women breastfeed their parents as a means of preventing them from starving to death. In the most frequently cited version, the woman is named Pero and her father is Cimon or Micon.[19] It was such a popular tale that it was frequently depicted in art, and a fresco that once adorned the wall of a *triclinium* in Pompeii (IX.2.5) featuring this scene is currently housed in the National Archaeological Museum of Naples.[20]

However, there are also several seemingly historical accounts of a woman visiting her imprisoned mother, who had been sentenced to death, in around 150 BCE. The prison guard could not bring himself to strangle her as ordered so decided to starve her to death instead, but he did allow her daughter to visit her in the interim. She was forbidden to bring her mother food and was searched by the prison guards to make sure that she was not attempting to sneak any in, but her mother did not starve because, he eventually realized, she was being nursed by her postpartum daughter. When he reported this act of daughterly devotion to his superiors, the woman's death sentence was remitted, and both mother and daughter were given maintenance grants for life.[21] Subsequently the site of the deed came to be considered sacred, so it was consecrated, and a temple to Pietas, the goddess of filial affection, was built on the spot – although this was eventually replaced by the building that would ultimately become the Theatre of Marcellus (construction was started by Caesar shortly before his death in 44 BCE, but it would be thirty years before the theatre was completed by Octavian and dedicated to his deceased nephew Marcellus). While we should not envisage Roman women breastfeeding their elderly parents as a matter of course, the idea that lay behind the myth was a popular and clearly resonant one. It was frequently referenced in the epitaphs of daughters who predeceased their parents, like that of Lysandre, set up by her mother Philonike and her father Eudemon, who bemoaned the fact that 'the breasts of my mother nourished me with their milk to no purpose at all, and to those breasts I cannot repay the favour of nourishment for their old age'.[22]

A Roman woman would be under the legal control of her father for the duration of her father's lifetime (unless she passed to the legal control of her husband upon marriage), and although her father's death would render her legally independent, and she could inherit an equal amount of his estate to any brothers – or the whole thing if she was an only child – she would still require the oversight of a guardian, perhaps another male relative or a close friend of the family, or even a family freedman. Her destiny was marriage, and once married, she would pass into the *ordo matronarum*, the 'order of matrons', an organized social network of married woman comprising perhaps as many as 1,400

individuals, and it was this social network that could – and often did –
organize collective action in order to protect its own interests.[23]

Once married, hopefully, she would become a mother and, assuming
she did not die in childbirth, enjoy the perks of motherhood for the rest
of her life. In private, she would wield influence over the family through
membership of the *consilium*, the family council, while in public she
would wield influence through the male members of her family: first
her father, then her husband, then her son, then – if she lived long
enough – her grandson. She would manage the household, trained by
her mother and advised by the tenets found in treatises on domestic
and estate management, including the *Household Management* of the
Classical Greek author Xenophon, translated into Latin by Cicero, or
the *On Agriculture* of the Carthaginian author Mago, translated into
Latin by Cato the Elder. In the absence of her husband, should he
be posted abroad as the governor of a province or the commander of
an army, she would manage the family's estates and the family itself,
since during the Republic it was not usual for wives to accompany
their husbands as they did during the Empire. She could even own
property outright, and live off the revenue it produced, like Varro's wife
Fundania, to whom he dedicated his treatise *On Agriculture*, an homage
to Cato's, so that she would know everything she needed to know in
order to run her farm effectively and ensure a decent income after his
death.

She would receive as much education as her family considered
appropriate and desirable, and she might aspire to be an intellectual,
albeit in a private rather than a public context. Several Republican
women were renowned poets, circulating in the orbits of creatives who
are still known to us today. Cornificia was the daughter of a man named
Quintus Cornificius and sister of a man likewise named Quintus
Cornificius, who climbed the *cursus honorum* to the position of praetor
and proconsul of the province of Africa, was elected augur and was,
like his sister, known for his poetry: clearly the pair were members of
a particularly literary family, and they moved in literary circles, being
acquainted with and referenced by Catullus (Cornificia's husband,

Camerius, was likewise mentioned).[24] While Cornificia's epigrams have unfortunately not survived to the present, they were still being disseminated, read and praised in the fourth century CE, four centuries after her death, and she even rates a mention by Saint Jerome in his *Chronicle*. He praises her work using the Latin adjective *insignis*, which can be translated somewhat neutrally as 'notable', but also more positively as 'remarkable', 'eminent', 'distinguished' and even 'extraordinary'.[25] The neoteric poet Catullus in turn describes the girlfriend of his friend Caecilius as 'a maiden more scholarly than the Sapphic muse'[26] – that is to say, Sappho – and providing enthusiastic and passionate feedback on and endorsement of Caecilius' poetic efforts. One Late Republican poetess's work has survived to the present: that of Sulpicia, the daughter of the patrician Servius Sulpicius Rufus and his wife Valeria, the sister of Marcus Valerius Messalla Corvinus, and related to Decimus Brutus, one of the ringleaders in the assassination of Caesar. As a member of the highest echelons of the Roman elite, she was seen in public dressed in double-dyed Tyrian purple, adorned with Indian pearls and drenched in Arabian perfume.[27] While her father wrote poetry in which he paraphrased Latin into Greek, Sulpicia wrote in Latin, her poems detailing her relationship with her fiancé and later husband, even including one on her feelings upon hearing that he had been caught in bed with a sex worker: 'this is the greatest cause of pain, that I may yield my place to an ignoble rival'.[28] An insight into Sulpicia's process can be found in the epitaph of her household's *lectrix*, 'female reader', Sulpicia Petale, who would have not only read aloud to her mistress but also, potentially, read Sulpicia's work in public to preserve her modesty.[29]

While not born into wealth and status, a woman might acquire both through the exercising of her talents. In the early to mid-first century BCE, Iaia of Cyzicus, who never married, preferred to concentrate on her art.[30] She painted portraits of women (two renowned works were a self-portrait, painted with the assistance of a mirror, and *Old Woman at Naples*), and she was both fast and brilliant, with her portraits coming to be regarded more highly than those of the best male artists working in the same period – Sopolis and Dionysius, whose work was displayed in numerous art galleries. Presumably her customers included members of the Late Republican senatorial families, as the people best placed to commission her and display the resulting portrait in one of their many homes. While there may not have been many female artists working in Rome, they seem to have been a popular subject for interior decoration, as two frescoes depicting them have so far been recovered in Pompeii.[31]

Yet just occasionally, we get a glimpse behind the curtain at a real woman, warts and all, and this shows us something quite different from the domestic goddesses their husbands praised to the skies in their *laudationes* and epitaphs. In a private letter that Cicero wrote to his friend Titus Pomponius Atticus on either 5 or 6 May 51 BCE, he related the details of a domestic dispute that he had witnessed between his brother Quintus and his wife, Pomponia, who also happened to be Atticus' sister – the marriage was clearly a turbulent one, ultimately ending in divorce five years later.[32] Cicero complained to Atticus about Pomponia's manner and the hostile way that she spoke to Quintus, explaining that 'her words and manner were so gratuitously rude'.[33] She refused to sit down and eat lunch with the brothers, or to spend the night with her husband when he attempted to initiate intimacies, leaving Cicero to harangue her brother into attempting to intervene and take her to task for her less than meritorious behaviour.

With the many examples, both positive and negative, that Fulvia had before her, who would she choose to be? Or would she perhaps eschew the general in favour of the specific, and look to her mother Sempronia, and her mother's sister Sempronia, both significant and influential women in their own ways – for better or for worse.

CHAPTER 2

FULVIA'S FAMILY

W E DO NOT KNOW the day on which, or even the year in which, Fulvia was born. This is simply not the sort of information that the Romans bothered to record for posterity during the Late Republic, except in the most exceptional of cases (for example, we know Antony's birthday – 14 January – because after his death it was declared *nefas*, a black day on the Roman calendar, but we do not know the year). Women were seldom if ever considered exceptional enough to warrant this attention. That is not to say that the Romans did not acknowledge or celebrate birthdays – after all, the most famous of the Vindolanda tablets (a collection of wooden tablets recovered from a garrison on Hadrian's Wall), and the earliest attested female handwriting in Latin, is an invitation from Claudia Severa to her friend Sulpicia Lepidina, requesting her presence at her birthday party.[1] It is simply that they were the sort of ordinary occurrence that did not tend to rate a specific mention in ancient literature. This dearth of information means that we must estimate Fulvia's age based on other details we have about her life, such as the dates of her first marriage, the order and dates of the births of her children and other activities. Thus, a birth date in the late 80s BCE or the early 70s BCE seems likely. She is referred to as being from Tusculum (modern Frascati in Lazio, about twelve miles south-east of Rome), an ancient Roman city down the Via Latina in the Alban Hills that was renowned for the number of consuls it had produced, so she was probably born at the family seat there.[2] According to legend, the city had been founded by Telegonus, the son of the Titan Circe and the Greek hero Odysseus.[3] The ancient geographer Strabo describes it as follows:

> A city with no mean equipment of buildings; and it is adorned by the plantings and villas encircling it, and particularly by those that extend below the city in the general direction of the city of Rome; for here Tusculum is a fertile and well-watered hill, which in many places rises gently into crests and admits of magnificently devised royal palaces.[4]

While today the ancient city lies in ruins, amenities including a forum, theatre, amphitheatre, fountain and acropolis have been excavated periodically since the nineteenth century.[5] At least thirty-six owners of Tusculan villas are known from the ancient literary evidence and over one hundred villa sites have been identified in the city's vicinity, attesting to the presence of many wealthy Roman families.[6] The famous orator Cicero was one prominent resident, and he considered himself at his happiest when in residence there, with his purpose-built sculpture gallery full of marble herms topped with bronze portraits that he called the Academy, so it is not surprising that he set his philosophical treatise *Tusculan Disputations*, written after the death of his beloved daughter Tullia in childbirth in 45 BCE, there.[7] The infamous general Lucullus, described as 'Xerxes in a toga' by his contemporaries on account of his lavish style of living, was another.[8]

Although it is extremely difficult to match any famous historical resident to any specific villa site with any degree of certainty, numerous details about the villas in this area have been preserved which enable us to reconstruct the kind of environment in which Fulvia would have spent her childhood when she and her family were away from their *domus*, or townhouse, in Rome. These abodes, solely devoted to *otium*, 'leisure', as opposed to *negotium*, 'business', contained well-stocked libraries, were decorated with collections of art including paintings and bronze and marble statues, and were enlivened with specialist birds in aviaries, animals in parks and fish in ponds. They were naturally and ecologically blessed with freshwater springs that served as sources for a number of the city of Rome's aqueducts. This seemingly idyllic way of life was not only thoroughly romanticized in antiquity; that romanticization has continued in the years since, such as in J. M. W. Turner's painting *Cicero at His Villa at Tusculum* (see fig 1).

Fulvia was the daughter of Marcus Fulvius Bambalio and Sempronia Tuditana. Both the Fulvii and the Sempronii Tuditani were ancient plebeian clans, and both had a long tradition of political and military activity in service of the Roman Republic. The Fulvii had the added benefit of being historically associated with the demi-god Hercules and his twelve labours. The earliest recorded case of a member of the Fulvii rising to the level of consul, the highest position available to a Roman under normal circumstances, is Lucius Fulvius Curvus in 322 BCE, and members of the family continued to occupy the highest echelons of the *cursus honorum* until 125 BCE.[9] This meant that the atrium of Fulvia's family home would have been full of portraits of distinguished ancestors, intended to serve as examples to their descendants, with the household shrine containing many death masks moulded from the faces of the illustrious deceased, brought out and worn at family funerals, and an extensive family tree naming all of these individuals scrolling across the wall. However, by the time of Fulvia's birth both prestigious families seem to have petered out, and Fulvia may well have been the last scion of both. Her father had been unable to rise to the lofty heights of his ancestors due to a speech impairment, hence his *cognomen* – *bambalio*, taken from the ancient Greek *bambalein*, meaning to stammer or stutter (literally, 'to clatter with one's teeth'). Generally, the *praenomen* would be used in private, amongst family members and close friends, and there were only a very small number of these names in circulation, while the family name and the additional descriptor, if you had one, would be used in public, and it would be these that would serve to differentiate you from everyone else with the same *praenomen* and *nomen*. Somewhat counter-intuitively, Roman *cognomina* are frequently unflattering, making reference to distinguishing physical or mental characteristics. So, every time anyone addressed Marcus Fulvius Bambalio in public, they were in effect reminding him of his speech impairment.

For a member of the Roman elite, expected to embark upon a political and/or military career that involved a considerable amount of public speaking, anything that negatively affected one's ability to communicate, such as a speech or hearing impairment, or even simply a poor memory, was highly disabling, and led people to cast aspersions on that person's intelligence.[10] Hence Cicero criticizing Fulvia's father not just on the grounds of his disordered speech, but also what he perceived to be his deficient intellect.[11] A Roman daughter was sometimes given a feminized version of her father's name, to differentiate her from her sisters and cousins, but since Fulvia seems to have had neither, it is not surprising that her father did not wish to inflict his insulting third name on his daughter and contribute to perpetuating it. Additionally, by the time Fulvia came to public prominence and her activities started to be documented in the historical record, it was already clear that she did not share her father's impairment, and was in fact a powerful and highly effective public speaker, so she is known only as Fulvia (strangely, modern scholars sometimes refer to her as Fulvia Flacca Bambula, although she was never addressed as such during her lifetime).

Fulvia's mother's family was likewise somewhat problematic, and for similar ableist reasons. While her maternal grandfather Sempronius Tuditanus had been elected consul in 129 BCE, had conquered the Istrians (the ancient inhabitants of the modern region of north-western Croatia and south-western Slovenia), and had authored thirteen books on the authority of magistrates, he had also been somewhat eccentric, preferring to dress in the sort of theatrical costumes worn in tragedies rather than the standard toga, and was in the habit of throwing coins to the audiences that gathered to hear him speak on the Rostra, the platform in the centre of the Forum.[12] While it was perfectly acceptable for members of the Roman elite to enjoy attending the theatre, it was not acceptable for them to aspire to acting as either a profession or a hobby for themselves, and those who did so were at best looked at askance and at worst declared infamous and blacklisted.[13] Even socializing with actors and actresses was considered suspect.

Cicero goes so far as to say that Tuditanus claimed to see visions, likening him to the mythological figures Ajax and Hercules, driven to madness by the vindictive goddesses Athena and Hera respectively.[14] He was, however, extremely wealthy, and that wealth seems to have made its way from his daughter to hers, making Fulvia an heiress. However, this intergenerational transfer of wealth did not go as smoothly as it could have done, since Sempronia's cousin Titus Longus attempted to have Tuditanus' will naming her as his beneficiary thrown out, under the terms of the *lex Voconia*, the Voconian Law, passed in 169 BCE, which prevented property valued at 100,000 sesterces (the minimum amount that served as the entry qualification to the equestrian order) from passing to women, and which would have enabled him as the next closest relative to seize it all.[15] It was not unusual for male relations, so-called friends, and acquaintances to attempt to take advantage of women they perceived to be vulnerable in this period, benefiting from the understandable reluctance of respectable women to participate in court cases and have to undergo the ordeal of testifying in public.

The historian Sallust, 86–35 BCE, an almost exact contemporary of Fulvia's, wrote an account of the Catilinarian Conspiracy, and in it he names as one of the conspirators a woman named Sempronia, the wife of Decimus Junius Brutus who had been elected consul in 77 BCE. Now, this Sempronia was probably not Fulvia's mother, but she may well have been Fulvia's mother's sister.[16] She was apparently favoured by fortune in both her birth and her appearance, and was also highly accomplished: intelligent, witty, charming, and conversant not just in Latin but also in Greek, she also composed poetry and was rather musically inclined, skilled at playing the lyre and dancing.[17] These were not unusual skills for a female member of the Roman elite to possess, as Cornelia Metella – the fifth and final wife of the famous general, statesman, and member of the First Triumvirate Pompey the Great, and born around 73 BCE so an exact contemporary of Fulvia – was likewise praised for her knowledge of literature, geometry and lyre playing.[18] A fresco from the Villa of Publius Fannius Synistor at Boscoreale, dated to around 40–30 BCE, depicts a Roman matron and child (or perhaps an enslaved person, due to the disparity in size between the two figures) playing the kithara together (see fig 2). The pair are lavishly dressed, swathed in purple fabrics and adorned with golden jewellery.[19]

However, Sallust is rather ambivalent about this particular beautiful and talented woman. He considers her to have disregarded what the Romans considered to be the traditional feminine virtue of *pudicitia*, a combination of modesty and chastity, ignored concern for her reputation, and crossed over into full-blown shamelessness. She spent money recklessly, racked up debts that she neglected to pay, and was even an accessory to murder.[20] He describes her as having 'perpetrated many deeds of masculine daring', and transgressing Roman gender norms was certainly something that Fulvia would do later in her life; in doing so, she may have been following the example set by her aunt and perhaps also her mother.[21]

Prior to marrying Fulvia's father, Sempronia had been married to a man who was probably named Lucius Pinarius Natta, and she had borne him a son, also named Lucius Pinarius Natta, so Fulvia had at least one elder sibling.[22] The Pinarii were an ancient patrician family who, like the Fulvii, were associated with the cult of Hercules, so this would have added an interesting dimension to Fulvia's extended family, especially once she married Antony, whose family claimed descent from the demi-god.[23] Depending on whether Sempronia had been widowed or divorced, Fulvia's half-brother Natta may or may not have lived alongside her in the house of Bambalio, as legally Roman children were the property of their fathers and tended to remain with them. But since it is estimated – based on the details we have of his career – that he was born around 100 BCE and she was born sometime around 80 BCE, he would have been significantly older than her, so may have been living independently by the time she was born, and as a result their relationship may not have been close. Of course, there is nothing to stop a young man doting on an unexpected baby sister, especially one that could prove useful to him once she grows up.

Natta went on to marry Caesar's niece Julia, and was the father of Caesar's great-nephew – and one of his heirs – Lucius Pinarius Scarpus, who would initially support Antony but eventually switch his allegiance to Octavian, so Fulvia was connected to Caesar by blood.[24] At a slightly further remove, Sempronia's cousin was the famous lawyer and orator Quintus Hortensius Hortalus, who was elected consul in 69 BCE; his daughter Hortensia, Fulvia's second cousin, was equally skilled at oratory, which she would publicly demonstrate in 43 BCE, to Fulvia's chagrin.[25] This branch of the family was also extremely wealthy, and Hortensius was renowned for his lavish lifestyle, which included an element of trend-setting: he served peacocks – formerly just an ornament in Roman aviaries – at the banquet he hosted to celebrate his elevation to the priesthood.[26]

Fulvia's parents did not remain married for long, and after their divorce Sempronia married for a third time. Her third husband was more in line with what was expected of a member of the Roman elite, and was on the cusp of a glittering political and military career. He was named Lucius Licinius Murena and, like Fulvia's father, his family originated from the ancient city in the Alban Hills, Lanuvium, that was famous for its grand temple dedicated to the goddess Juno Sospita, of which the portico and some fragments of terracotta decoration have survived.[27] Murena was, like Cicero, a 'new man' (that is, he did not have any ancestors who had reached the rank of consul), and was also, like Cicero, in the process of climbing the *cursus honorum*. He first served as *praefectus fabrum*, the officer in charge of military engineering, with oversight of workers in wood, stone and metal, then as quaestor (public official) in charge of public revenue and expenditure, in 74 BCE, then as a *legatus*, a high-ranking officer, on military campaigns in the Third Mithridatic War in Asia, Bithynia and Pontus in 73 BCE, then again in Pontus in 72 BCE, and then in Armenia in 69 BCE. He served under the aforementioned general Lucullus with distinction and was entrusted with leading the siege of the city of Amisus (modern Samsun in north Turkey).

Upon his return to Rome, he served as *praetor urbanus* ('urban praetor') in 65 BCE, and hosted a series of magnificent games for the people of the city to enjoy, including plays performed on a silver stage.[28] Then he left Rome again in 64 BCE and travelled north to Transalpine Gaul, where he served as proconsul for two years, before reaching the pinnacle of his career and being elected consul in 62 BCE. At this point, his luck ran out and he was accused of electoral bribery by Servius Sulpicius Rufus, his rival for the consulship, but he was defended in court by three powerful men: the inordinately wealthy Marcus Licinius Crassus, Hortensius and Cicero. The speech given by Cicero sometime in November 62 BCE survives in full, and it is thanks to this that we know a considerable amount about Murena and his career. Murena attended the trial dressed in rags, 'consumed by disease, worn out by his tears and his distress', to show how affected he had been by the allegations.[29] His prosecutor, Cato the Younger, attempted to cast aspersions on his moral character (to be expected in a corruption trial), but Cicero refuted his allegations that Murena was known to get stinking drunk and dance enthusiastically at uproarious parties: 'Nothing, then, can be said against Murena's private life; not one single word, gentlemen.'[30] He highlighted the fact that one of Murena's relations was a Vestal Virgin, and had given him her seat at the gladiatorial games – a very public and religiously loaded endorsement.[31] It was thanks to the successful defence and unanimous acquittal of Murena that Cicero became Rome's leading orator, finally surpassing his rival Hortensius.

While *consularis* ('consul's wife') was not an official position – something more akin to the British prime minister's or French president's spouse as opposed to the First Lady or Gentleman in the United States – as Murena's wife during the year of his consulship, Sempronia would have had special privileges. One notable one was the ability to reserve special seats for herself and her entourage, Fulvia included, at any gladiatorial games held in the Forum, and she also was responsible for hosting prestigious women-only religious rites such as the Bona Dea festival.[32]

Thus, as the daughter of wealthy and well-connected parents and the stepdaughter of a military hero and consul with exceedingly influential friends and allies, Fulvia was situated at the very heart of Roman political, military and social life from a young age, and directly connected to the Caesarian faction – and it would not be long before she began to reap the resulting benefits.[33]

CHAPTER 3

FULVIA'S CHILDHOOD

W HILE WE DO NOT know the specific details of Fulvia's infancy, childhood and adolescence, we can extrapolate some generalities based on the lives of other Roman women of her generation. There were a considerable number of old wives' tales in circulation regarding pregnancy and childbirth, with the Romans believing that a woman carrying a girl would have a more difficult pregnancy and labour, although girls would be born more swiftly than boys.[1] In the absence of anything resembling a hospital with a maternity ward, her mother would have laboured at home, seated on a birthing stool, attended by not just a midwife, but also female family members, friends, and the enslaved members of the household. Several marble reliefs depicting Roman childbirth have survived from antiquity, and these show it to have been a well-attended, almost public, process, with the mother and baby surrounded by women.

Since childbirth was considered to be as dangerous for women as battle was for men (and in fact, since pregnancy and childbirth were much more regular occurrences, perhaps we should consider it to have

A plaque depicting a parturition scene excavated at Ostia

been even more so), it is not surprising to see women who died in childbirth commemorated in heroic poses.

But Sempronia survived. As soon as Fulvia was born, she would have been rubbed with salt and bathed to remove all traces of the afterbirth, then examined to check that everything was in order, as while the Romans did not necessarily practise infanticide or exposure of infants as a matter of course, it was up to the *pater familias*, the male head of the household – in this case Marcus Fulvius Bambalio – to decide whether an infant would be invited to join the household. So, the midwife would have placed the tiny, swaddled bundle on the floor at his feet, presenting him with the opportunity to leave it there if he refused to accept the child into his household, or pick it up if he was happy to acknowledge her as his daughter. As a person living with an impairment, Bambalio may have been more compassionate than his peers. Since there are no records of him having any other children, he may have been somewhat disappointed that she was not a boy who could carry on the family name and restore the family's prestige. Or, as someone who had managed perfectly well without a political or military career himself – as many others whose lives are not generally recorded by ancient historians, such as Cicero's friend Atticus – he may not have cared a jot. Cicero, for one, was delighted with his daughter Tullia, who was an only child until her younger brother Marcus was born, when she was in her teens and married to her first husband, and father and daughter seem to have had a much closer relationship than did father and son. In any case, Fulvia would rise almost as high, and wield almost as much political and military influence, as any brother could have done (and seemingly more than her own half-brother Natta, who was more of a follower than a leader, and may have died as early as the late 50s). Judging by the fact that Bambalio and Antony were acquainted, Bambalio likely lived long enough to witness (and perhaps even benefit from) a significant portion of his daughter's triumph.

The Roman naming day was referred to as the *dies lustricus*, and the official ceremony the *lustratio*, during which girls were officially named on their eighth day of life, while boys were named one day later, on their ninth.[2] The reason for this was already lost in the mists of time in antiquity, and ancient authors themselves speculated. Plutarch suggested a variety of possible reasons.[3] One was that it was recognized that girls matured faster than boys. Another, perhaps inspired by Pythagorean philosophy, was that even numbers were considered female and odd numbers male. A third, likewise mathematically inclined, could also be connected with Roman naming conventions, since boys were normally given three names, and three multiplied by three equals nine, with the cubing implying perfection and completion, while girls were normally given two, and two cubed equals eight, with the cube here representing stability, which women were supposed to provide. Since Roman infancy and childhood were perilous, and mortality rates frighteningly high, for protection they were bedecked with an amulet – girls receiving a *lunula* in the shape of a crescent moon, boys receiving a *bulla* in the shape of a full moon. For children from wealthy families, these amulets were commonly made from precious metals such as gold. As the only child of her parents' marriage, and her father's only child and her mother's only daughter, Fulvia would have been treasured, even though she was not a son.

Although some commentators protested and insisted that mothers should breastfeed their own babies, it does not seem to have been common practice – women who did choose to breastfeed were lauded for doing so in their epitaphs.[4] Rather, it was the norm for women of Sempronia's class to engage the services of a wet nurse, and it had long been fashionable for that wet nurse to be of Greek origins, as it was believed that the baby would imbibe the much-lauded Greek culture along with the milk (and they would certainly learn the Greek language if that was what their primary caregiver spoke to them for the first few years of their life). Significant amounts of time and effort were expended on acquiring the best possible wet nurse, with close attention paid to the woman's character as well as her health, and during the period that she was nursing the child, which could last for up to three years, she was required to follow a strict regimen.[5] Fulvia would have been attended not only by her wet nurse but by a whole retinue of staff devoted to her welfare, such as nurses and pedagogues, and also enslaved children to be her 'milk-sisters' and playmates.[6] She would have formed lasting relationships with all of these, and they would have been with her throughout the highs and lows of her life. She would have been swaddled from directly after birth for a period of around two months to ensure that her limbs grew straight and strong, and when the swaddling bands were changed, she would have been bathed and massaged.[7] One additional aim of swaddling was to ensure the body developed in a visually pleasing way, and baby girls had their chests bound more tightly than their hips so that their adult bodies would conform to Roman beauty ideals. In addition to moulding her body, these staffers would have been responsible for moulding her mind and character, using examples taken from Greek mythology and Roman history of virtuous women – such as Lucretia, Verginia and Claudia Quinta – in order to inculcate Roman values.

No written descriptions of Fulvia's appearance survives, although some twentieth-century commentators opined rather boorishly that she must have been sufficiently appealing to inspire her three husbands to sleep with her, since she bore all three of them children reasonably promptly after their respective weddings. It has been suggested that the poet Catullus referred to her under the pseudonym of Quintia, just as he referred to her sister-in-law Clodia under the pseudonym of Lesbia.[8] He describes her as follows:

> Quintia is considered 'beautiful' by many. Me? I find her fair, tall, and well put together. While I note each of them I deny that the overall effect is 'beautiful' for she has no elegance, not so much of a speck of it in all her mighty form. Lesbia IS beautiful, she who is imbued with so much loveliness, that it seems she has stolen the share of every woman for herself.[9]

It is worth noting that here he is comparing Quintia directly to his paramour Lesbia, so of course she is going to be found wanting. However, during Fulvia's third marriage, to Antony, one of the freedmen (a formerly enslaved person who had been manumitted and granted Roman citizenship) of her first husband Clodius' family, the Sicilian teacher of Greek and Latin oratory Sextus Clodius – a man renowned for his sharp tongue – made a snide witticism at her expense. He said 'she tempts the point of my pen', meaning both that he was tempted to write a comic epigram about her and that he was tempted to stab her in the face with his stylus, since on this particular occasion one of her cheeks was swollen.[10] Not the most flattering insight into Fulvia's physical appearance – maybe on this occasion she was suffering from a toothache?

Simultaneously, Sextus was perhaps tapping into a seam of Classical Greek misogyny in which women were viewed as wax tablets ready and waiting to receive the imprint of men, with penises commensurately viewed as styli. So, in essence, Sextus was imagining Fulvia performing fellatio on him, hence her cheek becoming swollen because her mouth was full.[11] In favour of this interpretation is the fact that this is one rare occasion where Cicero seems to have entertained a modicum of sympathy towards her, since he criticized Antony for allowing Sextus so much leeway in making jokes at his and his associates' expense, even if he did to all intents and purposes say that Sextus was shooting fish in a barrel since, in his opinion, there was so much to joke about.

Roman mothers were in charge of their children's education during the early years of childhood.[12] Consequently, educating a daughter who would grow up to be a wife and mother responsible for educating her own children made sense.[13] Roman education not only comprised basics such as literacy and numeracy, but also, for members of the elite equestrian and senatorial classes, what was known as *paideia*, the sort of well-rounded liberal arts education that would turn a child into an ideal citizen. Considering the ease with which Fulvia would move in high society later in her life, and her successful endeavours in political and military matters, it is likely that she received an education that enabled her to go toe to toe with her male peers in debates and discussions. The age gap between Fulvia and her brother Natta was too large for her to have benefited from the expertise of his tutors, so she would have had her own, selected and purchased especially for her.

Atticus arranged both an enslaved *paedagogus* and a freedman *grammaticus*, Quintus Caecilius Epirota (who would later gain renown for being the first person to teach Virgil's poetry), for his only child, his daughter Caecilia Attica.[14] However, Epirota was dismissed after behaving inappropriately towards his charge as she aged.[15] Pompey's daughter Pompeia, whose mother Mucia was a friend of Fulvia's, likewise had a tutor who taught her Greek and read the *Iliad* with her.[16] This tutor may well have been Aristodemus of Nysa, who taught Mucia's two sons Gnaeus and Sextus grammar and rhetoric.[17] There is evidence that particularly valued members of certain households were loaned out to family members and friends as needed.[18]

It was thought by some that it was easier for women to retain a true Roman accent in their Latin speech – that is to say an old-fashioned one – since their relative social isolation meant that they would come into contact with fewer unfamiliar accents and dialects that might influence them, and they would not necessarily have undergone the oratorical training that their male relatives would have received that would have imparted a veneer of Greek-style sophistication. What this would have sounded like is unclear, although wistful comparisons with the mid-Republican playwrights Plautus and Naevius were made. Cicero writes of Lucius Licinius Crassus describing his mother Laelia's speech in such a way:

> The actual sound of her voice is so unaffected and natural that she seems to introduce no trace of display or affectation; and I consequently infer that that was how her father and her ancestors used to speak – not harshly... nor with a broad or countrified or jerky pronunciation, but neatly and evenly and smoothly.[19]

Laelia's speech was also praised by Quintilian, for, despite her unspoiled Roman accent, she apparently echoed her father's elegance.[20] She seems to have inculcated this quality in her own daughters and granddaughters.[21]

It may be that Bambalio, having struggled with his own speech, was determined that Fulvia would not, and took especial care to have her instructed in oratory and rhetoric, like her cousin Hortensia, although these were not typical subjects for girls.[22] Her stepfather Murena had famously been awarded an intellectual named Tyrannion as his prize for the successful capture of the city of Amisus and then promptly emancipated him, whereby he became a scholar in Rome, dividing his time between teaching and cataloguing the library of Apellicon that had been acquired by Sulla, so he may well have contributed to Fulvia's education.[23] The fact that Fulvia's two sons with Antony were given names loaded with mythological and historical resonance implies that she was familiar with Graeco-Roman literature and culture, both seminal works such as Homer's *Iliad* and *Odyssey* and the Epic Cycle, and the sort of Roman foundation myths that would be pulled together by Virgil to comprise his *Aeneid*, written in the years immediately following her death.

Additionally, in the case of daughters, it was considered crucial that they know how to successfully manage a household and everyone in it, as marriage was virtually inevitable. Fulvia would have been encouraged to follow Sempronia around as she went about her duties and learn from her example, overseeing the household staff of enslaved men and women, and emancipated men and women who still retained their connections to the family. Based on later accounts of Sempronia's continuing presence in Fulvia's life after her first marriage, especially at dramatic moments, it appears that the two were close.[24] Artistic representations of women and their children frequently show daughters aping their mothers in their hair and clothing choices, implying that the little girls were encouraged to be miniature versions of their mothers, as in one marble sculpture dating from around 50–40 BCE.

Roman children were encouraged to develop self-control, and girls in particular were encouraged to develop modesty, restraint and reserve. Judging by later accounts of her behaviour, which depict her as rather serious and thoughtful, and Antony as attempting to lighten her mood, Fulvia took at least some of these lessons to heart. The most important personal quality for a Roman girl to learn was *pudicitia*, 'sexual morality'.[25] While this was concerned first and foremost with virginity and chastity before marriage and fidelity after it, it also encompassed numerous other areas of a girl or woman's life. In order to display *pudicitia*, a woman did not necessarily need to remain inside her home at all times, but she definitely should not make unnecessary appearances in public, and when she did go out, she should do so only with certain people, and in a manner that involved walking, talking and dressing

A marble statue of a Roman woman and her daughter.

in a modest way. And the same was true of the reverse situation: if a woman was at home, she should only be visited by certain people, preferably other women rather than men, as being visited by men who were not members of either her or her husband's family could call her *pudicitia* into question. Many statues of Roman women are posed in such a way that their entire bodies, with the exception of their faces and hands, are swathed in the fabrics of their tunics and mantles – this is a demonstration of their *pudicitia*.

This issue of *pudicitia* and whether a girl or woman did or did not possess it lies at the heart of the later negative portrayals of Fulvia, as she was certainly not the type of girl or woman to only appear in public when absolutely necessary, nor was she the type of girl or woman to restrict her circle of acquaintance to predominantly female family members. When women went so far as to speak in public before an audience, it was a notable occasion. Valerius Maximus records several instances of 'women whose natural condition and the modesty of the matron's robe could not make them keep silent in the Forum and the courts of law'.[26] Of the women he mentions, he notes that Maesia of Sentinum 'bore a man's spirit under the form of a woman', and so earned the nickname Androgyne, and Carfania 'had impudence to spare'.[27] Unfortunately, we know nothing else about either of them.

Therefore, we might compare Fulvia to a young girl named Minicia Marcella, whose death was recorded in a letter sent from Pliny the Younger to his friend Aefulanus Marcellinus, and whose funerary altar (carved to match her mother's) has also survived. While this description dates to over a century after Fulvia's death, it offers an insight into the expectations placed upon young Roman girls:

> I never saw a girl so gay and lovable, so deserving of a longer life or even a life to last for ever. She had not yet reached the age of fourteen, and yet she combined the wisdom of age and dignity of womanhood with the sweetness and modesty of youth and innocence. She would cling to her father's neck, and embrace us, his friends, with modest affection; she loved

her nurses, her attendants and her teachers, each one for the service given her; she applied herself intelligently to her books and was moderate and restrained in her play. She bore her last illness with patient resignation and, indeed, with courage; she obeyed her doctors' orders, cheered her sister and father, and by sheer force of will carried on after her physical strength had failed her. This will power remained with her to the end, and neither the length of her illness nor fear of death could break it. So she has left us all the more sad reasons for lamenting our loss. Hers is a truly tragic and untimely end – death itself was not so cruel as the moment of its coming.[28]

Roman girls from the equestrian and senatorial classes were prepared for advantageous marriages from an early age.[29] These marriages were generally arranged by their fathers (hopefully after some consultation with their mothers and, in very enlightened households, with the girls themselves) as a means of directly benefiting him through the acquisition of political or financial clout.[30] While Bambalio did not have any political clout himself and, as someone who was not following a traditional career path up the *cursus honorum*, did not necessarily need to acquire it, marriage to his daughter would not have been desirable for an ambitious young Roman on those grounds. What Bambalio had going for him (and what Sempronia had going for her, independently of her husband) was wealth. Since Fulvia was the last scion of two wealthy families, and Roman daughters were not disinherited on the grounds of their gender but entitled to equal shares of their parents' wealth, her dowry and subsequent inheritance would have been substantial and very enticing for a young man hoping to embark on his career. The costs of pursuing a Roman political career were steep, and many Romans accrued enormous debts in the process, hoping to rise high enough that they would eventually be allocated a wealthy province that they could asset-strip to pay their creditors back in full.

Fulvia could anticipate her marriage occurring in her early to mid-teenage years, once she had entered puberty and started menstruating and was thus considered ready to bear children. Her contemporary Tullia, the daughter of Cicero and Terentia, was betrothed for the first time at the age of thirteen, while another contemporary, Caecilia Attica, the daughter of Atticus, was betrothed for the first time even earlier, at the age of six.[31] So it is likely that Fulvia's parents were thinking about arranging her betrothal and marriage by the mid to late 60s BCE, and looking around for suitable candidates. Roman senatorial and equestrian husbands were usually around ten years older than their prospective first wives, since they tended to marry only after they had taken their first steps on the *cursus honorum* and undertaken a period of military service or been to university. However, at times the age gaps could be considerable, as in the case of the marriage of Caesar's daughter Julia and Pompey the Great, which took place when Julia was around sixteen and Pompey was around forty-seven (it was his fourth marriage), or the marriage of Cicero and Publilia, which took place when Publilia was in her teens and Cicero in his sixties (it was his second marriage). Fulvia was lucky in this respect – her first husband, Publius Clodius Pulcher, was not so much older than she was. Betrothals were celebrated with a ceremony called a *sponsalium*, which was hosted by the bride's father, so Bambalio would have hosted one for Fulvia, and Clodius would have gifted Fulvia with a plain iron engagement ring.[32]

When Roman boys became men, at some point between the ages of fourteen and sixteen, there were formal proceedings. They shaved for the first time and dedicated their facial hair to the household gods. Then they took off their *toga praetexta*, the toga of childhood worn by both boys and girls with an apotropaic purple stripe along the edge, and exchanged it for the *toga virilis*, the toga of manhood worn only by men (the only adult women who wore togas were sex workers). They then went with their father, or another close male relative if their father was for some reason unavailable, down to the Forum to symbolize the fact that they were now an adult citizen and so able to vote in elections. For Roman girls, the transition to womanhood was less regimented. Once they began to menstruate, they were ready to be married, and once the marriage was arranged, on the night before the wedding, they would dedicate their *toga praetexta*, dolls and other childish things to the household gods. Many little girls played with dolls that were the ancient equivalent of Barbie, in the form of adult women with extensive wardrobes of clothing and jewellery, such as the one found in the sarcophagus of Crepereia Tryphaena, currently on display in Palazzo Massimo museum in Rome. However, some preferred to play with dolls modelled after the mythological warrior women the Amazons – perhaps Fulvia was one such bellicose little girl.[33] So it was, quite literally, getting married that turned a Roman girl into a Roman woman.[34] And in the case of Fulvia, it was her marriages that made her a woman that Roman authors considered worth writing about.

For most of the Republic, Roman marriages between citizens had been *cum manu*, 'with the power of *manus*', with the wife moving from the *patria potestas* of her father to the *patria potestas* of her husband, essentially transferring her from her father's family to her husband's family and rendering her – and her dowry – completely under her new husband's power.[35] However, in the last years of the Republic, the very time during which Fulvia was marrying her three husbands, things began to change and marriages were being contracted *sine manu*, 'without *manus*', meaning that the woman remained under the *patria potestas* of her father and part of his family. This was preferable by far, since it meant that if her father happened to die (and considering the age gap between husbands and wives, this was more than likely), she was no longer under the power of anyone and could legally manage her own financial affairs, albeit with the oversight of a tutor. Considering that Fulvia was an heiress twice over, it would have suited her family, and no doubt her, for her to keep control of her own finances. This would have enabled her to wield much more influence in all three of her marriages, and with respect to her children's futures. In Roman marriage portraits, the husband and wife are often depicted holding hands, a gesture known as *dextrarum iunctio*, as a symbol of marital *concordia*, 'concord'.

It was standard practice for elite women to enter marriage with a dowry, and something of a stereotype that a woman with a sizeable dowry would use it to dominate and henpeck her husband.[36] Bambalio would have set aside a considerable sum for Fulvia, especially since she was marrying into one of the most aristocratic families in Rome. It would likely have comprised land, property and probably even some portable components – family heirlooms such as silverware and jewellery. Cicero's first wife Terentia's dowry included rental properties on the Argiletum, a lane running past the Forum that was renowned for its bookshops, and on the Aventine Hill in Rome, as well as woodland and pastureland in Antium (an area south of Rome, near the modern Anzio) and a number of enslaved people.[37]

The Tivoli Hoard, named after its purported find-spot, which was the location of many luxury Roman villas, is a collection of silver dating to the mid-first century BCE that may have been buried in response to the upheaval of the civil wars. It comprises thirty pieces of tableware, each inscribed with the name 'Sattia, daughter of Lucius' and the weight of the item, which could have been part of the otherwise-unknown Sattia's dowry, with the inscriptions an attempt to safeguard the integrity of each piece.[38] A strict contract would have been drawn up to dictate exactly what should happen to the dowry's components under a range of circumstances. While the dowry passed to the husband, the proceeds from it were intended to keep the wife in the manner to which she was accustomed. If Fulvia was married *sine manu*, and the marriage ended in divorce or the death of her husband, the dowry would either revert back to her father or, if he predeceased her husband, to her, making her financially independent (subject to the technical oversight of a legal guardian). Some men even made their sons-in-law their legal heirs so as to facilitate passing their wealth on to their daughters in the event of their premature deaths – a means of protecting their inheritances from acquisitive distant relations.[39]

In the absence of formal ways to show off their position and prestige, women used informal ones such as their clothing and jewellery to communicate their wealth and status, not to mention their taste and sophistication. This applied both to living women and, sadly, to dead ones, as Pliny's description of the circumstances of Minicia Marcella's

Several pieces of silverware from the Tivoli Hoard

death and its aftermath makes clear – the money that would have been spent on her bridal trousseau was instead redirected to her funerary rites, essentially preparing her for a union with the god of the Underworld, Hades/Pluto, rather than her original fiancé. Archaeological evidence in the form of elaborate and luxurious burials for very young girls containing the accoutrements of the women they never grew up to be supports Pliny's ruminations.[40]

As a wealthy heiress, Fulvia would have been dressed in the finest bridal costume available in ancient Rome, its components sourced from the luxury boutiques that lined the Sacred Way, housing gold and silversmiths and jewellers in the centre of the city. The most distinctive part of it was the veil, the *flammeum*, which was a deep shade of yellow.[41] Pliny the Elder describes the colour in the same terms as he does egg yolk, which gives us a sense of just how warm and rich the yellow tone was.[42] This colour was worn exclusively by brides and the *flaminica Dialis*, the wife of the *flamen Dialis*, the priest of Jupiter, the most important religious role that a woman could aspire to, apart from being selected to be one of the six Vestal Virgins.[43] It is notable that the *flaminica Dialis* was not permitted to divorce her husband, and so she remained his wife and priestess for as long as they both lived, so this link represented a lasting marriage.

The veil would be placed on top of a wreath of flowers and herbs which the bride was expected to pick herself.[44] One of the herbs would be the aromatic marjoram, which was particularly associated with Venus, the goddess of love, sex and passion.[45] For the first time, the bride's hair would not be worn long and loose, but tied back with ribbons as it would be worn from now on for the rest of her life. It would be parted with a spearhead in preparation for being arranged into the *seni crines* ('six tresses') hairstyle, only worn by brides and Vestal Virgins.[46] The bride's tunic would have been especially woven on an upright loom, and tied with a chastity belt fastened with a Hercules knot for her husband to undo on the wedding night, to ensure many children would be forthcoming. Her shoes would, like her veil, be yellow. A fresco from the Villa of the Mysteries just outside Pompeii shows this ritual preparation for marriage (see fig 3). A female attendant begins the special arrangement of the bride's hair, while beside the seated bride Eros holds up a mirror to show her reflection. She is wearing a yellow gown, probably dyed with saffron, bound with a cloth belt that is tied in a Hercules knot.

What might Fulvia have hoped for from her marriage? Just because it had been arranged by her parents, it did not necessarily follow that she would have had no expectations of mutual affection – even passion – at all. One verse attributed to an anonymous Vestal Virgin proclaims, 'How happy married women are! O, may I die if marriage is not sweet!'[47] The poet Martial refers to his peer Sulpicia, whose erotic poetry focused on her husband of fifteen years Calenus, and advises: 'Let all girls who wish to please one man read Sulpicia. Let all husbands who wish to please one bride read Sulpicia... She tells of pure and lawful love, playful caprice and merriment. A good judge of her verses will say there was never a girl more roguish or more virtuous.'[48] In the one fragment of her poetry that survives, Sulpicia writes about her wish to be lying in bed with him post-coital, both of them replete and content.[49] In point of fact, it was believed that the female orgasm was necessary to ensure conception, so it was in the Roman husband's interest to satisfy his wife sexually if he wished to continue his line. Fulvia seems to have found happiness, satisfaction and fulfilment in her first marriage, and it set the standard for her subsequent marriages and the way that she chose to live the rest of her life.

CHAPTER 4

THE IDEAL
ROMAN WOMAN?

B EFORE WE EXPLORE FULVIA's life as a married women, let's look
at what expectations would have been placed on her by Roman
society – as for the Romans, there was such a thing as an 'ideal' woman,
and we know a considerable amount about who (or rather what)
they considered this ideal woman to be, because they wrote about
it. Extensively. There were three examples of women from ancient
Roman history (or rather mythology, as it is uncertain whether any
of these women truly existed) who were particularly feted, and these
were Lucretia, Verginia and Claudia Quinta.[1] All three were believed
to have embodied the supreme womanly virtues of *pudicitia* (modesty)
and *castitas* (chastity).

Lucretia is believed to have lived towards the end of the period
where Rome was still a monarchy, ruled by the Tarquin dynasty, and
her death is considered to have been the catalyst for the overthrow
of this dynasty and the establishment of the Republic in 509 BCE. I
say 'believed' because there are no contemporary historical sources that

record any of this. The definitive accounts of Lucretia were written by the Roman historian Livy and the Greek historian Dionysius of Halicarnassus some five hundred years later, towards the end of the first century BCE.[2] They were doing so at a time when female behaviour was coming under an increasing amount of scrutiny and being subjected to considerable formal legal restriction by the first Roman emperor Augustus (previously known as Octavian, Fulvia's enemy and the rival of her third husband, Antony).

According to the sources, Lucretia was the daughter of the magistrate Spurius Lucretius and the wife of Lucius Tarquinius Collatinus, and she was devoted to her husband and a paragon of female virtue. On one occasion, while off on a military campaign against the neighbouring Rutulians and laying siege to the city of Ardea about twenty-two miles south-east of Rome, a bored Collatinus entered into a drunken wager with several of his friends, one of whom, Sextus Tarquinius, was the son of the king Lucius Tarquinius Superbus. He bet that he had the most virtuous wife of all of them. Sure enough, after saddling their horses and taking the short ride home to Collatia, they found the blonde-haired and pale-skinned Lucretia weaving by lamplight (according to Ovid, she was fretting over Collatinus' absence and making a cloak to keep him warm on campaign), whereas all the other wives were taking advantage of the absence of their husbands to misbehave, enjoying an elaborate banquet with free-flowing wine.

Subsequently, Tarquin became consumed with jealousy, and desire both for Lucretia's virtue and for its destruction. He secretly returned to Collatinus' house, propositioned Lucretia and attempted to seduce her, alternating between threats of violence and declarations of love. When that failed, he resorted to blackmail and coercion: she could either have sex with him, or he would kill her and one of the household slaves and place their naked bodies in bed together, claiming that he had caught her in the act of committing adultery – as a relative of her husband, in Collatinus' absence, legally Tarquin was entitled to do this. If committing adultery was bad, committing adultery with an enslaved person was abhorrent. Under duress, Lucretia acquiesced. The day after the rape, dressed in funereal black, she informed her father and husband, in front of witnesses that included Lucius Junius Brutus (the legendary ancestor of Marcus Junius Brutus, one of the ringleaders in the conspiracy to assassinate Caesar), what had happened. She declared that while her body had sinned, her mind remained pure, and then, retrieving a knife she had hidden on her person in preparation, she stabbed herself to death.

Rather gruesomely, Brutus pulled the knife out of Lucretia's chest and all the men present swore an oath on the bloody and gory blade to drive the Tarquins out of Rome, abolish the monarchy and establish a Republic. They displayed the piteous spectacle of Lucretia's violated and bloodstained body in the Forum, stoking popular outrage against the Tarquins, and began a revolution. Their efforts were led by Brutus, and once they had met with success and established the Republic, he and Collatinus became the first pair of consuls. More than one ancient commentator praised Lucretia for being in possession of a manly soul inside a woman's body, and ordinary women were encouraged to view her as an example to follow.

Verginia is believed to have lived around fifty years later, by which time the Republic had devolved into an oligarchy ruled by the *decemvirs*, a council of ten, and her story is similar to Lucretia's. The historian Livy, where the account of this episode comes from, deliberately flags this similarity at the outset.[3] Verginia was the daughter of a plebeian Roman citizen and centurion named Lucius Verginius, and was engaged to the former tribune of the *plebs* Lucius Icilius when the patrician senator Appius Claudius Crassus Inregillensis Sabinus became enamoured of her. Just as Lucretia had rejected Tarquin, so too did Verginia reject Appius Claudius. And like Tarquin, Appius Claudius refused to accept this. He schemed with one of his clients, a man named Marcus Claudius, and had Marcus abduct Verginia while she was on her way to school, claiming that she was actually his slave. Since both Verginia's father and fiancé were well-known and well-respected men, this turned out not to be as straightforward as Appius Claudius had thought it would be, and the matter ended up in court.

Yet here Appius Claudius, sitting as judge, used his superior power and status to silence Lucius Verginius. Unable to plead his case, Verginius resorted to hacking Verginia to death with a meat cleaver he snatched up from a butcher's stall at the nearby shrine of Venus Cloacina (the goddess who presided over the Cloaca Maxima, Rome's great sewer) as he felt that killing her was the only way to protect her freedom and chastity.[4] Once again, the bloodstained body of a beautiful and blameless young woman was displayed to the crowd to engender sympathy and outrage and effect some sort of political change. On this occasion, it is notable that the reactions of the women in the crowd are included in the reports, which emphasize their anguish, tears, and cries of 'Is it on these terms that children are brought into the world? Are these the rewards of chastity?' Verginius and Icilius were then arrested, but their supporters rioted, overthrew the government and re-established the Republic.

Finally, Claudia Quinta was a woman – in some accounts an aristocratic matron, in others a Vestal Virgin – living at the time of the Second Punic War (218–201 BCE), Rome's second conflict with Carthage.[5] By 204 BCE, the war was not going well for Rome, the annual harvest had failed, and the omens and prodigies were dire. So, the Romans sought the help of Cybele, also known as Magna Mater, the 'Great Mother' goddess. Her cult statue was transferred from Asia Minor (modern Turkey) to Rome, but the ship that was transporting it ran aground on a sandbank in the Tiber. Claudia had been the victim of scurrilous gossip questioning her virtue, but she stepped forward and prayed to the goddess for help, with Ovid helpfully reconstructing her words for us:

> 'Thou fruitful Mother of the Gods, graciously accept thy suppliant's prayers on one condition. They say I am not chaste. If thou dost condemn me, I will confess my guilt; convicted by the verdict of a goddess, I will pay the penalty with my life. But if I am free of crime, give by thine act a proof of my innocency, and, chaste as thou art, do thou yield to my chaste hands.'[6]

Her prayers concluded, Claudia anointed herself with river water, then released the ship and towed it the rest of the way using her girdle, thereby proving not only her own personal piety, virtue and chastity, but also the goddess's willingness to come to Rome. Once the statue of the goddess (and the goddess herself, by Roman reckoning) was installed, Rome had a good harvest and managed to defeat the Carthaginians definitively. By way of thanks, Claudia's great deed was re-enacted at the Megalensia, the annual festival to the Great Mother held every 4–10 April, and a statue of her was set up in the vestibule of the Temple of Magna Mater on the Palatine Hill. It miraculously survived the burning of the temple not once but twice, first in 111 BCE and again in 3 CE.[7]

Conversely, there were women in ancient Roman history (or mythology) who were reviled for their vices, and feared for how they exposed Rome's vulnerabilities. First and foremost amongst these was Tarpeia, the daughter of Spurius Tarpeius, the commander of the citadel on the Capitoline Hill in the early years of Rome, in the eighth century BCE.[8] Tarpeia, as a Vestal Virgin, should have been a paragon of virtue and a figure whom all Roman womanhood could aspire to be like. Unfortunately, she was consumed by avarice, and betrayed Rome and the Romans to their enemies out of the base emotions of lust and greed – and what is worse is that she did this while enacting her religious duties. When the Sabine king Titus Tatius declared war on Rome in response to Romulus and the Romans' mass seizure of Sabine women to help populate their fledgling settlement, Tarpeia went outside to draw water from the spring of the Camenae for the purification of the Temple of Vesta.[9] Encountering Titus, she opened the Porta Pandana gate to let him and his army into the city. Explanations as to her motivation vary: she did so either because she desired Titus Tatius or because she desired the Sabine jewellery – the gold rings and bracelets that the soldiers wore on their left arms – going so far as to request 'what they bore on their arms' as payment for her assistance.[10] Unfortunately for her, she was not specific enough and the Sabines took her rather literally, proceeding to crush her to death under the weight of their immense shields. Not to be outdone in the pursuit of sheer pettiness, the Romans buried her at the site that subsequently became known as the Tarpeian Rock, a steep cliff on the south side of the Capitoline Hill, and proceeded to use this location as a method of execution for those convicted of capital crimes – not only other traitors but also the most notorious murderers, perjurers and larcenous slaves – hurling them from the top of the cliff down into the valley below.[11] They also depicted her fate on the reverse face of coins, variously showing her either being tortured by the Sabines and their shields or being buried up to her waist in a pile of them. The former design was issued on a silver denarius in 89 BCE by Lucius Titurius Sabinus, the latter on a silver denarius in 19 BCE by Augustus.[12]

Silver denarii depicting the fate of Tarpeia (the two on the left show the denarius issued by Lucius Titurius Sabinus, the two on the right that of Augustus)

It is important to note that ancient Roman historians did not view historiography the way that we do today – it was not necessarily a scholarly endeavour that was the product of hours of careful research and the close examination of sources and evidence in order to get as close to the factual accuracy of what happened as possible, but rather a means of using the past to inspire their contemporaries by providing moral exempla for them to follow. This was true of both men and women, and the three aforementioned virtuous women were held up as examples for women to follow (while Tarpeia was an example for them to avoid). There is some evidence that at least some of them did so in all seriousness. See for example a marble altar dedicated to the Great Mother goddess by a woman named Claudia Synthyche during the first century CE.[13] It was discovered on the bank of the Tiber in the early eighteenth

A marble altar dedicated to the Great Mother goddess by a woman named Claudia Synthyche, circa first century CE

century, and it references Claudia Quinta's triumph and bears a relief depicting it.[14] On the right of the relief we see Claudia Quinta – modestly covered from head to toe in the *stola* (a traditional long dress that was worn over a tunic, reaching from the shoulders down to the feet) and the *palla* (a mantle that was worn wrapped around the body and covering the head), the costume of the Roman matron – using her girdle to tow the ship bearing the cult statue of Cybele up the Tiber to Rome. Claudia Synthyche may have believed herself to be a descendant of Claudia Quinta, or she may simply have been inspired by the story.

How realistic, not to mention accurate, is this ideal? Surviving literary, documentary, archaeological and bioarchaeological evidence suggests that real women were far more complex and multifaceted than their male counterparts would have us believe. And indeed, not all men were necessarily desirous of a paragon of virtue: in one poem, the epigrammatist Martial declares to his wife, 'You may be Lucretia all day: at night I want Lais', calling to mind Jerry Hall's famous quote regarding the marital advice that she was given by her mother: 'To keep a man, you must be a maid in the living room, a cook in the kitchen and a whore in the bedroom.'[15]

Many epitaphs of women highlight the success with which the woman being commemorated fulfilled the traditional roles of wife, mother and housekeeper. One example from the second century BCE illustrates this perfectly in its brevity and simplicity:

> Friend, I have not much to say, stop and read it. This tomb, which is not fair, is for a fair woman. Her parents gave her the name Claudia. She loved her husband in her heart. She bore two sons, one of whom she left on the earth, the other beneath it. She was pleasant to talk with. She walked with grace. She kept the house. She worked in wool. That is all. You may go.[16]

The distillation of these virtues is expressed in the practice of using cinerary urns carved to look like wicker wool baskets (or bread baskets, in the case of the baker Eurysaces' wife Atistia, although this

A marble cinerary urn shaped like a wool basket, circa 10 BCE

has unfortunately been lost) to hold the ashes of respectable Roman matrons.[17]

However, other epitaphs such as the famous *Laudatio Turiae* and the *Laudatio Murdiae*, the latter commemorating a woman named Murdia and set up by her son, go much further in their coverage of these women's lives and works. What these 'ideal' women actually reveal are the ancient Roman male anxieties about women and their behaviour, hence the attempts to control and limit them that were enshrined in ancient Roman law through institutions like *patria potestas*, *manus* and guardianship. *Patria potestas*, the 'power of the father', was the power that the *pater familias*, the 'father of the family', exercised over his children (including adopted children) and descendants through the male line until his death, and it is often referred to as literal power over life and death. It was only upon the patriarch's death or decision to relinquish that power and allow emancipation that women could become *sui iuris*, 'independent'. Women remained under the *patria potestas* of their *pater familias* unless he transferred them to the control of their husband by way of marriage that included *manus*.

There were three types of Roman marriage, and the types that included entry into *manus* – the power that a husband held over his wife and all her property – were *confarreatio*, named after the sacramental loaf that was part of this religious ceremony; *coemptio*, 'purchase', which was a legal procedure that involved an imaginary sale; and *usus*, 'prescription', which was a more practical procedure in which a couple lived together without interruption for a period of one year (although this could be circumvented if the wife spent three consecutive nights away from her husband). By the end of the Republic, marriage with *manus* had become relatively uncommon, but women who were *sui iuris* and married without *manus* still required a guardian to oversee their affairs, which rather curtailed their independence.

Theoretically, men could use this power over women to enforce female morality, and ancient Roman historians and antiquarians delight in relating stories of men forcing women to pay the ultimate price for perceived transgressions. The Late Antique miscellanist Aulus

Gellius discusses a speech given by Cato the Elder in his capacity as censor with responsibility for enforcing senatorial morality in 184 BCE, entitled 'On the Dowry', in which he stated that a husband has the ultimate authority to punish his wife 'if she has done something perverse and awful', whether drinking wine without permission or committing adultery, and the penalties range in severity all the way up to and including killing her.[18] The inequality and incapacity that resulted were somewhat hypocritical, considering the uses that Roman men made of women, commandeering their superior social status, family connections, wealth and other resources – and in some cases even weaponizing these against them. For example, Cicero was happy to borrow money from a female friend of his named Caerellia, no matter how unseemly friends such as Atticus (about whom we shall hear more in due course) or other acquaintances thought being indebted to a woman was, and no matter how much he himself judged other men for borrowing money from women, simply because he desperately needed the cash.[19] In hostile accounts of specific and general female behaviour we often see the deliberate misconstruing of normal behaviour for the purpose of constructing an argument that hinges on character assassination. Returning to Caerellia, one presumably unanticipated consequence of her friendship and business relationship with Cicero was an accusation from Quintus Fufius Calenus, made in front of the entire Senate, that Cicero had debauched her, and that he had set aside a much younger wife in order to have his wicked way with a more mature mistress.[20] So even the fact that she was considerably older than Cicero at the time of the loan and their other business dealings (he was in his sixties, so she must have been in her seventies at the very least, or even eighties) did not spare her.

Additionally, we frequently see the coding of 'female' as negative, with men likening other men to women and accusing them of effeminacy in invective, much as one might use the terms 'bitch' or 'pussy' to excoriate a man for supposedly being unmanly today. Since the Romans were very keen on gender conformity, the reverse is also true. When men wanted to cast aspersions on a woman, she was frequently described as being unwomanly, as in not conforming to the ideal woman described above. The most extensive and detailed example of this in ancient Roman invective can be found in the orator Cicero's speech in defence of his protégé Marcus Caelius Rufus, generally referred to today as the *Pro Caelio*. Although Caelius was being prosecuted for his involvement in the murders of the members of an embassy from Alexandria who opposed the restoration of Egypt's dissolute King Ptolemy XII, Cicero argued that the prosecution was the result of a scheme hatched by a woman named Clodia with whom the young man had had an affair, and he claimed she was a woman scorned and proceeded to undertake a systematic character assassination of her.[21] Cicero's strategy worked, and Caelius was acquitted.

Clodia was Fulvia's sister-in-law, the older sister of her first husband Clodius, and it is clear that the two women had much in common, both in their apparently transgressive behaviour and in the way that behaviour was used against them. Considering that Fulvia was a woman who married three times, bore those three husbands five children who lived to adulthood, and ran a series not just of individual households but of extensive estates successfully, thereby fulfilling the primary duties expected of a Roman matron more than competently, negative assessments of her are clearly not entirely fair. But when it comes to their opinions of women, ancient Roman authors are frequently not entirely fair, and are often actively unfair for specific reasons. For example, the genre that someone was working in exerted a considerable amount of influence over both the broad brushstrokes and the minutiae of the portrayal – think of the pairing of the cruel mistress and enslaved beloved in Roman elegiac poetry, found in the work of Propertius, Tibullus and Ovid, in which they rhapsodize about their lovers Cynthia, Delia and Corinna respectively.

Regarding Fulvia, most of the references to her are found in historiography, and all but two of the ancient Roman authors who mention her do so in a negative and critical manner, although their negativity and criticism is not only about her, but also about the men that they are able to attack using her – namely her first husband, Clodius, and her third husband, Antony, and on occasion her brother-in-law Lucius Antonius Pietas, because the conduct of Roman women was considered to reflect either well or badly on their male relations. The possibility that women like Fulvia wielded undue influence over their men was an efficient way of criticizing not only the women for unwomanly conduct, but also the men for unmanly conduct. If the woman was dominant, it followed that the man was submissive, and this was a subversion, even perversion, of the natural order of things.[22] It is a crying shame that we are not in possession of a *Laudatio Fulviae*, an epitaph of Fulvia set up by her husband or one of her sons, that could give us a more three-dimensional portrait of this complex and complicated woman and offer us an alternative perspective on her motivations and actions, not only as a wife but also as a mother over the course of the next two decades. Because it was in her role as a wife and mother that Fulvia would truly excel.

CHAPTER 5

FULVIA AS A WIFE

Publius Clodius Pulcher (*CIRCA* 93–52 BCE) was beautiful by name and, if not exactly beautiful by nature, at least beautiful in appearance. His *cognomen*, *pulcher*, means 'beautiful/handsome' in Latin, and Cicero, for one, referred to him as *pulchellus*, 'pretty boy', in private correspondence addressed to his close friend Atticus.[1] While Cicero was perhaps simply being unpleasant, since he was no fan of Clodius, it is fair to say that Clodius was able to disguise himself as a woman convincingly enough in order to enter the Regia, the *pontifex maximus* (chief priest) Caesar's house during the women-only rites of the Bona Dea festival in 62 BCE, so he may well have been fine-featured.[2] It was probably this escapade, and the notoriety that resulted from it, that Fulvia had to thank for facilitating her marriage. Although at the conclusion of Clodius' trial for sacrilege, he was found not guilty, Cicero, who had testified against him and contested his alibi, believed that he had simply bribed the jury to ensure an acquittal.[3] There certainly seems to have been a general consensus that he was guilty, both at the time and in the years following, as over 150 years later the poet Juvenal mentioned the incident in his satire devoted to Roman women, saying that even people from Africa and India had heard of the escapade, and he commented on the apparently rather impressive size of Clodius' penis for good measure.[4]

It is possible that the taint of sacrilege (not to mention adultery, corruption and violence) that clung to Clodius afterwards made him unappealing as a possible spouse for the daughters of most of the Roman elite. In light of this, Fulvia's mother, Sempronia, and stepfather, Murena, saw an opportunity to make a match for Fulvia that was better than any her father, Bambalio, and his minimal connections and social cachet could manage.[5] Murena's links with Clodius went back to their service in the East under Lucullus in the Third Mithridatic War, during the late 70s and early 60s BCE, and in 64 BCE Clodius had served on Murena's staff in Transalpine Gaul, before being a prominent supporter in his election campaign for consul in 63 BCE. Still a teenager, Fulvia may well have been impressed and intrigued by Clodius, his racy reputation, and the fast and fashionable company he kept. Additionally, having witnessed her mother's tenure as wife of a consul during the upheaval of 63–62 BCE, starting with the Catilinarian Conspiracy and ending with the Bona Dea Scandal, and the soft power that could be wielded by the wife of an influential husband – as people sought to gain her favour as a discreet means of gaining his – Fulvia was no doubt pondering how she could make her marriage work just as well. For Clodius, the marriage offered not only close links with the current consul but also access to a considerable amount of money, in the form of Fulvia's dowry, that could be used to fund his political career. If he really had just spent a lot of money bribing the jurors at his trial to ensure his acquittal, an infusion of cash would have been most welcome.[6]

Clodius was a member of the ancient patrician aristocratic Claudian clan.[7] Many of his ancestors had served pivotal roles in Roman history from the very earliest years of the Republic in the late sixth century BCE. Perhaps the most famous was Appius Claudius Caecus, the highlights of whose career are known from an inscription that accompanied an honorific statue of him set up in the Forum during the Augustan

Principate.[8] He was elected censor in 312 BCE, consul in 307 BCE and 296 BCE, and commissioned the building of the Via Appia, the road leading from Rome to Capua, and the Aqua Appia, the city of Rome's first aqueduct. However, he was far from the only illustrious member of the family. According to Suetonius, the family held twenty-eight consulships, five dictatorships, seven censorships, six triumphs, and two ovations over the course of the Republic.[9] Thus Clodius' family name was quite literally inscribed into the very fabric of Roman history, culture and society. Perhaps it is not surprising that they were perceived by their peers as arrogant and superior.[10]

Clodius' father had been elected consul in 79 BCE, when Clodius, his youngest son, would have been about fourteen years old, but died several years later while abroad in the Roman province of Macedonia. It is possible that their father's death left the six siblings with something of a cash flow problem, at least in the short term, as Varro's *On Agriculture*, written in around 50 BCE, refers to the family as needing to economize in the wake of the patriarch's death, but this could be Varro having a bit of fun at their expense – temporarily strapped for cash they may have been, but they were still fabulously wealthy by Roman standards.[11] Their fortunes recovered quickly, and all three of Clodius' sisters made advantageous marriages to wealthy and influential men who were rapidly climbing the *cursus honorum* and would ultimately be elected consul. These men were able to facilitate the careers of their wives' brothers in their turn. Thus, Fulvia found herself located at the centre of a complex network containing members from all contemporary political factions and both sides of the approaching civil war between Caesar and Pompey, in addition to the connections that she already had through her own parents. And her contacts would have extended far beyond the senatorial and equestrian classes as a result of her freedmen and freedwomen, who could undertake a range of activities that senators and their family members were precluded from, and the enslaved people she could task with doing her bidding without question.

The Romans did not consider a wedding ceremony to be strictly necessary, but it was a good excuse for an elaborate series of festivities, and a way for the families in question to display their status, wealth and sophistication to their peers. It was especially useful in the run-up to elections for candidates standing for office, as it was a way of demonstrating whose votes they could rely upon when the time came. Since Fulvia was going to be marrying into one of the most ancient, prestigious and powerful families in the Republic, it stands to reason that her parents would have wanted to show her off.

While a Roman girl marrying for the first time was expected to be a virgin, a Roman groom was expected to be the opposite – sexually experienced enough to ensure the wedding night went smoothly.[12] It fell to the groom to pick an auspicious day for the wedding, make the appropriate preliminary sacrifices, and prepare to welcome the bride into his home by decorating the threshold of the residence with greenery.[13] It was this that would signal to all the neighbours that a wedding was under way, just as cypress boughs hung either side of the threshold would indicate that a death had occurred (one ancient explanation for this practice was that the scent of the cypress disguised the stench of decay).[14] The groom was also responsible for cutting the torches that would light the procession's way from the bride's childhood home to her marital one, carving at least five from whitethorn, hornbeam or hazel wood.[15] This was the extent of his preparation as, unlike the bride, the groom was not expected to wear a special ceremonial costume and just needed to make sure he had clean garments, preferably white. So it is likely that Clodius dressed in a freshly laundered and bleached toga, then donned a wreath and a garland, and waited with the rest of his household, family, friends and acquaintances for Fulvia to arrive.

For Fulvia, her wedding day would have been the most important day of her life so far. While she had been out in public with her mother during her stepfather's consulship, this was the first time she would be the centre of attention, not just in the eyes of her own extended family, but in front of the entire senatorial and equestrian class, in addition to any incidental plebeian rubberneckers. Someone – perhaps Sempronia, or her nurse – would have explained to her how important it was that she appear modest and chaste, showing a degree of apprehension about what was about to happen to confirm that modesty and chastity. She would have been encouraged to shed a tear or two, perhaps even lament a little bit, to demonstrate fear and reluctance regarding the imminent loss of her virginity.[16] This was a critical and foundational lesson in how women were expected to present themselves in public, when and why it was appropriate to show emotion, and the potential of a powerful performance to manipulate the audience. Clearly, Fulvia took this advice to heart, referring back to it on numerous occasions over the years, particularly at times when she was especially vulnerable.

The entire point of the wedding procession was for it to be public so that the community could bear witness to the marriage and the transfer of the bride from the home of her father to the home of her husband. This leading of the bride to the groom's house marked the legal start of the marriage, and proof that it had in fact taken place. While we do not know where Fulvia and either of her parents were living prior to her marriage (at the very least, Murena must have maintained a Roman residence where Sempronia was living and Fulvia could stay), we do know that Clodius owned a house on the Palatine Hill, Rome's most prestigious residential area. So wherever Fulvia's wedding procession started, it concluded with her winding her way through the streets on the Palatine, passing the homes of Rome's most important and influential, not to mention wealthiest, people, to a spot overlooking not only the Forum but the entire city of Rome. She was a living, breathing demonstration of how her family were quite literally going up in the world. She would have been unmissable in her saffron veil and shoes at the front of the lengthy torchlit procession, carrying three bronze coins as offerings – one for her husband, one for his household gods and one hidden for herself. She would have been accompanied by a crowd of women and children bearing baskets full of bread and wool-working supplies, symbolic of the labours she would be expected to undertake in her new role as a *matrona* and *mater familias*, and thronged by participants throwing walnuts, shouting the traditional salutations '*Talassio!*' and '*Feliciter!*' for good luck, and chanting bawdy songs composed specifically for the occasion – no doubt Clodius' recent escapades featured prominently in the lyrics. A terracotta urn from Sicily shows part of a wedding procession, with the bride, her mother and two attendants, one of whom would have been the *pronuba*, a woman who had only been married once and so stood as an example of female marital fidelity for the bride (see fig 4).[17]

Once Fulvia arrived at the threshold of Clodius' home, she would have been required to smear the doorposts with animal fat and decorate them with skeins of wool, then enter across a fleece spread on the floor.[18] However, she had to be very careful not to either kick or step on the threshold itself.[19] There was a tradition that lifting your foot high meant that you could expect to have the upper hand in the marriage, so she may have surreptitiously made sure to do that.[20] Once inside, Clodius would have presented her with fire and water before the pair reclined together on a special couch in the atrium, decorated with ivory and swathed in purple cloth embroidered with gold thread, to consume the wedding feast.[21] It was on this couch that, at the end of the evening, once it had been moved from the atrium to the bedchamber, the marriage would finally be consummated, and the couch retained as a souvenir and family heirloom. An example of this type of furniture was recovered from a villa on the Via Cassia just outside Rome (see fig 5).[22]

We can gain a sense of what an elite Roman wedding was like in this period thanks to the poet Catullus (*circa* 84–54 BCE), who wrote three *epithalamia*, wedding poems, perhaps influenced by the work of the Greek poet Sappho. Since he was the lover of one of Clodius' sisters until around 59 BCE, he may even have been present for Clodius and Fulvia's wedding (Catullus refers to Clodius in his poetry, calling him Lesbius, although he does not appear to have been a fan of this rival for the sister's attention).[23] Clearly, everything was done as well as it could have been, and the Roman gods of marriage Hymenaeus, Juno and Concordia had been sufficiently propitiated, as Fulvia fell pregnant, and her first child was a son, named Publius Claudius Pulcher (the original version of Clodius' name before he changed it to be more fashionable), and it was not long before she fell pregnant again – and this time the baby was a daughter, named Claudia. Considering that

Fulvia and Clodius were married for just under ten years, for most of which they lived together in Rome, yet only had two children together, it is possible that she suffered miscarriages and stillbirths like her contemporaries Julia Caesaris and Tullia Ciceronis. Yet she seems to have conceived and borne children immediately during each of her subsequent marriages with no problems, into her thirties and forties, so perhaps they simply practised some form of family planning or even resorted to the rudimentary methods of contraception known to the Romans, information that would have been passed on to Fulvia by either her mother or female members of her household staff such as her midwife and her wet nurse.[24]

In many respects, it is as difficult to get a sense of the historical Clodius as it is to get a sense of the historical Fulvia, for much the same reasons. No ancient biography of him has survived, and in the ancient accounts that we have, he is a character rather than a person – someone used as a foil, someone to be compared to and contrasted with.[25] One recent historian succinctly and memorably described him as 'a complete prick who pretty much used his wealth and privilege to do whatever he wanted, whenever he wanted', and that seems a fair assessment.[26] While Cicero is certainly not the most objective observer of Clodius' behaviour, the fact that he alleged on multiple occasions that Clodius burned down the Temple of the Nymphs on the Campus Martius (yet more sacrilege) to destroy the census records that would have attested to his electoral fraud, intimidated numerous people into selling him their property against their inclinations, and even built a wall in his residence blocking his sister's access into her own adjacent residence, indicates that there was a kernel of truth in the prevailing negative opinions of him held by many of his more conservative peers.[27] He was, at the very least, in possession of a massive sense of entitlement, as were his siblings, and it seems this may well have rubbed off on Fulvia over the course of their decade of marriage.

A tentative reconstruction of the part of the Palatine in which Fulvia and Clodius lived in the Late Republic places their house (probably inherited) across the street from the Cicero brothers' (newly arrived in the neighbourhood, as Cicero purchased his house in 62 BCE).[28] The houses in this area were built specifically to be seen, not just their exteriors but also their interiors, as part of ancient Rome's performative and agonistic society. Cicero's house, originally commissioned by the tribune of the *plebs* Marcus Livius Drusus in 91 BCE, was constructed in such a way as to enable the entire city population to see everything that he got up to during his tribunate. Although his architect offered to build it in such a way that he could be private, he responded that he preferred to be public: 'If you possess the skill you must build my house in such a way that whatever I do shall be seen by all.'[29] While this might be an extreme example (and this ease of access would lead to him being murdered there soon after), the Roman architect Vitruvius detailed certain features that an elite Roman house was expected to contain in order that the occupier could fulfil his political responsibilities appropriately:

> The common rooms are those into which, though uninvited, persons of the people can come by right, such as vestibules, courtyards, peristyles and other apartments of similar uses... For persons of high rank who hold office and magistracies, and whose duty it is to serve the state, we must provide princely vestibules, lofty halls and very spacious peristyles, plantations and broad avenues finished in a majestic manner.[30]

Considering Clodius' family's pre-eminent position at the heart of the Roman Republic over many centuries, his house undoubtedly would have been in possession of all of these features considered so necessary by Vitruvius.

Fulvia's new home was on the Clivus Victoriae (Victory Street), a street ascending from the Velabrum – the valley between the Forum and the Forum Boarium (the cattle market) – to the summit of the Palatine, on the north-west slope of the hill, overlooking the Forum. A bustling shopping district that produced the city's best smoked cheese and no doubt provided much of her household provisions,[31] it was in the vicinity of the Temple of Victory (hence the street name), the precinct of the Magna Mater (the Great Mother goddess), and the Porticus Catuli, a portico built by Quintus Lutatius Catulus using the spoils of his victory over the Cimbri tribe, serving as an open space planted with trees for leisurely strolling and shade from the hot Italian sun. One nearby resident, the immensely wealthy Lucius Cornelius Chrysogonus, a freedman of the dictator Sulla, partied constantly, and the sounds of lyre and flute music and general merry-making could be heard issuing from his home day and night.[32]

Neighbourly relations were no doubt fraught, and not just between Clodius and Fulvia and the Cicerones, as this was not the only feud that Clodius and Fulvia were drawn into during the years of their marriage. Their house adjoined that of the equestrian Quintus Seius Postumus, and when Clodius' offer to purchase the house was refused, he threatened to cut off Seius' light source, presumably by building up walls to block his windows, in retaliation for the slight. When Seius died in 58 BCE shortly after this altercation, and Clodius succeeded in buying his house at auction, albeit at an exorbitant price, Cicero accused Clodius of poisoning him.[33] Another nearby property, the house of Marcus Aemilius Scaurus, was acquired for 14.8 million sesterces in 53 BCE.[34] This house was famous for having the largest atrium in Rome, and its threshold was decorated with four black marble columns that had originally been used in Scaurus' temporary theatre on the Campus Martius. They were so large (thirty-eight Roman feet long) and heavy that Scaurus had to pay a sewer contractor security against possible damage to the drains caused by hauling them up to the Palatine.[35]

This meant that by 53 BCE, Clodius and Fulvia were living in one of the largest and grandest – perhaps even the largest and grandest – houses on the Palatine. Traces of this last property have been excavated, revealing an extensive basement with accommodation for more than fifty enslaved members of the household staff, as well as a shrine, a bathhouse, a garden, a pool and a nymphaeum (a monument consecrated to the nymphs).[36] The sprawling households of the wealthiest members of the Late Republican elite are attested through both literary and documentary evidence. While Cicero, as a 'new man', had a relatively small household staff based at his Palatine house, which frequently necessitated him borrowing or hiring additional staff from wealthier friends such as Atticus, his patrician peers such as Clodius were much better equipped.[37] Clodius' household would have included enslaved people and formerly enslaved people specially trained in administration (secretaries, book-keepers), personal care (maids, hairdressers, valets), transportation (litter-bearers), food and drink (chefs, sommeliers), entertainment (actors, musicians, dancers), health-care (physicians, midwives) and childcare (wet nurses, nannies, tutors). The degree and extent of specialization is made clear by the highly specific job titles referenced in the epitaphs found within several Late Republican household *columbaria* ('dovecotes', mass burial structures) that have been excavated around the city of Rome. One, known as the Monumentum Statiliorum, the *columbarium* of the Statilii Taurii, was located at the intersection of the Via Labicana and the Via Praenestina, inside the Porta Praenestina, and contained at least 633 burials; while another, known as the Monumentum Volusiorum, the *columbarium* of the Volusii Saturnini, was located on the Via Appia and contained at least 204 burials. Both give us an insight into the wealth and sophistication of the type of household that Fulvia was now responsible for overseeing.[38]

Life with Clodius would have been quite different from the life Fulvia had been living previously. Before her marriage, as a respectable maiden she would have been relatively sheltered – kept at home for much of the time, learning how to run a household, with her parents not allowing a breath of scandal to touch her name. But as soon as the wedding festivities ended, she moved to an entirely new house and an entirely new lifestyle. It was thought that men should take some responsibility for completing the education of their young wives and it is probable that Clodius did so as, unlike many Roman couples, Fulvia and Clodius spent most of their time together, presumably because they enjoyed each other's company immensely.[39] Since the normal way of things was for men to be outside in public and women to be inside in private, Fulvia's presence at her husband's side wherever he went would have been noteworthy – the very fact we know this about the couple at all is because Cicero thought that it was sufficiently unusual to see Clodius without Fulvia that it should arouse suspicion. But in fact, while the Roman conception of marriage was ideally one of mutual respect and admiration, domestic harmony and companionship, stronger feelings – particularly on the part of the husband – were viewed with considerable suspicion, as they implied a loss of self-control and, worst of all, the possibility that the woman might be the dominant partner and exerting undue influence. For example, Pompey the Great was criticized for what amounted to taking a honeymoon and spending too much time with his much younger wife Julia, the daughter of Julius Caesar.[40]

Based on literary references to Clodius' house on the Palatine Hill, it does seem to have been substantial, even before he started enlarging it at his neighbours' expense, and in line with what Vitruvius stated was appropriate for an aspiring politician. The 14.8 million sesterces that he reportedly spent on it would have been an enormous amount of money, even to someone from as wealthy a family as his.[41] He was required to open his doors early every morning for the *salutatio*, the formal process by which clients would visit their patron, receive his patronage and sometimes gifts, and escort him down to the Forum. There was certainly a performative aspect to this – the larger your train of clients, the more important and influential you were perceived to be – but in this period of constant civil unrest, frequently punctuated by outbreaks of violence and riots in the streets, a large entourage also provided personal protection. And Clodius was a man who needed a significant amount of personal protection, and ensured it by surrounding himself with gladiators and hired toughs.

As an aspiring politician's wife, Fulvia was expected to cultivate social networks of her own in order to further her husband's interests behind the scenes – and during his absences from Rome, such as Clodius' tenure as quaestor in Sicily in 61–60 BCE. When husbands were absent from Rome, it was the job of wives to be the point of contact for any of their clients that came seeking assistance, meaning that Fulvia would have become well acquainted with Clodius' political, diplomatic and economic interests. She undoubtedly looked to her mother as an example to follow in this respect, but perhaps she also looked to her husband's older sisters, particularly the eldest, Clodia Metelli.

Thanks to the invective of Cicero and the poetry of Catullus, today Clodia Metelli is one of the most infamous women of the Roman Republic. But in the early 60s BCE, this notoriety was still to come, and she would have been at least fifteen years older than Fulvia – no doubt seeming very impressive and sophisticated to her new young sister-in-law, with her luxury estate and beautiful gardens on the banks of the Tiber, and frequent trips to the seaside resort of Baiae. Perhaps Fulvia was inspired by Clodia's very active social life, and the literary salons that she hosted regularly. Clodia may have been the one who introduced Fulvia to Atticus, a close friend of hers, who would be a good friend to Fulvia in turn in her hour of need in 43 BCE.

Like Clodius and Fulvia, Clodia owned a house on the Palatine Hill, and no doubt the trio spent much time together in one residence or another. Probably also present much of the time was Clodia's daughter Caecilia Metella, who was close to Fulvia in age, at least until her marriage to Publius Cornelius Lentulus Spinther in 53 BCE (thanks to Metella, Cicero had another reason to hate the family that Fulvia had married into, as she had an affair with his daughter Tullia's husband, Publius Cornelius Dolabella, that resulted in Metella and Spinther's divorce in 45 BCE). Like her mother, Metella was immortalized in erotic poetry under a pseudonym: the poet Lucius Ticida wrote about her as Perilla.[42] And like her mother, she was politically active, and along with her aunt would become part of the Caesarian faction through her male intimates.[43] The upper echelons of ancient Roman society were a very small world indeed.

Since Clodius is known to have had an extensive retinue of Greek companions, in addition to what Cicero described as 'courtesans, eunuchs and strumpets', it is probable that Fulvia's days were now full of socializing with people that were considered not entirely respect-able – at least by the older and more conservative members of her acquaintance.[44] Their house would have been immensely crowded, full of conversation, debate, laughter, and even entertainment such as the recitation of poetry, the playing of music and singing.[45] More staid members of Roman high society such as the Cicerones would have looked askance at this; Quintus Cicero commented that Catiline (the ringleader of the Catilinarian Conspiracy of 63–62 BCE) had 'lived with actors and gladiators as his accomplices, the former in lust, the latter in crime', and there seems no reason to believe that Clodius would not have been held to the same standards.[46] It is perhaps not surprising that Fulvia's loom, which by rights should have been set up in the atrium and used on a daily basis to provide the household with woollen fabric for clothing, was left to gather dust as she turned her attention to matters beyond spinning and weaving.

CHAPTER 6

THE FIRST TRIBUNE

CLODIUS LEARNED EARLY IN his political and military career that it was possible to circumvent the usual procedures by appealing directly to the people and inciting mob violence. While serving on his brother-in-law Lucullus' staff in Asia during the Third Mithridatic War, his patrician sense of entitlement meant that he felt aggrieved by the fact that other officers had been given more responsibilities than him, so he provoked a mutiny.[1] Lucullus was removed from his military command and sent back to Rome, where he promptly divorced Clodius' sister on the grounds of her committing incest with her youngest brother, thereby blackening both his wife's name and that of her brother.[2] During Clodius' trial for sacrilege in May 61 BCE, Lucullus appeared for the prosecution at the trial, repeating his incest accusations and making the point that Clodius made a habit of breaking taboos.

Clodia's husband Metellus Celer died in early 59 BCE, and she promptly took advantage of her freedom by becoming involved in Clodius' political career and attempting to further his political agenda.

It is probable that she and Fulvia hatched many plans together on Clodius' behalf, and when Clodius invited his closest friends and advisors to a strategy meeting in the town of Solonium in Lanuvium, since Clodia was present, it is likely that Fulvia was too.[3] Later that year, Clodius decided to stand for election as tribune. There was a fundamental flaw in this plan, however: the tribunate was only open to men from plebeian families, and Clodius, being one of the Claudii, was a member of a patrician family. He sought to circumvent this restriction by having himself adopted by a plebeian, Publius Fonteius, making him a member of a plebeian family and therefore eligible. There was nothing even remotely sincere about the adoption: Clodius' new father was considerably younger than he was, and Clodius made no attempt to change his name or his children's names as was usual practice. But the following year, in 58 BCE, he stood for election and his attempt was successful. Clodius was now a tribune, and his approach to the tribunate was innovative, as he appealed directly to the urban *plebs*, proposing populist measures purposefully designed to benefit them and developing new methods of spreading information and mobilizing support, all of which made him incredibly powerful.[4]

The very first thing Clodius did with his new suite of political powers was to wreak revenge on Cicero for attempting to prosecute him for sacrilege. He drafted a bill that proposed exiling anyone who had ever put a Roman citizen to death without recourse to a popular vote, and the bill was voted into law.[5] This meant that Cicero had broken the law when he sentenced the Roman citizens involved in the Catilinarian Conspiracy to death in 63 BCE. He had to leave not only the city of Rome, but also Italy as well. His villas at Tusculum and Formiae were looted, and his newly acquired Palatine house, the symbol of his and his family's success, was plundered, stripped of its valuables and burned to the ground, with the year's two consuls looking on. One of them, Lucius Calpurnius Piso Caesoninus, permitted his mother-in-law Licinia to loot the house's columns for her own residence.[6] In an attempt to twist the knife even further, Clodius purchased what remained of Cicero's house and demolished it.

Clodius took advantage of the opportunity to kill two birds with one stone and settle a score with another of his enemies, Quintus Lutatius Catulus, whose Porticus Catuli happened to adjoin Cicero's house, and demolished that too. He then began construction on a new property on the site with a portico, in addition to an altar dedicated to the goddess Libertas (Liberty), with a cult statue sourced from Tanagra by his older brother Appius.[7] Fulvia's older half-brother Natta was the priest that carried out the rites required to dedicate the new altar, and he did so upon the request of his half-sister and their mother.[8] Unfortunately for him, the fact that he was relatively new to the role and therefore inexperienced meant that Cicero could argue, upon his return from exile in 57 BCE, that he had not done so correctly so the altar was not a proper altar and he should therefore have his ownership of the site reinstated. Clodius' construction was torn down, and the land was returned to Cicero so he could start to rebuild his house.

In the speech devoted to the issue of his attempts to recover his house that Cicero delivered before the College of Pontiffs, he flung all manner of muck at Clodius and Clodia, accusing the pair of conducting an incestuous relationship and using a number of creative double entendres to imply that Clodius had been performing oral sex on his sister, and that his friend and henchman Sextus Cloelius had been doing likewise.[9] Once Cicero's ownership of the land was reinstated, Clodius continued to harass him, unleashing his men on the builders working on the site, and setting fire to Cicero's house.

Clodius also now had the power to challenge the members of the First Triumvirate – Caesar, Pompey and Crassus – when they were not forthcoming with honours that he felt he had earned by supporting them. He served as something of a figurehead for senatorial opposition to the three men, particularly Caesar during his consulship. Clodius had an extensive entourage. While he could already boast of a considerable amount of support from young senators such as Curio and Antony, and an equestrian named Gellius who was so entrenched with the common people that he married a freedwoman to make a point, he also had freedmen and clients and other subordinates. Chief amongst these was

Sextus Cloelius, who was responsible for drafting Clodius' tribunician legislation, the terms of which won him considerable loyalty not only from the *plebs* but from his senatorial colleagues as well. This legislation was comprehensive. First, he restored the *collegia* ('colleges', organizations such as supper clubs and burial clubs) which had been suppressed since 64 BCE, and also allowed the establishment of new ones, enabling many freedmen and even enslaved individuals to join these groups. Second, he provided all Roman citizens with a monthly ration of five modii of grain, enabling them to have access to an essential staple foodstuff. Third, he altered the existing regulations for limiting or even prohibiting public gatherings. Fourth, he revised the means by which censors could remove people from the Senate, making it more difficult to exclude individuals and undermining the power of the censors. The first and second laws, and his personal oversight of their implementation, provided him with a mass following amongst the common people, known as the Clodiani, and he was able to rally them to provide vocal and even violent support or opposition as he saw fit. While his enemies such as Cicero denigrated his followers as bankrupt criminals, slaves, assassins, gladiators, beast-fighters and other deplorables, in reality many of them were shopkeepers, artisans and other ordinary Romans just trying to make a living.

Clodius' rivalry with his fellow senator Milo began in this fraught period, as their respective gangs frequently clashed in the streets of Rome. In 57 BCE, the Tiber became clogged with corpses after one altercation. In 56 BCE, since Clodius had been elected aedile, he was able to charge (somewhat hypocritically) Milo with criminal violence due to the actions of his entourage.[10] But this did not stop the clashes, with the gangs interrupting each other's speakers, spitting and throwing stones at one another, and coming to physical blows, while all throughout Milo's crew chanted yet more accusations of incest between Clodius and Clodia, to Clodius' (and no doubt Clodia's and Fulvia's) fury.[11] The significance of this political instability was underscored by a series of portents, as a blaze of light was seen crossing the sky from south to north, thunderbolts killed several citizens, a wolf was witnessed trotting through the city, an earthquake occurred, and soothsayers suggested that the reason for all the tumult was that someone was using a temple or some other consecrated site as a residence (a not-so-veiled reference to Cicero).[12] The following year, Milo returned the favour, indicting Sextus Cloelius on the same charges of criminal violence, although he was acquitted.[13] Cicero, no doubt still smarting from the pronouncements of the soothsayers, blamed Clodia and her influence for the acquittal.

The portents continued to worsen over the next couple of years. In 54 BCE, the Tiber flooded, burst its banks and inundated the lower levels of the city, destroying houses and washing many animals away.[14] The following year, sinister species such as owls and wolves were seen in the city, while dogs prowled and whined, some sacred statues started to sweat and others were struck by lightning.[15] Perhaps unsurprisingly, given the circumstances and the prevailing atmosphere of existential dread, Rome was an incredibly volatile and consequently unsafe place to be.[16] Even walking the streets could be dangerous if you attempted to do so without an armed bodyguard – Varro tells of an occasion when he and a group of friends went to the Temple of Tellus to meet with one of the temple's sacristans, only to be confronted by the priest's freedman, who informed them that he had been stabbed to death in the street earlier that day.[17] Unfortunately for the sacristan, the knifeman had mistaken him for somebody else.

Even friends and allies could come to potentially fatal blows: intriguingly, some years later, Cicero praised Antony for apparently having tried to murder Clodius around this time, chasing him through the Forum armed with a sword and into a bookshop, probably on the adjoining street known as the Argiletum (famed for its bookshops), where Clodius shut and barricaded himself inside a cupboard under the stairs until the danger had passed.[18] Since Cicero frequently implied that Antony was having an adulterous affair with Fulvia during her marriage to Clodius, his salacious explanation for the altercation was presumably that Antony was attempting to rid himself of his love rival.

In 53 BCE, matters between Clodius and Milo finally came to a head, when Clodius was standing for election to the praetorship while Milo was standing for election to the consulship. Since both men were likely to be successful in their election campaigns, they did as much as they could to try to sabotage each other. Milo, lacking Clodius' enormous intergenerational family fortune – readily supplemented by Fulvia's – was hugely in debt as a result of all the plays and gladiatorial shows that he had financed in order to gain the favour of the *plebs*, making his election to consul and the opportunities for enrichment that came along with it all the more necessary.[19] Targeted violence meant that the elections were postponed until the following year. Then, on 18 January 52 BCE, Milo murdered Clodius.

Once Clodius' body had been brought home, Fulvia, as his wife, was responsible for leading the mourning rites.[20] There was a strict format: first, you shrieked, then you moaned, alternating between load moans and quiet ones, all the while tearing at your hair, ripping at your clothes and beating your breasts. You might even bare them, thereby adding an erotic frisson to the proceedings – respectable women were usually covered from their necks down to their feet, rendering the opportunity to see their breasts (or any other part of their bodies) virtually impossible for anyone except their husbands.[21] Then, you transitioned to articulate speech, first calling and then singing lamentations to the deceased. This process would last some hours before gradually winding down, a way of controlling and managing grief.

However, rather than winding the proceedings down, Fulvia amped them up and deliberately distorted and disrupted all the traditional Roman funerary rites. As Publilius Syrus sagely observed, 'A woman's tear is the sauce of mischief.'[22] In a sense, as a wife, now a widow, she was the only one who *could* do this: aristocratic Roman men were expected to be masters of themselves, and in possession of absolute self-control, at all times. Additionally, many of them were adherents of Stoic philosophy, which discouraged feelings and displays of excessive emotion. While it was acceptable for women to lose control of themselves in the depths of their grief, men, on the other hand, were expected to exercise self-restraint, no matter who the deceased was to them.[23]

Of course, Fulvia had not lost control of herself, not in the least. She was acting in a manner calculated to best achieve her goal. There were historical precedents for this from both the monarchy and the early days of the Republic – upon the deaths of Lucretia and Verginia, their families had used the mourning ritual in a similar way, as a catalyst for instigating riots and a means to initiate personal revenge as well as institutional change. Somewhat more benignly, only the year before, upon the death from puerperal fever of Caesar's daughter Julia, the wife of Pompey the Great, her body had been taken from the Forum and buried on the Campus Martius to honour her father and husband, despite objections that to do so without a special decree was sacrilegious.[24] That this was all taking place in late January, at the darkest and coldest point of the year, close to the beginning of the Parentalia, the Roman festival concerned with honouring and appeasing the spirits of the departed so that they did not haunt you, would not have escaped people's notice.

In the turmoil that followed, Clodius' mob rampaged across the city. First, its members raced around the base of the Palatine Hill and attacked the Domus Anniana, Milo's ancestral home on the Cermalus, the south-western slope of the Palatine that faced the Circus Maximus, but were seen off by his household (Milo and his wife Fausta had not yet returned to Rome).[25] It was rumoured that he had been stockpiling shields.[26] From there, they headed to the Lucus Libitinae, a sacred grove containing the Temple of Venus Libitina, on the Esquiline Hill – probably in the vicinity of the cemetery, where the poor were buried in a mass grave and witches were believed to lurk on the lookout for decomposing body parts to use in their spells.[27] It also served as the headquarters of the *libitinarii*, the city's undertakers, and as a result it was a place where you could obtain all the equipment necessary for a funeral: here the rioters found the firewood they needed for Clodius' funerary pyre.[28] They swung by the homes of the consuls Scipio and Hypsaeus, and then Pompey's Domus Rostrata on the Carinae, and then returned to the Forum to cremate Clodius and enjoy an impromptu funerary banquet in his memory.

At some point over the next couple of days, they attacked the house of Marcus Aemilius Lepidus, who was serving as supreme magistrate on a temporary basis because the office of consul was vacant due to the postponed elections. Besieging him and his household, they furiously demanded elections, and at one point even gained entrance, trashing his atrium and destroying his *imagines* (his family's wax and terra-cotta funerary masks), his wife's wedding couch, and her loom with its weaving still on it – the epitome of disrespect – before they were driven off by a volley of arrows.[29] There are even accounts of the mob indiscriminately slaughtering anyone they came across who happened to be dressed in senatorial and equestrian garb, in case they were Milo.[30] Martial law was at last declared and Pompey was appointed sole consul for the purpose of quelling the violence, which he attempted to do by charging Milo with violence, bribery and electoral fraud. The whole of Rome was fixated on the subsequent case, eagerly anticipating each fresh development in the months leading up to the trial. Rumours circulated that Milo had also gone looking for Clodius and Fulvia's young son Publius, who had been in residence at the family's Alban villa near Bovillae, in the hope of murdering him too, but had taken out his frustration by torturing an enslaved person named Halicor for information and then killing three other household slaves instead.[31]

Since Publius was too young, Clodius' adult nephews, the sons of his older brother Appius, joined forces with Clodius' friend Antony to prepare the prosecution case.[32] While under normal circumstances women did not testify in court proceedings, they could do so with the support of their male relations. Clearly, the prosecution of Milo was a family affair, and Fulvia enlisted her mother Sempronia to testify alongside her.

The official mourning period for a bereaved wife was one year, and it would no doubt have suited Fulvia for her physical appearance to serve as a constant reminder of her loss in the lead-up to Milo's trial.[33] As a widow, Fulvia cut a striking and imposing figure as she made her way around Rome, immediately distinguishable by virtue of her clothing from married women whose husbands were still living. She may well have been inspired by her stepfather's appearance at his trial a decade earlier, or by the public appearances of Cicero's wife and daughter during his exile, although her mourning dress was entirely appropriate rather than a pointed gesture or affectation. Forswearing any jewellery and expensive and luxurious clothing, instead she wore ancient attire called a *ricinium*, a square garment folded over and pushed back from her face, instead of a *palla* covering her hair.[34] Near black in colour, probably woven from naturally dark wool, it stood out starkly from the white togas with purple stripes worn by the senators and other Roman citizens present at the trial.

Her visible state of mourning would have been reinforced by the decorations on the exterior of her property, with its threshold flanked by black cypress boughs to indicate that a death had taken place within, looming over the Forum for the entire one-hundred-day period between Clodius' death and Milo's trial.[35] In a very real way, the house and the smouldering site of the former Senate House were framing everything that went on.

Immediately after the murder and his pillaging of Clodius' Alban estate, Milo had started to think strategically and with one eye on self-preservation. He emancipated twelve slaves who had been the most heavily involved in the Battle of Bovillae, most likely to prevent them from being used against him – while enslaved people could be tortured into testifying against him, freedmen, as Roman citizens, could not be – although he claimed it was out of gratitude for them having saved his life.[36]

As early as 27 January, Milo and the tribune Marcus Caelius Rufus, Cicero's protégé and Clodia's nemesis, started claiming that Milo had only engaged with Clodius in self-defence, after Clodius attempted to ambush him.[37] This was publicly refuted by Quintus Metellus Scipio in a speech before the Senate a few weeks later, in the middle of February. Then, vindicating Milo's decision to emancipate his minions, the two younger Clodii demanded that Milo and his wife Fausta produce their slaves for interrogation, and in retaliation, Milo's side demanded that Clodius' slaves be likewise produced and interrogated – only eleven of them had been killed on that fateful day, so there were some survivors.

By the middle of March, Clodius' friend Titus Munatius Plancus had
come to an agreement with the freedman Marcus Aemilius Philemon,
who alleged that Milo had kept him and four other free men imprisoned for the last two months because they had witnessed the murder.[38]
At some point, a slave named Galata had been captured by Plancus
and his colleague Quintus Pompeius Rufus, and they claimed that he
had been apprehended in the act of murdering Clodius. Unfortunately,
before they could make him testify, Caelius and his fellow tribune
Manilius Cumanus abducted the slave and returned him to Milo.

The trial began on 4 April, held in public in the Forum, but the
first day of proceedings was interrupted by violence, leading Pompey
to declare that he would come to the Forum the following day and
ensure order by intimidating the rabble with an armed guard. On 5
April, the residents of Bovillae testified that during the storming of the
inn to capture Clodius the innkeeper had been murdered too, and that
Clodius had been dragged out of the inn and onto the public thorough-
fare.[39] Even more damningly, the Alban Virgins testified that a woman
had come to them to fulfil a vow on Milo's behalf because he had finally
succeeded in murdering Clodius.[40] Then, on 6 April, the final day of the
witness testimonies, it was Fulvia's turn. While the specific details of
Fulvia and Sempronia's speeches have not been preserved, it is clear that
the detailed reconstruction of the events of that day found in numerous
works of ancient historiography owes much to their testimonies.[41] It
is also important to note that Clodius and Fulvia's famous house may
well have been visible from the trial, with the speakers on the Rostra
gesturing towards it at opportune, particularly emotionally charged
moments.[42] According to Asconius, their testimonies and the tears they
shed while recounting them were key to Milo being found guilty of
murder by thirty-eight votes to thirteen: once again, Fulvia found tears
key to creating the desired impression in the minds of witnesses and
spectators.[43] Milo was exiled to Massilia (modern Marseilles), although
his henchman Marcus Saufeius, who actually stormed the inn and
committed the murder, was acquitted by one vote.[44] Even this early in
Fulvia's career, her public speaking skills and ability to work the crowd

seem to have been impressive. She had clearly learned a considerable amount from Clodius in their decade of marriage.

Upon Clodius' death, the majority of his estate would have passed to his children. Although under Roman law, since his father, paternal grandfather, and paternal great-grandfather were all dead, Clodius and Fulvia's son Publius Claudius Pulcher was now a *pater familias*, the head of his own household, in reality he was a young child, completely unequipped to manage his finances, business interests, and properties. So it is likely that Fulvia retained control of Clodius' estate on Publius' behalf, albeit with a degree of oversight from Clodius' brothers when they were not stationed abroad. But perhaps more importantly, Fulvia retained control of her late husband's rabble-rousing and intimidating followers. She took his place as their patron in the name of Clodius' son and heir, and even encouraged them to support her two subsequent husbands, thus helping further their political careers and interests.[45]

Fulvia's political apprenticeship was now complete. What would she do as a journeywoman?

CHAPTER 7

THE SECOND TRIBUNE

D URING THE YEARS OF the Republic, the Romans revered
the *univira*, the woman who married only once and who,
if widowed, remained single for the remainder of her life. She was
considered to bring good luck to the household.[1] Perhaps the most
famous example was Cornelia Africana, who lived around a century
before Fulvia. Her pedigree was impeccable and her connections
were formidable: she was the daughter of Publius Cornelius Scipio
Africanus, conqueror of Carthage in North Africa, the wife of Tiberius
Sempronius Gracchus, consul in 177 BCE and 163 BCE, and the mother
of the infamous Gracchi brothers, Tiberius and Gaius. As a wife, she
had excelled, bearing twelve children, although only three of them –
Tiberius, Gaius and Sempronia – lived to adulthood. She was under-
standably proud of her offspring, and on one occasion when another
matron was showing off her incomparable jewellery, went so far as to
wait until the children returned home in order to present them, smugly
stating that she considered them to be *her* jewels.[2] After the death of
her husband in 154 BCE, she took charge of his estate on behalf of

her children, refusing a proposal of marriage from King Ptolemy VIII Physcon of Egypt.[3] While she could have been a queen, she preferred to remain a matron.

Cornelia was honoured with a bronze statue depicting her in a seated position (apparently the fact that her sandals were strapless was considered especially noteworthy) on a marble base carved by the sculptor Tisicratis, a Greek artist working in Italy during the late second century BCE.[4] It is possible that it was modelled on the statue of the goddess Aphrodite carved by the revered Classical Greek sculptor Phidias, but it would in turn be used as a model for statues of other admirable Roman women who wished to emphasize their maternity.[5] It was set up first in the Portico of Metellus (the building was started in 146 BCE, and eventually dedicated in 131 BCE), and then when the Portico of Metellus was replaced with the Portico of Octavia (sometime after 27 BCE) the statue was retained, and it was here that it

The base of Cornelia's honorific statue, circa late second century BCE

was rediscovered in the late nineteenth century.[6] The prominent place-ment of the statue in the new building occurred soon after Fulvia's death, during Octavian's attempts at moral reform and his efforts to reinstate what he considered to be Rome's traditional values, and presumably because he wished to make the point that Cornelia and his sister Octavia were kindred spirits. While the statue itself has unfortu-nately not survived, its base has. Its inscription reads, simply, 'Cornelia, daughter of [Publius Cornelius Scipio] Africanus, [mother of] the Gracchi'.[7] She is commemorated entirely in association with her male relations.

Despite the clear differences between Cornelia and Fulvia, it is likely that they would have seen eye to eye on some things, at least. For example, in one of the two letters written by Cornelia to her younger son Gaius that have survived from antiquity, she opines, 'You will say it is a beautiful thing to get revenge on your enemies. This seems neither greater nor more beautiful to anyone than it does to me.'[8] In the wake of her elder son Tiberius' murder, she encouraged Gaius to avenge him, going so far as to hire mercenaries to assist him in doing so.[9] No doubt Fulvia would have agreed with that sentiment and that assist-ance, considering her actions following the death of her first husband Clodius. However, Cornelia followed it up with the proviso that this should be done 'only if it is possible to follow these aims and maintain the security of the state'.[10] Perhaps here Fulvia would have disagreed, but she would also have been justified in pointing out that Cornelia's Rome of the mid-second century BCE was a very different place to her Rome of the mid-first century BCE, which was rapidly descending into political and military chaos.

Fulvia evidently chose not to follow Cornelia's example and take the path of the *univira*, despite being an independent and wealthy (and independently wealthy) widow. Immediately after the traditional mourning period for Clodius was over, she remarried. Perhaps she chose to do so out of concern for her son Publius, in need of a male role model as he approached manhood. Perhaps she chose to do so out of concern for her own health, as the Hippocratic medical texts recommended that young widows remarry as quickly as possible in order to maintain a state of good health. Or perhaps she chose to do so because her reputation was at stake. One rather odd story recorded by Valerius Maximus, but found nowhere else, claims that in 52 BCE, a man named Gemellus hosted a banquet for one of the year's consuls, Metellus Scipio, and the tribunes. As part of the evening's entertainment, he set up a brothel to serve as the setting for an orgy between the men, a young man named Sentius Saturninus, and two women 'both famous for their fathers and husbands'. While the surviving manuscript names the two women as Munia and Flavia, it has been proposed that these are typographical errors and their names should be reconstructed as Mucia and Fulvia, as the accompanying description fits them better than the otherwise unknown Munia and Flavia.

Mucia Tertia was the daughter of a famous Republican lawyer, consul and *pontifex maximus* Quintus Mucius Scaevola, and the half-sister of two brothers who both reached the consulship, Quintus Metellus Celer (Clodia Metelli's husband) and Quintus Metellus Nepos. She may also have been a half-sister or stepsister to one or more of the Clodii. Between 79 BCE and 62 BCE she was married to Pompey, and after their divorce was married to Marcus Aemilius Scaurus (something that displeased her ex-husband greatly).[11] As Fulvia's sister-in-law's sister-in-law, the pair were likely well acquainted.

Like Fulvia and Clodia, Mucia was involved in Roman politics in this period.[12] Her ability to exert influence over her male relatives was used by none other than Cicero in his appeals to her brothers, and years later she would serve as a diplomatic emissary between her son Sextus Pompey and the Second Triumvirate.[13] So it is not surprising to see their names linked, but it is surprising to see them linked in this precise way. While Pompey did not offer an explanation for divorcing Mucia, there were whispers that she had committed adultery with Caesar while Pompey was away fighting in the Third Mithridatic War and dealing with the pirates that infested the eastern Mediterranean.[14] Suetonius, Caesar's biographer, claimed that Pompey would frequently refer to Caesar by the name Aegisthus – the man who had cuckolded Agamemnon, the King of Mycenae. This would make Pompey Agamemnon and Mucia Clytemnestra, an ominous comparison since Clytemnestra murdered Agamemnon upon his arrival home from the Trojan War.[15] These sources are all much later, however, and none of Mucia's contemporaries cast aspersions on her, nor were there any rumours of infidelity during her marriage to Scaurus.[16]

Like Mucia, Fulvia would fall victim to accusations of, if not precisely marital infidelity, then certainly marital irregularities, long past the point at which they were supposed to have occurred – in the form of Cicero's attacks on Antony, Curio and Clodius in 44 and 43 BCE. It is possible that what we see in Valerius Maximus' account is some latent anxiety about the involvement of women in Roman politics – the guest list of Gemellus' supposed orgy comprises a consul and two tribunes with a partner provided for each. In view of this, perhaps Fulvia chose to remarry out of a desire to continue to involve herself in politics, a much easier thing to do as the wife of an up-and-coming mover and shaker than as a single woman, no matter how notorious her former husband. Had she remained single and attempted to involve herself as a wealthy woman of leisure in the Roman political scene, she may have found herself on the receiving end of vicious gossip and even slander from her more traditional peers, just as her sister-in-law Clodia had several years earlier. Clodia's penchant for regular trips to the luxurious seaside resort of Baiae, hosting of risqué and indulgent parties, and ownership of pleasure gardens overlooking the spot in the Tiber where handsome young men happened to like to swim, combined with her attempts at providing a degree of financial and political patronage to up-and-comers like Marcus Caelius had resulted in her being publicly verbally eviscerated by Cicero as 'a shameless and wanton courtesan' and the 'Medea of the Palatine'.[17] So-called slut-shaming is not just a modern phenomenon.[18]

We have an insight into how a single mature woman with personal assets such as beauty, wealth, status and connections might conduct herself on the Roman marriage market from an episode recorded in Plutarch's biography of Lucius Cornelius Sulla Felix ('Lucky').

The dictator was attending a bout of gladiatorial games and found himself sitting near a beautiful woman named Valeria, whose father was Marcus Valerius Messalla Niger the consul and censor, brother was the consul and augur Marcus Valerius Messalla Rufus, maternal uncle was the famous orator Quintus Hortensius Hortalus (Fulvia's mother Sempronia's cousin), and she was also related to the chief Vestal Virgin Caecilia Metella Balearica. An impeccable pedigree and set of connections. When she passed behind him, she reached out and pulled a thread of wool from his toga. Feeling this, he looked around in surprise, only to be met with Valeria's self-assured response: 'There's no reason to be surprised, Dictator. I only want to have a little bit of your good luck for myself.'[19] Taken with her, he made discreet enquiries and, clearly pleased with what he heard, began negotiations for what would be his fifth and final marriage. Clearly, Valeria's assertive and flirtatious behaviour was acceptable because of her age and the degree of independence that she knew as a divorcée – a teenage virgin doing likewise would have been roundly excoriated by all and sundry, as would her parents for raising her to be so wanton. Thus we might envisage Fulvia taking the bull by the horns and facilitating arrangements for her second marriage in a similarly direct manner, riding high on her public profile in the wake of her testimony at Clodius' trial.

Fulvia's choice, Gaius Scribonius Curio, was born around 84 BCE, making him about a decade her senior at the very most. While not from an ancient patrician aristocratic family like Clodius, Curio was from a more recent plebeian aristocratic one, definitely on the front line of Roman politics and incredibly well connected. His father, also called Gaius Scribonius Curio, had been elected consul in 76 BCE and censor in 61 BCE, while Curio himself had already been elected as quaestor in 54 BCE and spent several years serving in the province of Asia (modern Turkey). Curio had been closely aligned with Clodius, as both he and his father had defended Clodius in the Senate in the wake of the Bona Dea affair and the accusations of sacrilege made against him in 62 BCE. Cicero referred to him at this time as 'Little Miss Curio' and described him rather dismissively as a 'goateed youngblood'.[20]

But from 59 BCE, Curio's high-profile public opposition to the First Triumvirate and their proposed legislation, perhaps inspired by his father's feelings about them, put him on the same side as Cicero, and the pair struck up a friendship. Clearly Cicero was not the only one who appreciated Curio's efforts, as he was apparently complimented in the Forum and applauded in the theatre.[21] It is a sign of Curio's standing and influence at this time that a conspiracy to assassinate Pompey, known as the Vettius Affair in reference to the putative assassin, Lucius Vettius, was considered to have been put together by Caesar in an attempt to blacken his reputation.[22]

An insight into Curio's personality can be found in the work of the historian Velleius Paterculus: 'Curio was a man of noble birth, eloquent, reckless, prodigal alike of his own fortune and chastity and of those of other people, a man of the utmost cleverness in perversity, who used his gifted tongue for the subversion of the state. No wealth and no pleasures sufficed to satiate his appetites.'[23] So not too far removed from Clodius in many respects – perhaps Fulvia had a 'type', and these were personal qualities that she found particularly appealing. Caelius described him as having an 'easy manner'.[24] He was certainly personable enough to maintain friendships with Clodius and Antony, and with Cicero, who detested them both, and somehow managed to stay on good terms with Clodius despite campaigning for Cicero's recall from exile.

While prior to Curio's marriage to Fulvia, he did not have the financial resources of his contemporary Scaurus (Mucia's new husband, who while serving as aedile in 55 BCE had the advantage of possessing a wealthy father, mother and stepfather who could supplement his income and assist him with the expenditure necessary for constructing a temporary theatre and hosting elaborate games), he did have ingenuity on his side. In 52 BCE, he built two large wooden theatres, each of which was balanced on a revolving pivot.[25] In the morning, a play was performed in each theatre, with the theatres facing in opposite directions so that the actors performing one play did not drown out the actors performing the other. Then, once the plays had concluded, the theatres

revolved and combined to form an amphitheatre in which gladiatorial games and athletic competitions were put on. He even had twenty
African panthers left over to pass on to Marcus Caelius for his games
in 50 BCE.[26] After the inaugural performances, and the proven success
of the theatre's revolutions, many spectators would actually choose
to remain in their seats during the transition (Pliny the Elder, who
recorded this incredible architectural and engineering accomplishment,
actually calls this 'madness', although in an admiring way). Thus Curio
was able to organize a particularly successful and, more importantly,
memorable set of funeral games for his father, who had died early in 53
BCE.[27] His agent Rupa had wanted to organize the games while Curio
was still away from Rome, but Cicero and his friends encouraged him
to wait for Curio's return, and Cicero even tried to dissuade him from
hosting games at all, claiming that the public were bored of them.[28] The
fact that his games were funeral games even allowed Curio to circumvent a recently passed law (the *lex Tullia*, passed by Cicero in fact) that
forbade candidates for office hosting games in the two years prior to
the elections that they wanted to stand in. This meant that when the
time came for Curio to stand for election to the tribunate in 50 BCE,
his name was on everyone's lips. His revolving theatres may also have
been the very things that fired Fulvia's imagination when it came to
the possibilities of their union: here was a political animal and, perhaps
more importantly, a showman whose ability to seize the moment and
flair for the dramatic matched her own – someone she could work with.
He was clearly a man who would benefit from the access to Clodius'
followers that Fulvia could provide.

Fulvia and Curio married around 50 BCE, and although their marriage
was to prove short-lived, it did get off to a promising start. After having
lived with the volatile Clodius for the better part of a decade, Fulvia
must have found the more easy-going Curio refreshing. She added to
the couple's newly-wed lustre by falling pregnant immediately, going
on to bear her third child and Curio's first, named Gaius Scribonius
Curio like his father and grandfather. They divided their time between
their home in Rome and Curio's villas in Alba Longa and Cumae.[29]

Curio's political career began building momentum with his election to the tribunate in 51 BCE and the pontificate in the same year. Like Clodius, he campaigned on a populist platform and was very popular with the urban *plebs*. However, by this point in time he appeared to have become a supporter of Pompey, which meant it surprised everyone when he abruptly changed sides and threw in his lot with Caesar.[30] Later commentators would claim that Caesar bribed him in order to gain his support, paying off debts that would presumably have included the costs incurred by the construction of his audacious revolving theatres. However, the role of his friendship with Antony, given Antony's staunch support of Caesar, should not be overlooked. The pair had been working together closely during Curio's tribunate, planning to get Antony elected to the position of augur and laying the groundwork for his campaign for the tribunate the following year.[31] Cicero would later accuse Curio of inciting his friends to commit violence in order to achieve these ends.[32]

Unfortunately, Curio then became embroiled in the civil war between Julius Caesar and Pompey the Great. As the two Roman magnates struggled for political and military supremacy, with neither willing to give way to the other, politics in Rome became strongly polarized. While over the course of Curio's tribunate he had attempted to undertake a programme of populist legislation, he was stymied by senatorial opposition. It was subsequently declared by Velleius Paterculus that he 'more than anyone else, applied the flaming torch which kindled the civil war and all the evils which followed for twenty consecutive years'.[33] Curio was afraid of how vulnerable he would be at the end of his term in office, once he was no longer considered sacrosanct and thus could be politically and even physically accosted. He gave a speech denouncing Pompey to the Senate, then he left Fulvia and his newborn son in Rome to travel to Ravenna to meet up with Caesar. Curio then returned to Rome with a message from Caesar demanding either that both he and Pompey disarm or that Caesar's actions be acknowledged and approved. This did not go down well, and two of the tribunes for the following year,

Antony and Quintus Cassius Longinus, were both expelled from the Senate, and all three returned to Caesar.

Legally, Caesar was expected to set aside his *imperium* – essentially giving up his military command, which was only valid in Gaul, and laying down arms – if he wished to return to Rome and stand for election to consul. He refused to do so while Pompey retained his own *imperium*, and instead advanced from the province of Cisalpine Gaul into Italy with the Thirteenth Legion in early January 49 BCE. Upon Caesar's crossing of the unofficial boundary and border provided by the River Rubicon, which was interpreted as a declaration of war, there was a mass exodus of people from the city of Rome. Pompey and his supporters gathered up their households and all their portable possessions and headed to Macedonia and Thrace. Many of Fulvia's neighbours on the Palatine Hill would have been part of this vacation, making offerings to the gods to try to ensure a safe journey, while those that remained battened down the hatches and prepared themselves for a siege as the worst-case scenario. Cicero's wife Terentia and his daughter Tullia, for example, remained but were undoubtedly anxious about the treatment that would be meted out to them.

Caesar bestowed *imperium* upon Curio, which meant he could command an army, and so he went to campaign in Sicily in the service of Caesar. We can gain an insight into the way that Roman women were assumed or expected to feel about their husbands' military service from one of Propertius' elegies, in which he envisages a woman named Arethusa writing to her husband Lycotas, apologizing for the blotches where the ink on the papyrus is stained with tears, but taking him to task for abandoning her.[34] 'Is this the husband's loyalty and are these the bridal gifts you pledged when all innocent I succumbed to your embraces?' she asks, and well we might imagine Fulvia expressing similar sentiments to Curio, with their newborn wailing in her arms, either before or after his departure from Rome.[35] The poet Ovid, who was exiled from Rome to Tomis (modern Constanţa in Romania) after offending Octavian some years later, described the atmosphere in his home on the day of his departure: 'My loving wife was in my arms as I wept, herself weeping more bitterly, tears raining constantly over her innocent cheeks... Wherever you had looked was the sound of mourning and lamentation, and within the house was the semblance of a funeral with its loud outcries. Men and women, children too, grieved at this funeral of mine; in my home every corner had its tears.'[36] While Ovid had not been condemned to actual death, exile amounted to social death, and he would indeed die in Tomis a decade later.

Caesar tasked Curio with seizing the strategically important province of Sicily after its governors had fled. He initially found success there, securing the province's grain supply without a fight as Cato, who was the provincial governor at the time, did not have sufficient troops to hold the island and had no wish to subject it to prolonged military action. This enabled Caesar to continue feeding the inhabitants of Rome, seeing off famine, and possession of the strategically placed island province enabled him to control the shipping lanes of the central Mediterranean. However, Curio then decided to invade Africa. Just as Propertius has his heroine Arethusa comment on the ominous portents of her and Lycoris' wedding torches having been lit from a funeral pyre and sprinkled with water from the River Styx, so might Fulvia have followed the reports of Curio's campaign's progress with a sinking feeling in her stomach, dreading every message received first from Sicily and then Africa.[37]

The prospect of dying miles from home in some random corner of the ancient Mediterranean, far away from your loved ones, was something that clearly preyed on the minds of men in this volatile period. Who could they trust to provide them with appropriate funerary rites and a decent burial under such fraught circumstances? The poet Tibullus wrote first about deliberately avoiding military service so that he could remain at home in the arms of his lover Delia, and told his patron Marcus Valerius Messalla Corvinus (Valeria's second consular brother) that while *he* might want military victory and the accompanying glory that would result from decorating the façade of his home with the spoils of war, as far as Tibullus himself was concerned, 'Begone, ye trumpets and ensigns!'[38] In a second poem, written while he was sick, he frets, 'No mother have I here to gather the burned bones to her grieving bosom; no sister to lavish Assyrian perfumes on my ashes and weep with hair dishevelled by my tomb. Nor anywhere is Delia, who, ere from the city she let me go, inquired, they say, of every god', and imagines all the ways in which Delia might intercede with the gods on his behalf.[39] No doubt this was a scenario that Curio recognized as a possibility, and hoped that Fulvia was supplicating herself in front of the household gods.

Yet while Curio's campaign started well, he was up against an opponent who had two reasons to hate him and wish him dead. First, King Juba of Numidia was a member of the Pompeian faction, and categorically not a Caesarian sympathizer (Caesar had actually once physically attacked him and publicly humiliated him by yanking on his beard during one of his diplomatic visits to Rome). Second, and more personally, Juba justifiably held against him the fact that Curio, during the year of his tribunate, had attempted to confiscate his kingdom. After defeating Pompey's general Publius Attius Varus and Juba at the Battle of Utica, Curio became overconfident and was in turn defeated by Juba's general Saburra at the Battle of the Bagradas River, after he walked straight into a trap that had been set for him. Juba's army not only destroyed Curio's, but also succeeded in seizing a huge amount of treasure.

Curio chose to fight to the death rather than face Caesar as a failure. Saburra underlined his victory by decapitating Curio and presenting his severed head to King Juba as a trophy. Widowed for the second time in three years, Fulvia was once again unable to give a deceased husband a proper funeral, but on this occasion there was no opportunity for her to exact revenge on those responsible.[40]

In this, Fulvia had a lot in common with another woman named Cornelia: Cornelia Metella, daughter of Metellus Scipio, who had been married first to Publius Licinius Crassus, son of Crassus the triumvir, and second to Pompey. Both of her husbands had died under brutal circumstances far from home, with Crassus falling in the Battle of Carrhae along with his father and three legions in Parthia in 53 BCE, and Pompey being murdered on a beach in Egypt in 48 BCE.[41] In point of fact, there are clear parallels between the deaths of Crassus Senior and Pompey, and the death of Curio. Crassus Senior was decapitated, and his severed head was subsequently brought to the wedding of the Parthian king Orodes II's son and heir Pacorus to the Armenian king Artavasdes II's sister at the Armenian capital city of Artashat. As part of the wedding festivities, the guests enjoyed a performance of the famous Greek tragedian Euripides' *Bacchae*, and one of the actors, Jason of Tralles, used the head as a prop, substituting it for the ersatz head of Pentheus.[42] There is also a story that molten gold was poured into his mouth to symbolize his thirst for wealth, a grisly method of execution that was repurposed by George R. R. Martin in his first *Song of Ice and Fire* novel *A Game of Thrones*.[43] Pompey was likewise decapitated, and his severed head was kept by Ptolemy XIII and his advisors in order to be presented to Caesar upon his arrival in Egypt a short while later.

The poet Lucan makes much of the fact that Cornelia was unable to administer the standard funerary rites for either husband, and portrays her reproaching the goddess Fortuna for this double blow, in a manner that we might envisage Fulvia doing, albeit with slightly less self-pity:

Unworthy then was I to kindle my husband's pyre, to bend over the cold limbs, and throw myself upon the body; unworthy to burn my torn tresses, to gather the limbs of Magnus scattered in the sea, to pour a flood of tears into every wound, and to fill my bosom with the bones and warm ashes, with the purpose of sprinkling in the temples of the gods whatever I might gather from the extinguished flame. The pyre burns on with no funeral honours; perhaps some Egyptian hand proffered this service which the dead resents. Well is it that the remains of the Crassi lie unburied; the fire that was granted to Pompey shows greater spite on the part of Heaven. Shall my sad lot ever repeat itself? Shall I never be allowed to give due burial to a husband? Shall I never mourn over an urn that contains ashes? But what need is there of a grave, or why does grief require any trappings? Do I not, undutiful wife, carry Pompey in my whole breast? Does not his image cling to my inmost heart? Let a wife who intends to survive her husband seek his ashes.[44]

So Fulvia found herself suddenly and dramatically widowed with a young son whose interests she needed to safeguard. Other Roman women were lionized for collapsing in danger of death or even killing themselves rather than face living on without their husbands, but that was a self-indulgent luxury that Fulvia could ill afford in the midst of a civil war.[45] Just as she had chosen to remarry quickly upon Clodius' death, and to remarry an ally of her deceased husband, so she chose to remarry quickly again, and remarry not only an ally of her deceased husband but the man who was perhaps his best friend, despite the famous Roman maxims that 'frequent re-marriage gives room for the evil tongue' and 'the woman who marries many is disliked by many'.[46]

Curio and Marcus Antonius had been close companions since childhood. Plutarch details their youthful misadventures and indiscretions, citing Curio as having been a bad influence on Antony, leading him into drinking, womanizing, and such excessive spending that Antony ended up in significant debt to the tune of tens of thousands of sesterces, debts to which Curio stood as guarantor until his father found out and banned the pair from seeing each other.[47] They had been so close, in fact, that at one point they were accused of having a homosexual relationship, something that their equality in social rank precluded.[48]

Curio had used his popularity and influence over the people of the city of Rome to ensure Antony's election to the tribunate the year after he served his term, so it was perhaps with this great favour in mind that Antony sought to look after his widow and child. This type of action was not unusual: when one of Crassus' brothers had died, he married his bereaved sister-in-law.[49] An added bonus was the fact that Fulvia and Antony's marriage was supported by Caesar – who, having known Fulvia since she was a child due to their shared relatives, was well acquainted with her personal qualities and thought that her influence would steady Antony. However, the circumstances were somewhat controversial, with Fulvia being a recent widow and Antony divorcing his wife Antonia, who was also his first cousin, for adultery so he was able to marry Fulvia.

This practice of something akin to wife-swapping, which may seem somewhat unsavoury to us today, was a fairly normal practice in Republican Rome. It was not unusual for betrothals and marriages to be made to suit the prevailing polit- ical alliances of the day, and then equally quickly unmade through

A marble portrait bust of Marcus Antonius

divorce as soon as an alternative match became expedient. Quintus Hortensius Hortalus, the Late Republic's leading advocate and orator prior to the rise of Cicero, was such an admirer of Marcus Porcius Cato Uticensis (Cato the Younger) that in 56 BCE he begged to marry Cato's twenty-year-old daughter Porcia and father a son who would share the two men's blood. Cato turned down his request, wishing his daughter to remain married to her husband Marcus Calpurnius Bibulus, by whom she had three children, but proceeded to offer Hortensius his own wife Marcia instead, mollifying Hortensius with the fact that any children produced would be siblings to Cato's three children by Marcia. She was considered by both men, and later commentators, to be 'noble soil for the production of children'.[50] While we do not know Marcia's thoughts on the situation, Marcia's father agreed to the match, Cato divorced her, and she married Hortensius, indeed bearing him the child he longed for. The poet Lucian envisages Marcia begging Cato to remarry her upon Hortensius' death rather than seeking to further his political agenda by marrying her to someone else.[51] While we do not know Marcia's thoughts on this either, the couple did, in fact, remarry

– and, since Marcia had inherited Hortensius' vast estate, Cato became considerably richer than he had been.

An alternative example of an attempt at politically advantageous wife-swapping and childbearing, albeit a far less successful one, can be found in the marriage of Fulvia's friend and reputed orgy partner Mucia and Scaurus, following the former's divorce from Pompey. Scaurus was under the impression that marrying Pompey's former wife would be politically and socially advantageous for him, linking him with Pompey via any children he had with Mucia – being half-siblings to her three children with Pompey. He was, however, mistaken, with Pompey taking considerable offence at his presumption and only offering him a token amount of support during his trial in the summer of 54 BCE.[52]

Still only in her late twenties or early thirties, Fulvia had twice been widowed prematurely by violence, a fact that was not lost on observers. Cicero snidely warned Antony to take care not to follow in the footsteps of Clodius and Curio, 'since you have that in your house which proved fatal to them both'.[53]

CHAPTER 8

THE THIRD TRIBUNE

FULVIA'S MARRIAGE TO ANTONY was ever so slightly scandalous
because Antony was, in fact, ever so slightly scandalous. We are
remarkably well informed about Antony's misspent youth because
Cicero used it as ammunition against him in his *Philippics*, a series
of fourteen speeches he delivered and pamphlets he disseminated
in the period 44–43 BCE in the wake of the assassination of Caesar,
when his and Antony's feud was at its height.[1] Plutarch also used it as
context in his biography of Antony, written in the late first century CE.
Unfortunately, in one of the tragedies of ancient manuscript transmis-
sion, Antony's attempts to respond to this mudslinging, and explain
and justify himself – such as his treatise *On His Own Drunkenness* –
have not survived.[2]

While Antony came from a prestigious plebeian senatorial family
that claimed descent from Anton, one of the sons of the Graeco-Roman
demigod Herakles/Hercules, by the time of his birth they had fallen
on hard times. This might have had something to do with Antony's
father's rather short-sighted tendency to give the family silver away

to friends in a spot of financial bother.[3] Upon the death of his father, Antony had to actually refuse his inheritance because all that came with it was debt, rendering him a bankrupt before he was even an adult.[4] He then proceeded to accumulate a substantial amount of debt of his own during his escapades with Curio.[5] It is possible that this precarious financial situation led Antony to align himself with a woman named Fadia, the daughter of the wealthy freedman Quintus Fadius Gallus and thus far below his social station, before contracting marriage with his first cousin Antonia Hybrida (while his peers referred to his relationship with Fadia as marriage, it could simply have been one of concubinage, with them attempting to cast aspersions).[6] Cicero would later accuse him of marrying Fulvia to alleviate a debt of six million sesterces.

Antony also had a long-term relationship with a mime actress and dancer named Volumnia Cytheris, the freedwoman of a man named Publius Volumnius Eutrapelus (like Fadia, she was sometimes referred to as Antony's wife).[7] He was not the only member of his social and political circle to spend quality time with her: one of his contemporaries, Gallus, wrote her four books of love poetry before she threw him over for Antony, and another, either Marcus or Decimus Junius Brutus, two of the future assassins of Caesar, made overtures to her too.[8] Even Cicero enjoyed her company at a dinner party hosted by Volumnius. Although he managed to restrain himself from attempting to initiate any intimacies, he was delighted to have the opportunity to gossip about her with his friends.[9] After all, politicking did not take place only in public, in the Forum or the Senate House, but also in private, in the baths and at banquets.

There was a significant amount of homosocial bonding going on amongst the members of the Caesarian faction in the late 50s and early 40s BCE as they attempted to shore up their political position, and just as Fulvia herself had been an important element of this via her marriages, so was Cytheris through her extramarital liaisons with the Republic's movers and shakers. Consequently, Cytheris was unusually prominent for a courtesan, accompanying Antony in public during his tribuneship in 49 BCE, positioned ahead of Antony's mother Julia in his retinue as an indicator of just how much things were in flux during Caesar's war with Pompey.[10] It suited Cicero to present Cytheris as Antony's second wife during his marriage to Antonia Hybrida, and then during his marriage to Fulvia, as a means of blackening Antony's name and casting aspersions on his moral character, despite the fact that relationships with courtesans were a normal part of life in high society. He had used similar means against Gaius Verres in his prosecution speech against him in 70 BCE, drawing attention to the prominence of Verres' mistress Chelidon and her influence over his decision-making during Verres' tenure as governor of Sicily.[11] What did Fulvia think about this? Considering that Clodius, Curio and Antony had all been part of the same social circle for years, and certainly Clodius had been accused of having an entourage filled with performers such as actors and actresses, of which Cytheris may well have been one, it is likely that the women were acquainted before Fulvia's marriage to Antony.

Roman men were not expected to be faithful to their wives, and extramarital relationships with enslaved people, formerly enslaved people and others lower down the social hierarchy were standard practice. None of these individuals were on the same level as a wife, however, especially not one who was a member of the senatorial and equestrian elite. In fact, Cicero claims that on 3 May 49 BCE, Antony was not only accompanied by Cytheris, but also seven litters' worth of girlfriends and boyfriends, so he seems to have had a very lively and extremely varied extramarital sex life.[12] Of course, Antony was not alone in this. Around this time, Caesar, who had been married to his third or fourth wife Calpurnia since 59 BCE, was having an affair with Servilia, seduced a number of other married women, and would shortly commence an affair with Cleopatra, Queen of Egypt.[13] His sexual escapades with both women and men were so well known that his soldiers sang bawdy songs about them during his famous Quadruple Triumph in 46 BCE – the military victories over Gaul, Pontus, Africa and Egypt – and a few fragments of these have survived to amuse us to this day.[14] So senatorial wives were well acquainted with their husbands' proclivities, and seemingly chose to ignore them for the most part.

But Cytheris clearly occupied a significant place in Antony's heart, something which was recognized by his contemporaries, as is made clear by the fact that when Cicero's wife Terentia sought Antony's assistance in allowing Cicero to return to Italy and become reconciled with Caesar in 47 BCE, she asked Cytheris to act as an intermediary.[15] Did this happen before Antony married Fulvia, or afterwards? At first glance, the former scenario would make more sense, since if Antony was already married to Fulvia, surely Terentia would have gone to her for help before going to Cytheris? Yet perhaps Terentia recognized that Fulvia was unlikely to be receptive to assisting her first husband's sworn enemy, or perhaps Cytheris simply wielded more influence over Antony than Fulvia at this point in time. Whatever the chronology of these intertwined relationships, a senatorial woman whose sister was a Vestal Virgin meeting with a courtesan and begging her to intercede on her and her consular husband's behalf was highly irregular, so it is likely that upon marrying Antony, Fulvia watched Cytheris closely, waiting for an opportunity to neutralize her. And it is probable that she also took careful note of the women in her social circle who sought Cytheris' assistance rather than her own, biding her time while she planned how best to deal with them.

As devastating as being widowed by violence twice in three years would have been, Fulvia was more fortunate than her female peers whose marriages ended in divorce: unlike them, she was able to retain custody of all three of her children – Publius, Claudia and Gaius. Had her marriages to Clodius and Curio ended through divorce, no matter who was at fault or why, both ex-husbands would have been legally entitled to the children, and had they been so inclined, or so vindictive, they could have prevented her from ever seeing them at all. The children of elite Roman families could experience a considerable amount of upheaval, enduring not only their parents' numerous marriages, divorces, bereavements and remarriages, but also having to adjust to the presence of new half-siblings and step-siblings.[16] Since Antony would have retained custody of his and Antonia Hybrida's daughter, Antonia Prima (born sometime in the 50s BCE, so of an age with Publius and Claudia), Fulvia would have found herself donning the mantle of stepmother, a position that was fraught with negative associations.[17] At the very least, stepmothers expected to encounter resentment or hostility from their newly acquired stepchildren.[18]

This is an instance where, considering the vitriol that Fulvia's actions during her marriage to Antony tend to receive from ancient authors, it is surprising we do not see the sexist and misogynistic Roman attitudes towards stepmothers brought to bear as a means of blackening her character. Many other Roman stepmothers were accused of a variety of types of cruelty towards and mistreatment of their stepchildren, extending all the way to murder, and since commentators were keen to emphasize how unwomanly Fulvia was, attacking her maternal instincts would have been an easy win for her detractors. Thus we can entertain the possibility that Fulvia was an exemplary stepmother to Antonia Prima, as any deviation would have been eagerly seized upon as a stick to beat her with. Just as she was likely involved in arranging the marriage of Claudia to Octavian to strengthen the bonds between Antony and his foremost political rival and ally in 44 BCE, so, around the same time, was she likely involved in arranging the betrothal of Antonia Prima to the son of another of Antony's key allies in this period – Lepidus, Caesar's replacement as *pontifex maximus* and the future third triumvir. While Claudia was allocated the higher-profile match, that may not have been due to favouritism, but simply because she was older and therefore in a position to marry immediately rather than need an extended betrothal in order to reach an appropriate age (probably around twelve years old, at least). The betrothal stood until around 36 BCE, after Fulvia's death, when Lepidus had ceased to be politically significant. Antony then arranged a different marriage for Antonia Prima with one of his eastern allies, the obscenely wealthy Pythodoros of Tralles. Their daughter Pythodorida would ultimately become Queen of Pontus and Cappadocia.

Not long after the amalgamation of Antonia Prima with Fulvia's brood, there was another addition. True to form, just as had been the case in her first and second marriages, soon after Fulvia embarked

upon her third she fell pregnant, and in around 47 BCE she gave birth
to her third – and, as far as we know, Antony's first – son. The baby
was named Marcus Antonius, after his father, but was known by the
additional name (*cognomen*) Antyllus, to differentiate the two. This was
in all likelihood a corruption of Antonillus, literally 'Little Antony' or
'Antony Junior'. As Antony's eldest son, Antyllus was his legal and
political heir, and was featured prominently on Antony's coinage in the
following years. While Antony occupied the primary position on the
obverse faces, Antyllus occupied the reverse, and assuming we can trust
these portraits as reasonably faithful likenesses of the pair, he closely
resembled his father.[19]

*A gold aureus depicting Marcus Antonius and his eldest son, Marcus
Antonius Antyllus*

Antyllus' importance was further recognized by his betrothal to
Octavian's daughter Julia, the first Roman emperor's only biological
child, in 37 BCE.[20] As Antyllus aged, he began to accompany his father
on his sojourns in the eastern Mediterranean, and spent much of his
time in Alexandria, where he had his own retinue, including a team
of personal physicians. One of these, Philotas, shared anecdotes about
Antyllus that ended up in Plutarch's biography of Antony, and they
give us an insight into the way that he was raised and treated those
around him. It seems he followed his father and grandfather's example
and bestowed lavish gifts upon his friends and acquaintances.[21]

So, Fulvia and her three children moved out of Clodius' house
on the Palatine Hill and into Antony's (her eldest son Publius was
probably still slightly too young to live independently, even though it
is probable that Clodius' estate had passed to him upon his father's
death in 52 BCE), where he had at least one child living with him, his

first daughter Antonia Prima (he apparently had children with Fadia, but nothing about them, not even their names, has been recorded). At this point in time, Antony also lived on the Palatine Hill, a stone's throw away from Fulvia.[22] His house was quite a sizeable residence, so the blended family could have lived there comfortably for a time.[23] However, upon the death of Pompey the Great in Egypt in 48 BCE, a public auction of his estate was announced via the traditional practice of planting a lance in front of the Temple of Jupiter Stator (Jupiter the Sustainer) at the foot of the Palatine Hill, roughly where the Arch of Titus stands today. Antony purchased one of his properties, the Domus Rostrata, at a knockdown price, remarking that he had gone from being 'beggar one day, rich the next'.[24] This residence was on the Carinae, the western end of the southern spur of the Esquiline Hill (in the vicinity of the Basilica of San Pietro in Vincoli today), an area in which several buildings resembled the keels of ships.[25] It seems that Pompey had appreciated this and decided to adopt it as a decorative theme: the Domus Rostrata was so named because its façade was embellished with the rostra from the pirate ships that he had defeated during his extraordinary command over the Mediterranean in 67 BCE. It also came with beautiful gardens,[26] and was situated near the ancient temple of the earth goddess Tellus.[27]

The fact that the house had passed to Antony rather than Pompey's son Sextus was a rather sore spot with the latter, and he continued to be snide about it when dealing with Antony for some years afterwards.[28] But like Antony's Palatine house, this one would be passed to one of Octavian's henchmen after his death – in this case the emperor's stepson and future successor, Tiberius – and it too likely burned down, albeit later, during the Great Fire of 64 CE during the reign of the emperor Nero (Antony's great-great-grandson).[29]

Did the family move across the city and take up residence on the Carinae instead of the Palatine? The way that Cicero harangued Antony about the house and the way he behaved while living there suggests that Antony may have treated it as something akin to a gentleman's club or even a fraternity house, hosting non-stop drinking and gambling parties with unsavoury members of his social circle such as Cytheris and her fellow mimes Hippias and Sergius, who were rapidly making their way through the contents of Pompey's renowned wine cellar. Cicero had plenty to say about their supposed degradation of such hallowed ground. If so, it was perhaps not the most suitable place for his wife and young family. It would have made sense for them to remain on the Palatine, and for Antony to divide his time between the two residences, having one foot in the prestigious neighbourhood of the Palatine and the other in the trendy neighbourhood of the Carinae, one of the most fashionable quarters of the city.

In any case, in moving from Clodius' Palatine house to Antony's, Fulvia would no doubt have been relieved to have the opportunity to depart from a house that had seen so much tragedy to another, in search of a fresh start. Even if she did not herself reside in the Domus Rostrata, she was still technically mistress of it, and it was one of the finest residences in the city. She may also have felt somewhat smug about possessing the house of one of her first husband's political enemies, a house that Clodius had at one point threatened to demolish as he had done Cicero's.[30] She was no doubt instrumental in assessing the contents and deciding to dispose of Pompey's collection of silver plate, his expensive purple soft furnishings, and his furniture, with a view to cherry-picking the pieces that she liked and replacing those she did not with items more to her own taste.

———

By 44 BCE, Antony's sustained support for Caesar had paid off and he was elected consul alongside the dictator. Little did he know that he would soon be taking Caesar's place as the pre-eminent man in Rome, with Fulvia by his side as the pre-eminent woman.

For Caesar, the Ides (15th) of March 44 BCE began like any other day – although, had he been paying more attention, he might have noticed that something was not quite right.[31] It was gloomy (the poet Virgil would subsequently succumb to the pathetic fallacy and imbue the weather with impending doom). First thing in the morning, his wife Calpurnia shared with him that she had had a troubling dream in which their house had collapsed, and he had been wounded and then approached her, streaming with blood, in order to take refuge. Caesar, too, had had a strange dream, in which he had been raised up into the sky until he could grasp the hand of the god Jupiter. Hearing this, Calpurnia begged him not to attend the planned meeting of the Senate, scheduled to take place that morning in an antechamber within the vast complex of the Portico of Pompey because the Senate House in the Forum was currently undergoing construction work. On the agenda was his impending Parthian campaign, for which he was planning to depart a mere three days later. In the face of her severe distress, Caesar acquiesced, and agreed to send Antony to cancel the meeting, but the senator Decimus Brutus (the most significant conspirator behind the ringleaders Marcus Junius Brutus and Gaius Cassius Longinus) managed to change his mind. The Etruscan diviner and soothsayer Spurinna lurked, muttering ambiguous warnings.

It has to be said, the conspirators were fortunate: they succeeded in their plan to assassinate Caesar in spite of their level of preparation and competence rather than because of it. The plot was so vast, and so many people had come to be included (although we know the names of only twenty conspirators today, some estimate as many as seventy were involved, since Junius Brutus believed that this would make it a legitimate act of tyrant removal rather than an illegitimate murder), that it was hardly a secret, and several people attempted to warn Caesar of what awaited him as he made his way through the city. Someone went to his home to intercept him, only to find he had already left. Another handed him a wax tablet with an account of the conspiracy etched upon it as he passed, but he did not stop to read it. A man named Artemidorus actually went to the meeting of the Senate to intervene, but arrived too late.

There were gladiatorial games happening at the same time as the Senate meeting, so burly, tooled-up ruffians were lingering in the colonnade of the portico, waiting for a prearranged sign from Decimus Brutus to barricade the entrances and exits. Antony, walking alongside

Caesar, was intercepted at the door by another conspirator, Gaius Trebonius, on a pretext. While many of the conspirators thought that Antony should be assassinated as well, Junius Brutus reiterated that Caesar was a tyrant that needed to be removed, and since they were not aiming at a full-scale purge, Antony should be spared.[32]

The ominous signs continued to proliferate. As Caesar oversaw the auspices which traditionally opened a meeting of the Senate, the sacrifices went awry. The first victim had no heart, a sign of impending death. The second was missing the upper part of its entrails. Yet still he pressed on, having no patience for portents.

With Caesar isolated inside the room, separated from companions who would otherwise have come to his aid, unprotected and unarmed, the conspirators struck. Each attempted to stab him at least once (another point Junius Brutus had been firm about), but in the chaos they managed to injure each other as well. Although Caesar initially fought back, he soon accepted the inevitable, pulled his toga over his head, and died at the feet of a statue of his former friend, colleague, son-in-law, rival and enemy, Pompey. It was at this point, with Caesar lying dead at their feet, that the conspirators realized they were not entirely sure what to do next. As Cicero comments, 'That deed was done with the courage of men but the strategy of children.'[33] They had been so wrapped up in their own personal hatred of Caesar that they had rather assumed that his death would be met with rejoicing, but it turned out that the opposite was true. Many of the Senate and most of the people had loved Caesar, and there were rather more of them than there were conspirators.

As word spread about what had happened, the gladiatorial games ceased, the theatre emptied, and people began to plunder the markets. The conspirators marched to the Forum, bloody knives in their hands, and proclaimed what they had done, only to be met with appalled silence. One of them even waved a *pileus*, a cap traditionally bestowed upon enslaved people upon their emancipation from enslavement as a sign of their liberty, and this undoubtedly seemed a bit rich to the urban *plebs* looking on in horror and disgust at the spectacle the senators were making of themselves. Meanwhile, three enslaved people placed Caesar's body on a litter and carried it home to Calpurnia.

Antony, now the sole consul, had to tread very carefully in the wake of Caesar's death. Once he saw the brutalized body and realized what had happened, he shed his toga and fled home to the Domus Rostrata in disguise, fearful (not unjustifiably) that he would be next – although Cicero was not involved in the conspiracy, he opined later to anyone who would listen that Antony should have been removed too.[34] If Fulvia and the children were not present at that location, he would have undoubtedly sent word to them, whether they were at the house on the Palatine or one of the couple's other residences, warning them to guard themselves.

Antony's friend Lepidus, Caesar's Master of the Horse, recognized his ultimate authority as the remaining consul, and supported him by transferring troops across the Tiber to the Campus Martius (the 'Field of Mars', a meeting and mustering place outside the *pomerium*), ready and waiting for orders. He was given all of Caesar's papers by Calpurnia, and with these in hand, summoned the remainder of the Senate to meet at daybreak the following day at the nearby Temple of Tellus to debate the next steps. He attended this meeting wearing armour under his toga. He had the unenviable task of having to appease not only both the anti- and pro-Caesarian factions of the Senate, but also Caesar's soldiers and veterans, and the urban *plebs*. There was also the question of whether, if Caesar had been a tyrant, as the conspirators insisted he was, should all of his orders be followed now? He had, after all, allocated magistracies and other positions such as provincial gover-norships for the next few years, and the people he had selected were unsurprisingly most unwilling to give up their appointments out of some misguided notion of liberty. So, at first, Antony struck a concilia-tory note: he acknowledged the legitimacy of the so-called Liberators' actions – they had removed a tyrant, not murdered a rival – yet he retained Caesar's appointments and his agenda.

On 17 March, he even invited one of the conspiracy's ringleaders, Cassius, to dine at his home, offering his young son Antyllus as a hostage as surety for Cassius' safety. While there was a long history of Romans offering hostages to ensure good behaviour during diplomatic negotiations between hostile parties, what was unprecedented about this situation was the age of the hostage involved: Antyllus could not have been older than two at the time.[35] While Antony could have acted unilaterally as Antyllus' *pater familias*, given his openness to female influence throughout his life and political career it seems highly unlikely that he made the decision to do this with no input from Fulvia at all, nor any regard for her feelings. Yet there is no way that she was neutral or even unconcerned about placing her youngest child in this vulnerable situation: after all, only two days prior, Cassius and his cronies had brutally murdered someone. She would have been helpless against casting her mind back to the events of 52 BCE, and the threats against her son Publius from Milo and his gang, and despaired at such a thing happening again. While Antyllus was not the only child hostage on this occasion, his companion and fellow hostage Marcus Lepidus was ten years old, and thus slightly more able to attempt to protect himself or at least try to escape if it became necessary. He also benefited from the added layer of protection of being nephew to both Brutus and Cassius (they and the boy's father, the future triumvir Marcus Lepidus, were married to three sisters, daughters of Caesar's mistress Servilia). Antyllus could boast no such family relationship with the Liberators to insulate him from the threat of retaliatory violence, and although he would have undoubtedly been accompanied by enslaved persons such as his nurse, they would have been little defence against military men with weapons. Consequently, Fulvia's presence at dinner that evening is highly likely, as she would hardly have made herself scarce, and her participation would have gone some way to reassuring Cassius of Antony's good intentions. The occasion passed without event, and the next day Antyllus was restored to his mother, safe and sound. Cicero would later offer a rare word of praise for both Antony and Antyllus for their joint effort on behalf of the Republic.[36]

However, when the time came for Caesar's funeral, Antony took a leaf out of Fulvia's book of vengeance. Just as she had publicly displayed

Clodius' body in the Forum, calling attention to the violence done to him, so did Antony publicly display Caesar's, going one better and having a mannequin made up and rotating it to give the crowd a better view of the twenty-three stab wounds. He delivered an emotional speech, employing the tactic of stochastic terrorism against the Liberators by demonizing them, and in the process incited the crowd to riot and rampage through the city. Just as the crowd in 52 BCE had seized Clodius' body and cremated it in the Forum, so did this crowd seize Caesar's and cremate it on the spot, the site of the pyre subsequently serving as the foundations of the Temple of the Deified Caesar that can still be seen in the Forum today (visitors even leave flowers and other offerings there *in memoriam*). And just as the crowd at Clodius' funeral had burned down the Senate House, so too did the crowd at Caesar's.

In the immediate aftermath of Caesar's assassination, Antony was the most powerful and influential man in Rome. He immediately relieved the Temple of Ops on the Capitoline Hill of the 700 million sesterces that Caesar had deposited there.[37] There was a lot to do, and Fulvia was determined to help him do it. We are fortunate that Cicero's letters to family members, friends and acquaintances during this tumultuous period have survived, as he treated them to a running commentary regarding his disapproval of the way that the couple were managing the day-to-day business of the Republic. According to him, Fulvia was far too prominent, and was actually transacting political business on Antony's behalf from the women's quarters of their Palatine home. Living nearby, he would have had an unobstructed view of the comings and goings from the house. Unlike that paragon of Roman womanhood Lucretia, Fulvia was not restricting herself to spinning and weaving but rather engaging in international diplomacy.[38] She was especially close with one of Rome's eastern client kings, Deiotarus of Galatia in Asia Minor. He had unfortunately been deposed, and efforts were under way to reinstate him. 'No doubt he deserves any kingdom we can give him,' Cicero sniffed in a letter to his close friend Atticus on 22 April, 'but not through Fulvia.'[39] An agreement was reached between Deiotarus and Fulvia regarding the transfer (one might even

say bribe) of an astronomical amount of money – ten million sesterces
– to Antony.[40]

In comparing Fulvia to Lucretia, Cicero was in turn implying that
Antony was like Tarquin, but making him out to be even worse than
one of Rome's ancient and unlamented kings, railing bitterly 'what king
ever had the unmitigated impudence to put up all benefits, grants, and
rights in his realm for sale? Exemptions, citizen rights, rewards – are
there any that he has not sold to individuals or communities or whole
provinces? Nothing base or sordid is told of Tarquin: but in [Antony's]
house gold was weighed and money counted amongst the women's
wool baskets.'[41]

It was also imperative that Antony consolidate his influence over
Caesar's soldiers and veterans. In order to do so, he undertook a tour
of Italy, and Fulvia accompanied him.[42] This was unexpected, as in this
period Roman women had no formal contact with the military and
no involvement in military matters. During the Republic, women did
not even tend to accompany their husbands on their postings abroad,
but rather stayed at home in Rome, with couples often separated for
years at a time. This had started to change during the civil wars of the
first century BCE, starting with the dictator Sulla's wife Caecilia Metella
accompanying him to Athens, and then Pompey's wife Cornelia accompanying him to Egypt, but while civil unrest and strife had become the
norm, it was still not considered normal. The fact that women were
appearing in proximity to legions was yet one more sign that things
had gone horribly awry.

After travelling down the entire length of the Via Appia, a journey
of around two weeks' duration, the couple arrived at Brundisium
(modern Brindisi), the port that served as the gateway to the eastern
Mediterranean and was of huge strategic importance throughout the
Republican civil wars. Once there, Antony ordered that the politically
disloyal and mutinous soldiers be subjected to decimation.[43] While
Caesar had threatened the Ninth Legion with this punishment during
his war against Pompey, he had restricted it to the ringleaders of the
mutiny rather than all of the soldiers.

Decimation was an ancient military disciplinary measure in which a cohort (around 480 soldiers) was divided into groups of ten, the members of each group drew lots, and then one soldier would be executed by the other nine via a method such as stoning, clubbing or stabbing. Antony ordered the unlucky centurions to come to his residence and had them beaten to death in front of Fulvia.[44] During this brutal process, she was not only present but apparently close enough that the blood splashed her face.[45] The Romans considered blood a polluting substance, so Fulvia would have required some kind of subsequent purification. There was no reason for her to be present for this event unless she wished to be and had requested to be. It was perhaps an additional layer of punishment for the soldiers to be subjected to this humiliating treatment not only in front of their commander, but also his wife. But Roman women were not necessarily able to be kept insulated from interpersonal violence in this period – let us not forget that Milo's wife Fausta was present at the Battle of Bovillae, and it is unlikely in the extreme that she avoided seeing her husband and his henchmen brutally murder Clodius and most of his entourage.

Interestingly, it seems to have been around this time that Antony finally parted ways with Cytheris, evicting her from the Domus Rostrata, taking his house keys back from her and assuring Fulvia of his newfound marital fidelity.[46] We can gain an insight into the interpersonal dynamics of Fulvia's relationship with Antony around this time from an anecdote that survives in several places.[47] When attempts were made by the Liberators and their allies in 43 BCE to have Antony declared a public enemy for abusing his position and powers, he went into hiding. On one occasion he returned to Rome late at night, hidden inside a carriage that drove up to his front door. Hiding his face and disguising his voice, he told his doorman that he was a courier who had come with a message for the lady of the house. He was admitted into Fulvia's presence, and he passed her the letter. As Fulvia read its declaration of love and promises of fidelity, she began to cry, upon which Antony cast off his disguise and swept her up in an embrace.[48] Cicero relates this story primarily in order to lambast Antony for being so frivolous at such a dangerous time, but also to depict him as a slavish lover in thrall to a domineering woman. Plutarch, however, uses it as a means of showing how Antony sought to soothe Fulvia at an extremely difficult and dangerous time for them both.[49]

While Antony was on the run, Fulvia and his mother Julia did their utmost to lobby his peers in the Senate on his behalf, dressing themselves in mourning garb and going from house to house, Antony's infant offspring in tow to elicit an extra level of sympathy, arguing that it was illegal to have someone unilaterally declared a public enemy.[50] Antyllus' presence on this occasion would undoubtedly have served to remind people of Antony's willingness to put his son in danger for the sake of the Republic the previous year, and made them more amenable. This period must have been extremely difficult for Fulvia, undoubtedly putting her in mind, once again, of the tumultuous events of a decade prior, when Clodius had been murdered and rumours abounded that Milo was coming for her son Publius next. Just as there had been then, now there were threats against her children.[51]

With Antony gone from Rome and on the run, her father Bambalio either dead or of no real use, and her brother Natta and stepfather Murena likewise also either dead or no longer politically influential, Fulvia was without powerful male protection. She became a target, with people bombarding her with spurious lawsuits, and successfully seeking to seize her property and possessions. It was common at this time for people to attempt to take advantage of women who were perceived to be vulnerable – the *Laudatio Turiae* inscription we encountered earlier gives another example of a fatherless and husbandless woman forced to fend off avaricious enemies at a time of political turmoil. Luckily for Fulvia, at this point her friend Atticus stepped in.[52] He was completely neutral, having chosen neither to pursue a political career nor to align himself with one political faction over any others, and so could accompany her to all the lawsuits with which she was being bombarded. He was also fabulously wealthy, and was able to help her complete the purchase of an estate that she had begun before all the trouble but now did not have the money to conclude and was not able to secure a loan

1. *J. M. W. Turner's painting 'Cicero at his Villa at Tusculum', on display at Ascott House, near Leighton Buzzard, owned by the National Trust.*

2. A fresco from the Villa of Publius Fannius Synistor at Boscoreale, dated to around 40–30 BCE and currently housed in the Metropolitan Museum of Art.

3. A fresco from the Villa of the Mysteries just outside Pompeii shows a ritual preparation for marriage.

4. *A polychromy terracotta urn from Sicily shows part of a wedding procession.*

5. *An ivory couch recovered from a villa on the Via Cassia just outside Rome, on display at the Metropolitan Museum of Art in New York.*

6. *A beautiful mosaic from the Casa della Matrona ignota at Pompeii depicting a wealthy matron and her parure, which can be seen in the National Archaeological Museum of Naples.*

7. 'The Vengeance of Fulvia' by Francisco Maura y Montaner, 1888.

8. 'Fulvia with the Head of Cicero' by Pavel Svedomsky, 1898.

9. (Top left) 'Agreement between Camilla and Turnus' by Francesco de Mura (1696–1782).

10. (Top right) Hypsicratea depicted in an illuminated manuscript, c. 1410.

11. (Left) Woman holding a shield in a contemporaneous fresco from the Villa of Publius Fannius Synistor, Boscoreale, currently housed in the Metropolitan Museum of Art.

12. *The Tomb of Caecilia Metelli, Rome.*

13. *'Tu Marcellus Eris', or 'Virgil Reading the Aeneid before Augustus, Livia, and Octavia' by Jean–Auguste–Dominique Ingres, 1812.*

14. *'Agrippina Landing at Brindisium with the Ashes of Germanicus' by Gavin Hamilton, 1765–72.*

15. *A scene from HBO's Rome with Polly Walker as Atia and James Purefoy as Antony.*

to facilitate. He loaned her the money without requiring interest or even a legal contract.

Since it was around this time that Fulvia gave birth to her last child – her fourth (and Antony's second) son, Iullus Antonius – she no doubt appreciated Atticus' support, both moral and financial, even more than she would have done otherwise. The choice of the unusual name Iullus, a variation of Iulus, the son of the Trojan hero Aeneas and grandson of the goddess Venus, was a nod to Antony's deceased benefactor Caesar, and his connection to the Julian family through his mother Julia.[53] It was also a means of emphasizing Antony's relationship with Caesar in the face of competition from Octavian, Caesar's posthumously adopted son and legal heir. However, it may also have been a subtle reference to the fact that Fulvia's nephew Scarpus was Caesar's great-nephew, as Natta was married to Caesar's niece. Scarpus had been close to Caesar, the dictator having named him as one of his secondary heirs in his will and leaving him a bequest of one-eighth of his property, although Scarpus had tactfully turned the inheritance over to Octavian.[54] Scarpus was closely aligned with Antony, his uncle by marriage, rather than Octavian, his cousin, during this time. He served under Antony during the civil wars against the Liberators, and was subsequently allotted the governorship of Cyrenaica with control of its mint, through which he issued coins bearing his and Antony's images.

We can get an insight into the thoughts and feelings of a couple separated for political reasons, with the husband exiled and the wife left behind to cope without him, albeit from the husband's perspective, by reading Ovid's letters from Tomis to his wife, whom he does not name, back in Rome. While Ovid's wife could have accompanied him, and did in fact beg to be allowed to do so, he preferred for her to remain behind to defend his property, as the vultures started circling, and represent his interests, just as Cicero's wife Terentia did during his exile.[55] Ovid's wife was not sanguine about her situation, however, and as time went on seems to have begun to complain bitterly to Ovid about the shame of being an exile's wife, about how embarrassing she now found social interaction, avoiding eye contact and blushing profusely, and even declared that she was no longer proud of him or of being married to him.[56] Just as Cicero and Terentia's marriage buckled under the strain of separation, so too did Ovid and his wife's, with him responding in kind, criticizing her lack of success in affecting his recall and finding fault in her shyness and timidity.[57]

No one could ever accuse Fulvia of shyness or timidity. Under these circumstances, her bravura and assertiveness were a distinct advantage. Before long, her lobbying paid off, and Cicero's initiative to have Antony declared a public enemy failed. The danger having passed, Antony was able to return to Rome, and what he did next surprised everyone: he entered into an alliance with his deadly rivals Octavian and Lepidus.

CHAPTER 9

THE TRIUMVIR

W‍HAT WE KNOW TODAY as the Second Triumvirate, an alliance between Antony, Octavian, and Marcus Aemilius Lepidus, was formalized by the *lex Titia*, the Titian Law, on 27 November 43 BCE.[1] To consolidate the coalition, and link Antony and Octavian by marriage, Fulvia's daughter Claudia, now a young teenager, was betrothed to Octavian, just as Caesar's daughter Julia had been betrothed to Pompey.[2] This may have been Fulvia's idea, as mothers and other female relations and friends were often responsible for initiating conversations about and attempts at matchmaking between young couples – when Cicero's daughter Tullia was looking for a husband, Terentia and her friends Pontidia, Servilia and Postumia put together a list of three candidates. To make the alliance between the two principal heirs of Caesar as public as possible, it is likely that Octavian and Claudia had a lavish wedding. Then, Claudia moved across the Palatine to Octavian's house, which had once belonged to Fulvia's cousin Hortensius and was a rather humble abode, lacking marble columns and mosaic pavements, so probably rather different to the standard of living that Claudia was used to.[3]

At some point in the period 43–41 BCE, Antony had a series of coins issued at mints in Rome, Lugdunum (modern Lyon) and Phrygia. Perhaps first struck to celebrate his birthday, and then reissued periodically over the next few years by both Antony and his subordinates, they depict a curious figure on the obverse face.[4] This figure, a woman with her hair arranged in the fashionable *nodus* coiffure that is often seen on female portraits that survive from the Late Republic and Early Principate, bears a pair of wings that has led to her identification as the goddess Victoria, or Victory.[5] The *nodus* was a hairstyle that Ovid recommended for women with round faces, since pulling the hair up into a bun would show the ears.[6] It is possible that this portrait is of Fulvia in the guise of Victory, whether in hopeful anticipation of Antony's planned military campaign against the Parthian empire, or in recognition of her continuing efforts on his behalf.[7] The reason that this identification has been proposed is that goddesses tended to be depicted in far more idealized and stylized ways than this, and this portrayal does not conform precisely to any contemporary representation of Victory in Roman art. If so, this would make Fulvia the first living woman to appear on a Roman coin. The renaming of the Phrygian city of Eumeneia (modern Işıklı) to Fulviana in this period may have been an additional boon bestowed on Fulvia, although the new name does not seem to have been used for very long.

Over the course of the year that followed Caesar's assassination, diplomatic relations between Antony and the Liberators deteriorated, with many of the conspirators leaving Rome for the provinces and

beginning to amass armies there – such as Brutus and Cassius in Greece. Simultaneously, Antony and Octavian were initially at odds (Antony attempted to deprive Octavian of his inheritance, Octavian slandered Antony to Caesar's veterans and soldiers, Antony accused Octavian of trying to murder him), as both men wished to be seen as Caesar's successor

A bronze as *depicting Nike/Victory*

and so take on his mantle. Tensions escalated to the point where they declared war on each other (Octavian went so far as to temporarily align himself with Decimus Brutus against Antony, despite his involvement in the conspiracy), culminating in the inconclusive Battle of Mutina on 21 April 43 BCE. They were, however, eventually able to set aside their differences in favour of what they both considered to be the greater good: avenging Caesar's death. But vengeance was expensive, and by late 43 BCE, in order to fund their war against the assassins of Caesar, the triumvirate found they needed money.

Following in the footsteps of political predecessors such as Sulla (who had, in fact, proscribed Antony's grandfather, another famous orator), they decided to undertake a series of proscriptions, drawing up a list of two thousand enemies whom they could put to death and seize the estates of – Antony dictated the list while he was dining one evening.[8] Fulvia apparently had sufficient influence to add some names of her own. Why did she do this? Ancient commentators attributed her actions to sheer greed and avarice, but it is worth bearing in mind that it had been less than a year since she was relieved of much of her own property and possessions, so it is possible that she saw an opportunity to regain what she had lost. The names she added may even have been those of people who had targeted her, and this was her opportunity for revenge and restitution. So, when she is accused of taking the opportunity to have a man named Caesetius Rufus proscribed because he owned a property adjacent to one of hers that she had coveted but he had refused to sell to her, there is perhaps more to the story. When Rufus' murderer interrupted a dinner party and brought his head to Antony in order to cross the name off the list and claim his reward, Antony denied all knowledge and sent the man on to Fulvia.[9] She received the head and ordered it be displayed outside the property, presumably as a warning to others.[10]

For a woman who had twice seen her family targeted by violence and her children's lives threatened, and had been deprived of all her male protectors, it would have made sense to cultivate a reputation as a dangerous and merciless enemy. While the famous saying 'Let them hate as long as they fear me' (*oderint dum metuant*) is often attributed to the emperor Caligula (Antony's great-grandson, incidentally), it actually goes back to the Latin playwright Accius and his *Atreus*, written around 140 BCE, and was used by Cicero in relation to Antony's behaviour in this period. The same maxim could be applied to Fulvia, and for much the same reason.

The proscriptions marked a decisive turning point regarding people's feelings about the triumvirs and their associates – the presence of extrajudicial hit squads marauding with impunity on the streets of Rome succeeded only in alienating many of their supporters, and led to an increase in support for Brutus and Cassius, and Pompey's son Sextus Pompey, who not only offered a place of refuge for the proscribed on Sicily, but also rewards for those who assisted them that were twice those offered by the triumvirate for those who executed them.[11]

It is certainly worth noting that, for all that ancient commentators liked to present Fulvia as avaricious, tapping into an ancient Roman stereotype that women were greedy and out for what they could get from men, in the normal way of things what women were supposedly obsessed with was fine jewellery and clothing. One key motivator for the sumptuary laws that were frequently passed during the Republican period – one by Caesar as recently as 46 BCE – was the belief that women would waste all their available money on such fripperies. Recall the anecdote of the mother of the Gracchi brothers, Cornelia's friend, boasting of her jewels, only for Cornelia to parade her children and refer to them as *her* jewels. Within recent memory, Caesar had famously gifted his mistress Servilia with a pearl worth six million sesterces, perhaps as compensation for the end of their romantic relationship upon his marriage to the much younger Calpurnia in 59 BCE.[12] Conversely, the wife in the *Laudatio Turiae* gave her husband all her jewellery, including the gold and the pearl pieces, to fund his escape from Rome, something that her husband was keen to make everyone aware of, going so far as to describe her as having 'tor[n] them off [her] body' in her eagerness to support him, to emphasize how exceptional she was.[13]

One such wealthy matron and her parure can be seen in a beautiful mosaic that was once in position in the centre of the floor of a room in the Casa della Matrona ignota (VI.15.14) at Pompeii (see fig 6).[14] The woman's dark hair is centrally parted, pulled back from her face, and arranged in a bun at the nape of her neck in the rather severe style favoured by Republican matrons in this period, yet she is wearing a robe richly embroidered with golden thread, pearls in gold settings hang from her pierced ears, and a pearl necklace is draped around her neck.

So might Fulvia have looked, right down to the serious expression, yet she is never envisaged as conforming to the stereotype and coveting jewellery of any kind. Only property, and power. This could have been a means of emphasizing how fundamentally unfeminine she appeared to her contemporaries, not valuing supposedly female things like pearls, but there may well be a grain of truth in this presentation of her preference for less ephemeral and more lasting trappings of wealth and status. (Relatively) impoverished senatorial and equestrian women were not unknown, and while many ancient commentators were very enthusiastic about the *idea* of old-fashioned Republican virtuous poverty in comparison to new-fangled Republican decadent riches, it is worth remembering that these commentators were all astronomically wealthy themselves.[15] Fulvia's actions here contrast sharply with those of Octavian and Antony, accused of proscribing people in order to acquire their Corinthian bronze vases.[16]

The most famous name on the triumvirs' list, both in antiquity and today, was Cicero. He, his son, his brother and his nephew were all proscribed, and of the four, only his son Marcus escaped because he happened to be abroad at the time. But Cicero's inclusion was not simply about the triumvirs' need for money or their desire to neutralize their opposition. Antony's enmity to Cicero went back a long way: twenty years before, in the wake of the Catilinarian Conspiracy of 63 BCE, Antony's stepfather Cornelius Lentulus had been one of the conspirators that Cicero had summarily executed without trial. While the pair had had some semblance of a working relationship in the years

since, it undoubtedly preyed on Antony's mind, and the minds of his
mother and his brothers, to whom he was very close both personally
and politically. Then there was the fact that Cicero had been open
about his wish that the assassins of Caesar had assassinated Antony
too – he also repeatedly called for his assassination after the event – and
had pushed for Antony to be exiled, and his *Philippics* made this even
more personal. In later years, the question of whether Cicero should
have attempted to gain a pardon from Antony in exchange for burning
all his writings, first proposed by Antony's friend Gaius Asinius Pollio,
would become a popular exercise for tutors to set their students of
rhetoric.[17]

Fulvia, too, had her reasons for hating Cicero. He had publicly
humiliated her sister-in-law Clodia in his *Pro Caelio* speech in 56 BCE,
and in the process had cast aspersions on Clodius and the veracity of
his and Fulvia's marriage by accusing the siblings of incest and Fulvia
of adultery with Antony. He had not only opposed Clodius politically,
but after his murder had defended his murderer and Fulvia's son's
attempted murderer. He had publicly insulted her father and another
of her sons, and had publicly excoriated Antony using numerous jibes
about their marriage and Fulvia herself.

Having fled Rome in an attempt to get to safety, on 7 December
43 BCE Cicero decided to break his journey at one of his seaside villas.
As his ship came into land, crows swooped down from a nearby temple
dedicated to the god Apollo and swirled around him, later coming to
perch on the windowsill of his bedroom, with one even going so far as
to land on his couch and peck at him while he napped.[18] Once he felt
restored, he headed back to his ship, but his assassins were close behind
him and, having been told his whereabouts by one of the household
staff, managed to intercept him in the woods. There they murdered him.
On Antony's orders, his head and hands were cut off and brought back
to Rome so that they could be displayed on the Rostra in the Forum,
a stark warning to anyone who might be tempted to take up Cicero's
mantle. It is at this point that one of the most infamous episodes in
Fulvia's life and career seems to have occurred. When Cicero's head was

presented to her, she reportedly spat on it, then retrieved a hairpin from her elaborate coiffure and proceeded to stab his tongue.

This bloodthirsty instance captured the imaginations not only of ancient commentators, but also numerous artists in later historical periods. These recreations range in their interpretation of the scene. There is the relatively restrained *The Vengeance of Fulvia* by Francisco Maura y Montaner, painted in 1888, in which Fulvia simply bends at the waist to inspect the head being presented to her on a plate (see fig 7). There are the more dynamic Gregorio Lazzarini (1692), Francesco Maria Bassi (before 1728) and Bartolomeo Pinelli (1781) works in which Fulvia is depicted in the act of desecrating Cicero's head, hairpin in hand. And, most lurid of all, there is *Fulvia with the Head of Cicero* by Pavel Svedomsky (1898), which depicts the aftermath of the desecration, with Fulvia reclining languidly beside the mouldering head of Cicero, gazing at it in fiendish and sated glee (see fig 8).

What to make of these allegations? Roman hairpins are ubiquitous on archaeological excavations and in museum exhibitions, and it is easy to see that, however elaborately and ornately decorated, when cast in metal or carved in bone they could be quite lengthy and wickedly sharp. Women, otherwise unarmed, do seem to have used them as weapons when the occasion called for it.[19]

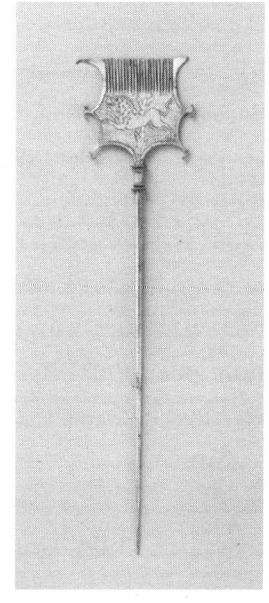

This vignette of an unforgiving woman arming herself with a hairpin and using it to wreak vengeance on someone who has wronged her appears in Apuleius' novel *Metamorphoses* (also known as *The Golden Ass*), written in the latter part of the second century CE. However, here he writes his character Charite as doing so while her victim is alive. Thrasyllus has murdered her husband Tlepolemus and brutalized her, so she drugs his wine and while he is unconscious she gouges out his eyes.[20] 'I shall pour a libation on my Tlepolemus' tomb with

A silver hairpin

the gore from your eyes, and I shall dedicate those eyes as a funeral offering to his sacred ghost,' she says, and once she has accomplished what she set out to do, she ends her life at her husband's tomb.[21]

But Fulvia was hardly at risk from Cicero's decomposing head. If she did take out her frustrations on it in the manner described, might she have been treating it more in the manner of a *kolossos*, or voodoo doll, and attempting to bind it so it could no longer slander her and her nearest and dearest? Many ancient Roman curse tablets contain detailed instructions about the process of cursing and binding someone via the medium of stabbing a representation of them with pins and needles. Just as Cicero had once accused Fulvia of being a curse upon her husbands, she was now reflecting that back onto him, and regaining her power and finally gaining the upper hand.[22]

She was not alone in wanting revenge. For example, Diodorus Siculus records an unsavoury incident that took place during the First Punic War (264–241 BCE), when, after the Roman general Marcus Atilius Regulus died while imprisoned by the Carthaginians, his bereaved wife Marcia, believing that he had died of neglect while in captivity, ordered her sons to mistreat their Carthaginian prisoners in turn. Bodostor and Hamilcar were subsequently confined in such a small space that they were forced to contort their bodies like serpents, and were deprived of food for days at a time. When Bodostor died under these circumstances, Hamilcar was left alone with his rotting corpse, provided with just enough food to keep him alive and suffering, while trying to avoid his compatriot's effluvia.[23] Once word spread via gossip from the household staff to the tribunes about what was going on, the Atilii were excoriated for bringing shame on Rome and threatened with prosecution on a capital charge. Marcia's sons finally stood up to their mother, rebuked her, and released Hamilcar.

Similarly, after the murders of Cicero, his brother Quintus and his nephew Quintus the Younger, Antony handed over the Tullius family freedman Philologos, who had betrayed the Cicerones, to Quintus' wife Pomponia so that she could exact her revenge upon him for his perfidy. She reportedly tortured him extensively, going so far as to force him to cut off pieces of his own flesh, bit by bit, then roasting them and making him eat them.[24] While Plutarch does not praise her for her bloodthirsty actions, he does not exactly go out of his way to criticize her either.

The focus on Fulvia, and the maximizing of her role in the proscriptions, simultaneously serves to minimize Octavian's role in the entire process. As Cicero's one-time protégé, yet the member of the triumvirate who added Cicero's name to the list, he was especially culpable.[25] It is possible that one of the sources that ancient historians used for this period was Octavian's memoirs, and of course, when writing his account of events many years later, in the mid-20s BCE, it would have suited him to deflect the blame onto the now long-dead Fulvia.[26]

By the standards of the day, it is not hard to see why Antony and Fulvia thought Cicero had it coming. But inevitably their feud did not end with Cicero's death. Later that year, Brutus murdered Antony's youngest brother, Gaius, whom he had been holding captive in Macedonia, by way of revenge. Just over a decade later it was Cicero's son Marcus, elected suffect consul in 30 BCE, to whom Octavian delegated the pleasure of announcing Antony's death to the Senate and enacting a string of punitive measures against his memory. Marcus would revoke Antony's honours, have all his statues torn down, and decree that no member of the family could ever again bear the name Marcus.

We can appreciate the turmoil that the proscriptions caused for the wives and other female relations of the men proscribed, and the efforts they went to on their menfolk's behalf, because several examples of specific women's experiences have survived, in both literary and documentary forms. These are the most extensive and comprehensive accounts of ordinary women's experiences not just in this period, but in any period of ancient Roman history. The unprecedented circumstances meant that for later commentators, such as the historian Appian, women's perspectives on events were finally worth recording alongside those of men.[27] Having said that, for the most part the women's own names are not recorded, perhaps in accordance with the belief that respectable women should not be mentioned or drawn attention to in public discourse.

Many women's stories were recorded because their love for and loyalty to their proscribed male relations such as husbands and sons was considered admirable. The wife of Ligurius succeeded in hiding her husband for a time, until the couple were betrayed by an enslaved woman that they had trusted. After her husband was beheaded in front of her, Ligurius' wife followed the men toting his head all the way to the triumvirs, begging them to punish her: 'I sheltered him; those who give shelter are to share the punishment!' Unfortunately for her, the triumvirs were moved so they spared her life, leaving her to resort to having to starve herself to death rather than live without Ligurius.[28]

For other women, the outcomes were happier. Acilius' wife used her jewellery to bribe the soldiers who came in search of her husband, and convinced them to charter a ship upon which he could escape to Sextus Pompey in Sicily.[29] Similarly, Virginius' wife chartered a ship to carry them and all their money to Sicily, and when she and her husband were separated, rather than absconding with all their worldly goods, she made sure to leave a messenger to tell him where she had gone so that he could join her anon.[30] Lucius Cornelius Lentulus Cruscellio's wife Sulpicia begged to accompany him on his journey to Sicily, but he refused to allow her to undertake such a dangerous journey and fled in secret. Once there, he sent word back to her that he had arrived safely, and she promptly escaped from under the watchful eye of her mother and went to join him. She travelled alone except for two enslaved companions, and all three of them underwent an arduous journey so that she might be reunited with her husband.[31] In a similar vein, Apuleius' wife told him that if he attempted to leave Rome without her, she would testify against him, so they departed together, and her presence, along with their household's, went some way towards helping him escape notice.[32]

Some wives proved to be ingenious in their ability to help their husbands evade notice: Antius' wife wrapped him up in a clothes bag and had him carried off by porters; Rheginus' wife first hid him in a sewer and then disguised him as a charcoal dealer, complete with beast of burden; Quintus Lucretius Vespillo's wife Turia hid her husband in their attic, between the planks of their double roof.[33] Titus Vinius' wife Tanusia concealed her husband in a chest at the home of one of their freedmen, Philopoemen, and pretended that he had already been killed. Then she availed upon Octavia to intercede with Octavian on their behalf. She confronted him, admitted what she had done, and then opened the chest with a flourish, revealing her husband. Octavian, astonished by her gumption, not only removed her husband's name from the list but also granted Philopoemen entry to the equestrian order.[34] Less ingenious, but no less impressive, Coponius' wife apparently had sex with Antony in exchange for her husband's safety.[35]

Finally, and perhaps most surprisingly, Antony's mother Julia publicly defied her son by openly sheltering her brother, whom Antony had added to the list as revenge for his uncle voting in favour of him being declared a public enemy earlier in the year. When the enforcers attempted to remove him from her house, she hurried to the Forum and accosted Antony and his colleagues, announcing, 'I denounce myself to you, triumvir, for having received [my brother] under my roof and for still keeping him, and I shall keep him till you kill us both together, for it is decreed that those who give shelter shall suffer the same punishment.'[36] Since Antony was obviously not going to order his mother's decapitation, he resorted to criticizing her conduct as a mother, but also praised her conduct as a sister and removed his uncle's name from the list.

However, some women's stories were recorded for the opposite reason: so that their betrayals might be set down in stone to shame them for all eternity. Septimius' wife, who had been having an affair with a friend of Antony's, sought to actively murder her husband and convinced her lover to ask Antony to add his name to the list. When Septimius learned he had been proscribed, he fled home to what he believed were the loving arms of his wife, only to have her lock all the doors and detain him until the enforcers could come to arrest him. On the same day that her husband was beheaded, she celebrated her wedding to her lover.[37] And Fulvius' freedwoman, upon whom he had bestowed freedom and a generous dowry to facilitate her marriage because she had been his mistress, betrayed him to the enforcers due to her jealousy over his wife. Less overtly malignant, but still culpable, Salassus' wife betrayed him to the enforcers out of fear.[38]

The most vivid and dramatic account of a woman's experience at this time, and as close to the source as it is possible for us to get, comes from the *Laudatio Turiae* inscription. In it, the bereaved husband describes how his wife continuously petitioned the triumvirs to have his name removed from the list of the proscribed so that he could return from exile. She eventually met with success when Octavian finally agreed that his citizenship could be restored to him. Unfortunately, Octavian was not in Rome at the time, so the wife took this information to Lepidus, expecting him to oblige her. Instead, he instructed his lictors (attendants who doubled up as bodyguards and enforcers) to remove her from his presence. According to the husband, 'not only were you lifted up, you were also dragged and carried off like a slave. Your body was covered with bruises… [and] you had to endure Lepidus' insulting words and cruel wounds.'[39] Eventually the wife managed to shame Lepidus into cooperating.

We might have expected Fulvia to have some sympathy for her peers, considering her own experiences during her marriage to Clodius as well as earlier in her marriage to Antony, but perhaps her suffering on those occasions – and the lack of assistance that had been forthcoming – had hardened her heart and inured her to the suffering of others. While Rome's senatorial and equestrian women were not included in the proscriptions, 1,400 of them were ordered to pay a higher rate of tax on their property as their contribution to the war effort. Just as is the case today, wealthy Romans did everything they could to avoid and evade taxation, and women were no exception. The most prominent amongst them made delegations to the female relatives of the triumvirs, hoping to convince them to intercede with the men on their behalf. While Octavian's sister Octavia and Antony's mother Julia met with them and agreed to take their part, their pleas to Fulvia, who was considerably more influential than Octavia or Julia, fell on deaf ears. The most powerful of all the triumviral women flatly refused to help them, and had them thrown out of her house. Why did Fulvia act in this way? She was presumably amongst the 1,400 women who would have been liable for the tax – or perhaps she was exempt due to her relationship to Antony and Octavian, so did not care about it. Alternatively, maybe she was prepared to comply with the tax, not only because she understood the rationale for setting it but also because it gave her an opportunity to make a gesture of sacrifice for the good of the Republic, which would be yet another example of her inclination towards public performance.

One of the ringleaders of the delegation was Hortensia, Fulvia's second cousin, and she gave a public speech that is one of the few given by a woman to have survived:

> As was fitting for women of our rank addressing a petition to you, we had recourse to your womenfolk; but what was not fitting was the treatment we received at the hands of Fulvia, and we have been driven by her to come to the Forum. You have already taken away our fathers and sons and husbands and brothers, on a charge that you were wronged at their hands; if you also take away our money, you will reduce us to a wretched condition unbecoming our birth, our character, and our female nature. If you maintain that you have been wronged at our hands too, as you say you were by our husbands, then proscribe us as you did them. But if we women have not voted any of you public enemies, have not torn down your houses, destroyed your army, or led another one against you; if we have not hindered you in obtaining offices and honours, why do we share the penalties when we had no part in the wrongdoing?
>
> Why should we pay taxes when we have no access to the offices or the honours or the military commands or the entire political process, which you have now brought to such a sorry state by your rivalries? Because, according to you, there is a war

on? When have there not been wars, and when have women ever paid taxes? ... Let war with the Celts or the Parthians come, and we will not prove inferior to our mothers in ensuring safety; but for civil wars may we never pay a contribution, nor ever help you against each other. We did not pay tax in the time of Caesar or Pompey, and neither Marius nor Cinna forced us to, nor even Sulla, and he governed the country as a tyrant. You, on the other hand, maintain that you are restoring ordered government.[40]

The triumvirs were outraged that mere women had dared to oppose them when men had the good sense to stay silent, and their first response to this was to have the women brutalized, ordering their attendants to forcibly remove them.[41] However, the response of the crowd of spectators who had gathered to watch the fracas was so negative, appalled as they were at the sight of respectable Roman matrons being physically manhandled by thugs, that they were forced into submission. Whether the triumvirs acquiesced to their demands because of the power of Hortensia's words – or because of the sheer embarrassment of being publicly accosted by a delegation of respectable Roman matrons in the Forum – is unclear, but the following day they reduced the number of women being taxed from 1,400 to 400.[42] Relations between Antony and Fulvia must have been strained after this. So it was perhaps a relief for both of them that, after the final defeat of Brutus and Cassius at the Battle of Philippi in October 42 BCE, Antony had to depart from Rome, heading east to start the process of tidying up the provinces and client kingdoms that had been left in disarray by the so-called Liberators and their military campaigns.

In 41 BCE, the two consuls were Publius Servilius and Lucius Antonius, Antony's surviving younger brother, but it was claimed that Publius Servilius was consul in name only, and that Fulvia was really the one running the show in Rome, due to her singular position as the wife of Antony and the mother-in-law of Octavian.[43] Even more powerful than either consul, it was claimed that she was essentially the third member of the triumvirate, having managed to marginalize Lepidus. While this may have been yet more double character assassination, depicting Fulvia as inappropriately masculine and Lucius (and the rest of his circle) as inappropriately feminine and in her thrall, it was not unheard of for women to wield influence over the Senate.

A few years earlier, on 7 June 44 BCE, Cicero had visited Brutus at his villa at Antium, and in a letter to Atticus recounted what had happened there at a family council attended by himself, Brutus, Brutus' mother Servilia, his wife Porcia, his sister Junia Tertia, and a number of others. When Cicero criticized Brutus' clumsy handling of the aftermath of the assassination of Caesar, Servilia sprang to her son's defence, having no compunction about putting Cicero in his place – he had not, after all, been trusted to know about the conspiracy, let alone participate in the assassination itself. She also promised to get a grain commission removed from a senatorial decree, and Cicero related this in his letter so matter-of-factly that it is clear some degree of intervention in senatorial business was not an unusual occurrence, whether for Servilia herself or for powerful women more generally.[44] This presumably involved approaching and lobbying influential senators known to be amenable to such measures, just as wives, daughters, mothers, sisters and other female relations did when their menfolk were absent and *in extremis*, such as in exile, but under more normal circumstances.

But perhaps Lucius really was something of a pushover: Velleius Paterculus rather dismissively describes him as sharing all the faults of his older brother but possessing none of the virtues which Antony occasionally showed.[45] Fulvia continued to be associated with military matters, supposedly managing to withhold permission for Lucius to be awarded a triumph for his military victories over the Alpine tribes, and then when she eventually acquiesced, ensuring it was voted for unanimously.[46] When Lucius finally had his moment, on the first day of the year and therefore the first day of his consulship, a deliberate linking of these two forms of authority and achievement, it was Fulvia who presented herself prominently to the crowd.[47] We hear nothing of his mother or his wife, assuming he had one at this point in time – there

is no record of him ever having had any children. While his contemporaries may have murmured that Lucius' victory over a handful of recal-
citrant tribes did not warrant a triumph, he proudly proclaimed (or
boasted) that he had captured more golden crowns from his defeated
enemies – expressing their loyalty and seeking his patronage – than
even the famous Republican general Marius.[48] Considering the Roman
belief that the first day of the year set the tone for what followed,
it should come as no surprise that, before the year was out, Lucius
and Fulvia would find themselves as reluctant allies, embroiled in the
Perusine War.

CHAPTER 10

FULVIA'S WAR

Apart from Fulvia's treatment of Cicero's severed head, nowhere is the Roman hypocrisy when it comes to dealing with her more apparent than in the ancient historians' coverage of perhaps the most famous single episode from her storied career: the Perusine War (41–40 BCE). It is entirely fair to criticize Fulvia for her unnecessary desecration of Cicero's head (assuming that such an event did, in fact, occur), even if her motivations, given her and Cicero's long-standing enmity, are somewhat understandable. Indeed, as we have seen, other Roman women who resorted to mutilation and torture were likewise criticized. So far, so reasonable. But as far as Fulvia's war-mongering is concerned, she has been unfairly targeted in comparison to other Roman women.

In the winter of 41–40 BCE, Antony was away from Italy, travelling through the eastern Mediterranean, first overseeing Rome's territorial acquisitions there in his capacity as triumvir with responsibility for the eastern provinces, then laying the groundwork for his proposed military campaign against Rome's neighbour and old enemy, the

Parthian empire. This was a mission inherited from Caesar, and was intended to avenge the defeat and massacre of Crassus and his legions at the Battle of Carrhae, and the loss of legionary standards, in 53 BCE. Antony enjoyed first an affair with the Cappadocian princess Glaphyra, and then another with the Egyptian queen Cleopatra, before finally accepting an invitation from Cleopatra to spend an extended period with her in Alexandria. During this time, his erstwhile ally Octavian sought to take advantage of his absence and marginalize him, confiscating land from landowners and reallocating it for the foundation of colonies of Roman veterans from over thirty legions, thereby garnering their loyalty to himself alone rather than himself and Antony jointly.[1]

The fact that there was considerable upheaval in Italy at this time is attested by references in the Latin poetry written contemporaneously, such as Virgil's *Eclogues*, Propertius' *Elegies* and Horace's *Epistles*.[2] Virgil has one character, a goat herder named Meliboeus, complain to his companion Tityrus of them being 'outcasts from [their] country' and heartsick over 'unrest on all sides in the land', and another, a smallholder named Moeris, lament 'we have lived to see the day – an evil never dreamed – when a stranger, holder of our little farm, could say: "This is mine; begone, old tenants!"'[3] It is hardly surprising that Italian landowners from forty separate cities spread across Campania, Samnium, Umbria, Picenum, Etruria and the north of Italy would be hostile to Octavian's actions, and they had a considerable amount of public support.[4] The proposed confiscations triggered an agricultural crisis with the knock-on effect of a famine, exacerbated by Sextus Pompey's naval blockade of Italy which prevented provisions from Sardinia, Sicily, Spain and Africa reaching the stricken region.

In the face of the veterans' enthusiasm and their impatience for the foundation of the colonies, Fulvia and Lucius were left with few options. Their attempts at diplomacy with Octavian went nowhere, and then Octavian antagonized Fulvia – and disrespected Antony – further. First, he divorced her daughter Claudia, sending her back home to Fulvia claiming that he had never actually consummated the marriage.[5] It seems that he subscribed to Juvenal's adage: 'Give up on any hope of

harmony if your mother-in-law is alive.'[6] Then he wrote and disseminated obscene and insulting poetry about Fulvia herself. Octavian
went so far as to claim that she had propositioned him, relying on the
well-worn stereotype of the rampant older woman constantly seeking
the attention of younger men, and stated that he would rather go to
war with her than have sex with her:

> Because Antony fucks Glaphyra, Fulvia is determined to
> punish *me* by making me fuck her in turn. I fuck Fulvia? What
> if Manius begged me to sodomize him, would I do it? I think
> not, if I were in my right mind. 'Either fuck me or let us fight,'
> says she. Ah, but my cock is dearer to me than life itself. Let
> the trumpets sound.[7]

This text was still circulating almost one hundred and fifty years later,
when it was quoted by the poet Martial, and several decades later than
that, when the imperial biographer Suetonius stated that a collection
of Octavian's epigrams had survived to that point in time, allowing him
to read them.[8] This would seem to indicate that it was widely disseminated both during Fulvia's life and after her death, as Octavian sought
to establish his reputation as a macho man at her expense, since he
had been on the receiving end of equally gendered insults and wished
to change the conversation. His divorce of Claudia, probably undertaken in a fit of pique, backfired, as it led people to suspect that he was
incapable of consummating the marriage (or perhaps even bedding a
woman at all).

Octavian's ineptitude, to put it kindly, when it came to battle
was well known, as even his closest friends Agrippa and Maecenas
recounted how he had fled from the Battle of Philippi in 42 BCE
claiming illness and spent three days hiding in the marshes, leaving
Antony to decisively defeat the assassins of Caesar, end that portion
of the civil war, and gain all the credit.[9] His enemy, the piratical Sextus
Pompey, had described him as 'womanish'.[10] The Antonius brothers
also had plenty to say on the subject, with Antony sticking the knife in

by claiming that Octavian had engineered his adoption by Caesar as a result of performing sexual favours for him, and Lucius twisting it by claiming that, after having been thoroughly used by Caesar, Octavian had sold himself to one of Caesar's close associates, the author of military treatises Aulus Hirtius, for 30,000 sesterces, and that he depilated the hair on his legs.[11] Lucius had long had Antony's back, as had their younger brother Gaius, murdered by Brutus in 42 BCE in retaliation for the proscription of Cicero: unlike other sets of siblings at this time who found themselves on opposite sides of the political divide, for better or worse the Antonii came as a package deal.[12]

But however transparent Octavian's motives may have been, his aspersions would have been especially humiliating for Fulvia. Despite the fact that Fulvia was still relatively young – probably not more than forty years old – and had only recently given birth to her fifth child, so was clearly still fertile, she began to fall victim to the entrenched Roman sexist and ageist attitudes towards women.[13] Here Octavian was telling everyone not only that she was sexually unfulfilled, but that she had failed in a desperate attempt to cuckold Antony. It mattered not whether there was any truth to the allegations, and it is clear that some people believed them. Meanwhile, at this point in time, the famously virile Antony had recently concluded an affair with the eastern courtesan Glaphyra, going so far as to bestow the kingdom of Cappadocia upon her son Archelaus as a sign of his regard for her.[14] He was now openly carrying on another with Cleopatra, Queen of Egypt, which would result in the birth of twins before the end of 40 BCE. As a result, many of Fulvia's motivations and actions were being undermined – dismissively attributed by her peers to jealousy and vain attempts to recapture Antony's attention, since his agent Manius had supposedly informed her about his extramarital relationships.

In response, Fulvia resorted to attempting to tug on the veterans' heartstrings, parading her and Antony's young sons, Marcus Antonius Antyllus (by now around six years old) and Iullus Antonius (around two years old) in front of them, and pointing out how much greater a general Antony was than Octavian, with the Caesarean faction's victory over the so-called Liberators, the assassins of Caesar, at the Battle of Philippi entirely due to the former.[15] She was also implying military continuity, with Antony's sons taking his place once they were grown up and capable of commanding armies themselves (let us not forget that Octavian owed his own military position to his adoptive father, Caesar).[16] Her actions inspired Lucius to do something similar a little while later, bringing the little boys with him when he and Octavian left Rome to perform the foundation rites for the new colonies – but then claiming that Octavian was planning to ambush him and the boys en route, and fleeing to the protection of a nearby colony comprising Antony's veterans, who were outraged at the insult to their patron and his family.[17]

Thus Fulvia and Lucius sought to protect Antony's interests, raising eight legions and occupying first Rome and then Perusia (modern Perugia in Umbria), which brought them into direct conflict with Octavian in what is known today as the Perusine War. The truth of this conflict is difficult to establish from the ancient literary sources – which, written with the benefit of considerable hindsight, are entirely hostile to Fulvia and, to a lesser extent, Lucius. Fulvia is accused of starting the war in a desperate attempt to turn Antony's attention away from Cleopatra and back towards herself.[18]

Fulvia and her children decamped to Praeneste (modern Palestrina), along with a number of senators, equestrians and their families.[19] Praeneste was set into the Apennines, around twenty-three miles east-south-east of Rome, and was strategically located as it controlled the route between the regions of Latium and Campania. It had been loyal to Marius rather than Sulla during that period of civil war (83–82 BCE), leading to the latter sacking it in 82 BCE, then rebuilding the city and colonizing it with his veterans. Therefore, the Perusine War was not the first time Praeneste had been pulled into a disagreement between rival warlords. It was renowned for its immense Sanctuary of Fortuna Primigenia, founded in 204 BCE, much of which still survives in the fabric of the modern town, and no doubt the goddess's favour was much sought after. Fulvia claimed that she had withdrawn there out of fear for her children, as

Antony and Octavian's triumviral colleague Lepidus had expressed some anxiety over their safety.[20] From there, she enlisted the help of Antony's friends Ventidius, Asinius, Ateius and Calenus to encourage Lucius to return to Italy from Gaul, and raised an army for him to lead.[21] Fulvia was accused of bribing soldiers and also of advising Lucius to declare war on Octavian.[22] Lucius and his legions occupied the city of Perusia, and Octavian, his generals Marcus Vipsanius Agrippa and Salvidienus Rufus, and his legions laid siege to it.

Just as later sources sought to minimize Octavian's role in the proscriptions of 43 BCE, so did they try and minimize the Perusine War, and present it as a relatively insignificant and bloodless conflict, as opposed to a brutal civil war on Italian soil. Yet there is fascinating documentary and archaeological evidence for the siege, and for the psychological warfare that was waged during it, in the form of the lead sling bullets shot across the city walls by both sides that have been recovered in archaeological excavations.[23] (Recall Milo, the murderer of Fulvia's first husband Clodius? He took advantage of the civil war between Caesar and Pompey in 49 BCE to return from his exile in Massilia illegally, stirred up trouble in Campania, and was shot in the head with a sling bullet during a siege – no doubt his many enemies, Fulvia included, thought good riddance.)

These lead sling bullets were known as the *glandes perusinae* ('acorns of Perusia', although while *glans* can be translated as 'acorn', it can also be translated as 'head of penis'), and a selection of them are on permanent display at the National Archaeological Museum of Umbria in Perugia. The bullets bear insulting inscriptions directed at all the principal participants in the conflict, including Fulvia, and are highly sexualised in nature. One missile declares, 'I'm aiming for Fulvia's clitoris!' (*peto landicam Fulviae*) with the addition of an engraving of a lightning bolt, and another demands 'Fulvia, spread those arse cheeks!' (*Fulvia culum pandite*).[24] References to the clitoris were the crassest and crudest of ancient Roman obscenities: the clitoris itself was considered the ugliest part of the female genitalia – an enlarged clitoris was associated with female hypersexuality and nymphomania – so referring to the clitoris

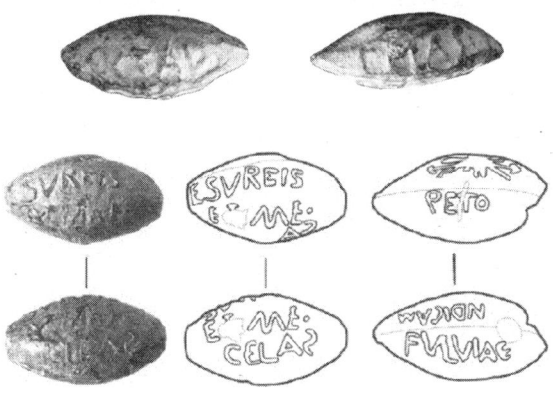

Lead sling bullets from the Siege of Perusia, 41–40 BCE

of a respectable Roman matron like Fulvia was the epitome of disrespect, and the sentiment ties in nicely with that of Octavian's offensive poetry and his presentation of Fulvia as a sex-crazed hag. Clearly someone, potentially even Octavian himself, was briefing the soldiers comprehensively and making sure that they kept to the company line.

It seems from these inscriptions that Fulvia was considered by the soldiers to be on a par with her male allies and enemies, who were likewise subjected to sexualized insults and taunts. Lucius was insulted regarding his hair loss, clearly evident on the coins he minted and issued and in striking contrast to his hirsute elder brother, denigratingly referred to as 'Baldy', and instructed to 'spread them cheeks' (*L. Antoni calve, culum pandite*).[25] Octavian was instructed to 'take this, you bitch' (*Octavia accipe*) and 'sit on this, you gape-assed Octavian' (*sede, laxe Octavi*), implying that he had been on the receiving end of so much anal sex that it had permanently damaged him.[26] Courtesy of one bullet that is housed in the Ashmolean Museum, he was greeted cheerfully before being informed 'you suck cock' (*salve Octavi, felas*) by the Tenth Legion Equestris.[27] Additionally, in referring to him as Octavian rather than his adopted name of Gaius Julius Caesar, the Antonian forces were calling into question the entire basis of his political and military authority: his posthumous adoption by his great-uncle, the dictator Gaius Julius Caesar.

According to Cassius Dio, at least, Fulvia did involve herself in the military campaign – strategizing, giving orders, and handing out the military watchwords to the soldiers on duty.[28] She apparently even wore a sword.[29] Thus although Praeneste was not under siege like Perusia, we might imagine her striding along the city's terraces, surveying the territory below in the manner of an *imperator* (commander), even if she could never technically be declared one, in the manner of the woman holding a shield in a contemporaneous fresco from the Villa of Publius Fannius Synistor (see fig 9).[30]

After some time, the Antonian forces were starved into submission, and Octavian's army stormed Perusia. Present alongside Lucius was Tiberius Claudius Nero, his wife Livia Drusilla, and their infant son Tiberius, which gives us an insight into the experiences of women other than Fulvia who were caught up in this episode.[31] When the city fell, they had a harrowing experience, escaping first to Praeneste, and from there to Naples, where they boarded a ship to Sextus Pompey in Sicily.[32] Travelling the length of the Italian peninsula under those conditions, toting one child and pregnant with another, must have been terrifying.

Octavian either lost control of his troops or chose to permit them to sack the city and burn it to the ground. The defeated forces were then treated with extreme brutality, with hundreds of senators and equestrians reportedly consecrated to the deceased Caesar and then sacrificed on his altar on the anniversary of Caesar's death on the Ides of March.[33] Amongst their number was a man named Tiberius Cannutius, who had been a strong supporter of Octavian and enemy of Antony during his tribuneship in 44 BCE. Several sources imply that the rationale for this treatment was that the Perusians were Etruscans, so not *real* Romans, despite their Roman citizenship.[34] In an attempt to absolve Octavian of the responsibility for the city's fall, Velleius Paterculus named the local dignitary Cestius Macedonicus as being responsible for starting the conflagration, setting fire to his house and all its contents before falling on his sword and throwing himself into the flames.[35] The poet Propertius, who originated from the area, wrote of the trauma of the war and its aftermath:

What is my rank, whence my lineage, and where my home,
Tullus, you ask in our eternal friendship's name. If you know
Perusia, grave of our countrymen who fell in the days of Italy's
agony, when discord at Rome took hold of her citizens – soil
of Etruria, especially to me do you bring grief, for you have
borne the abandoned limbs of my kinsman with not a handful
of earth to cover his poor bones – there neighbouring Umbria,
bordering on the plains below, a country rich in fertile fields,
gave me birth.[36]

Once defeated, Lucius proceeded to grovel to Octavian, claiming he
had not been acting out of self-interest, but rather only a concern for
the Republic:

I was aware that Fulvia was a proponent of monarchic government, but as far as I was concerned, I collaborated with my
brother's forces in order to destroy all of you. And now if my
brother comes to abolish the monarchic regime, I will go to join
him, either openly or secretly, and, on behalf of our country, I
will renew my struggle against you, even though you have now
become my benefactor. On the other hand, if he too is merely
choosing and setting apart people to share sole rule with him,
I will fight on your side against him, as long as I think that you
are not also trying to establish a monarchy. For I will always set
the interests of my country above favour and family.[37]

By claiming that Fulvia was in favour of a return to monarchy –
presumably one in which Antony was crowned king with her reigning
alongside him as his queen – Lucius was betraying her, blaming her, and
invoking the very fears that had led to Caesar's assassination in 44 BCE.

Having no brothers himself, Octavian admired Lucius' filial
devotion (in time, he would gain the nickname 'Pietas' for it).[38] He
released Lucius, who proceeded to leave Italy and take up an administrative position in the western province of Hispania (modern Spain),

which saw him wielding more authority than the province's governors. This is the last we hear of him, and it is assumed that he died soon afterwards, presumably of natural causes since there was no scandal. Then, Octavian turned his attention to Fulvia. He allowed her and her children, and Antony's mother Julia, to depart from Praeneste, and they travelled south to Dicaearchia and on to Brundisium in the company of Lucius Munatius Plancus, one of Antony's most loyal supporters, and three legions of cavalry.[39] From there, Fulvia and the children sailed to Greece with five warships, while Julia took refuge in Sicily with Octavian's enemy Sextus Pompey instead.[40] The fact that Sextus then sent Julia to Antony in the company of the leading figures of his entourage along with a convoy of warships, and sought to ally himself and his faction with Antony, implies that the political situation was rather more complex and multifaceted than a spurned wife causing trouble. It also suggests that, at least at this point in time, there was a possibility that Antony and Sextus might join forces and work together to neutralize Octavian. Fulvia may even have instigated this diplomatic embassy, and others, as she was in communication with the proconsul Titus Sextius, encouraging him to resume control of Roman Africa, a command he had held from 44 until 41 BCE before relinquishing it.[41]

The peace and quiet of Antony's sojourn in Alexandria having been disturbed by a spate of increasingly irate correspondence from across the Mediterranean, he finally departed from Egypt and sailed at the head of two hundred ships back to Italy. Breaking his voyage to collect some of his friends who were fleeing Octavian's wrath, he was confronted with their version of events, which heaped the blame on Fulvia. Concurrently, Octavian returned to Rome and made a ceremonial entry into the city, clad in the triumphal dress of the purple-dyed and richly embroidered *toga picta* and sporting a laurel crown on his head, and perhaps even receiving his second acclamation as *imperator* (his first had been received in 43 BCE, after the Battle of Mutina).[42]

Meanwhile, Fulvia sailed from Italy to Greece with her children, landing at either Athens and travelling from there to Sicyon, situated in the northern Peloponnese, or putting in at Sicyon itself, after just over a week at sea.[43] Sicyon was famous for its philosophers, poets and artists, chief amongst them the Classical sculptor Lysippus, head of the Sicyonian school and renowned for his bronze statues. He had bestowed upon his home town a magnificent one of the personification of Opportunity, portrayed as a young man with his hair worn long in front but short at the back – to demonstrate that opportunity cannot be seized once it has passed – holding a razor in his hand to represent that success and failure are balanced upon a razor's edge, his own be-winged feet balancing on tiptoes on a sphere.[44] But there would be no further opportunities for Fulvia to seize and bend to her once-formidable will. By this time, she was very ill. No specific diagnosis is recorded, beyond that she became depressed as a result of Antony's criticism of her actions in Italy, and his anger exacerbated her condition.[45] Perhaps she sought help at the local sanctuary to Asklepios, the Greek god of medicine, which had a direct connection to the far more famous sanctuary at Epidauros, no doubt a powerful marketing tool for the desperate and desperately ill; the Sicyonians claimed that a local woman named Nicagora had brought the god in the form of a snake to them directly from there, in a cart drawn by mules.[46] Here Fulvia would have undertaken an incubation ritual, spending the night under a painting depicting the gods Dream and Sleep lulling a lion, alongside the huge bone of a mysterious sea monster (interestingly, Sicyon was famed for its conger eels that were at least as large as men), and hoping for a visit from Asklepios himself and his intercession on her behalf.[47]

Either Antony did not believe that Fulvia was deathly ill, or in the moment he simply did not care. He abandoned her in Sicyon in high dudgeon and returned to Italy to meet with Octavian without even telling her he was leaving or saying goodbye. In fact, he may not even have bothered to see her in person, instead communicating his displeasure via messenger. It was at this point that Fulvia died.

The contradiction in terms that was the woman warrior found its way into the most important piece of Roman literature produced at this time. In the period 29–19 BCE, Virgil composed the *Aeneid*, an epic poem that tells the story of the Trojan prince Aeneas' journey from Troy to Italy, where he founded the Roman Julian clan, the family to which Caesar and his great-nephew and adopted son Octavian belonged. It contains many allusions to the recent historical events that Virgil had lived through and the historical figures responsible for them, such as Octavian, Antony and Cleopatra. At one point in the poem, he extols the virtues of the mythical warrior maiden Camilla, a princess of the Italic Volsci tribe, and despite the fact that she is fighting on the side of Turnus against Aeneas:

> To crown the array comes Camilla, of Volscian race, leading her troop of horse, and squadrons gay with brass – a warrior maid, never having trained her woman's hands to Minerva's distaff or basket of wool, but hardy to bear the brunt of battle and in speed of foot to outstrip the winds. She might have flown over the topmost blades of unmown corn, and not bruised the tender ears in her course; or sped her way over mid sea, poised above the swelling wave, and not dipped her swift feet in the flood. All the youth, streaming from house and field, and thronging matrons marvel, and gaze at her as she goes; agape with wonder at how the glory of royal purple drapes her smooth shoulders, how the clasp entwines her hair with gold, how her own hands bear a Lycian quiver and the pastoral myrtle tipped with steel.[48]

Camilla is described here as a *bellatrix*, 'warrior maid'.[49] She does not cover her body modestly from head to toe, with the *stola* and *palla* of a respectable Roman matron, nor does she spend her time indoors spinning and weaving textiles for use by the members of her household. Rather, she wears military costume covered by a purple cloak and wields weapons – a lance and a quiver – that she has been training to use since she was a child. Her entrance is presented as akin to that of a great Republican commander, and the crowd of onlookers are amazed by her.[50] This is how she is depicted in later works of art, such as *Agreement between Camilla and Turnus* by Francesco de Mura in the eighteenth century (see fig 10).

It is thought that Camilla is Virgil's invention, although perhaps based on or inspired by a combination of Italic folklore and the Greek tales of the Amazons.[51] He explicitly compares her with the Amazon queen Penthesilea, also described as a *bellatrix* when she appears earlier in the poem.[52] In her, he envisages a highly experienced and competent commander and soldier, capable of leading a combination of male and female troops, and as someone who conforms to traditional heroic behaviour, including her interest in the spoils of war that ultimately causes her downfall.[53] Like Fulvia, Camilla is not one to spend her time on the traditional women's work of spinning and weaving. But unlike Fulvia, her martial prowess is praised rather than criticized. Since Fulvia had only been dead a decade at the start of Virgil's endeavours, and many of her peers (not to mention her enemies, such as Octavian himself) were still alive when the poem began to circulate, the irony of this would not have been lost on them.

The *Aeneid* is myth – fiction, even. Yet in the historical sources of the time we find a number of Fulvia's contemporaries are, like Camilla, praised for their fighting spirit, especially when it is displayed in defence of their husbands and their interests, while she is vilified.

Valerius Maximus praised Hypsicratea, the queen consort of King Mithridates VI of Pontus, for cutting her hair, adopting masculine dress and weapons, and riding off after her husband to accompany him when he was on campaign against the Romans during the Third Mithridatic War (73–63 BCE).[54] Elsewhere, she is described as riding a Persian steed and being dressed and armed like a Persian man – she may have been a member of Mithridates' cavalry.[55] She was at his side in 67 BCE when he was victorious against Pompey at the Battle of Zela, and again in 66 BCE when he was defeated by Pompey in a surprise night-time attack on his camp near Dasteira, north of the source of the Euphrates River, not far from the Armenian border. She even joined him on the run afterwards, riding through the mountains and into

Armenia, and then on to Colchis and the Caucasus mountain range. Since Valerius was friends with Pompey's son Sextus, it is likely that he had contact with people that had known the couple personally and could provide first-hand information about them and their escapades, giving this remarkable tale the ring of truth.

After Mithridates' death in 63 BCE, there is some evidence that Hypsicratea became first a prisoner of war, then a companion of Caesar, under the assumed identity of the historian Hypsicrates of Amisus, who reportedly lived to be ninety-two years old and was known as an authority on two subjects: the fortifications of the Bosporan Kingdom and the Amazons of the Caucasus region.[56] Her willingness to share Mithridates' privations was given as an example of selfless marital love, and remained a popular tale for centuries, with many illustrations included in illuminated manuscripts and on medallions during the medieval period (see fig 11).[57] But admittedly, she was a barbarian, not a Roman woman, and thus held to a different set of standards.

Moving to Rome itself, the wife commemorated by her husband in the *Laudatio Turiae* inscription is commended by him because during his exile, when his wife and mother were living alone in the house on the Palatine Hill that had once belonged to Milo and had been confiscated and sold upon his exile for the murder of Clodius, Milo and his goons had attempted to break in and reacquire the house by force, but she had fought them off. He says 'bravely you drove them back and defended our house'.[58] Presumably she did so by commanding the household staff to arm themselves and fight back against the intruders, serving as something of a general.

And Porcia, the daughter of Cato the Younger and the wife of Marcus Junius Brutus – one of the ringleaders in the assassination of Caesar – is described in admiring terms as being 'of no womanish spirit'. Apparently, when she learned of Brutus' plan to assassinate Caesar, she sought to encourage and reassure him. She requested that a knife be brought to her so that she could trim her fingernails, then used it to stab herself in the thigh. When Brutus scolded her for her carelessness, she told him that she had done it on purpose: 'What I did was no accident;

in the plight we are in it was the surest token of my love for you. I wanted to try out how coolly I could kill myself with steel if your plan did not turn out as you hope.'[59] There are several conflicting accounts of Porcia's death the following year. While she probably simply died of illness in the summer of 43 BCE, thus before the Battle of Philippi during which Brutus perished in 42 BCE, there persists a version of her death in which, upon hearing of Brutus' death, she was prevented from laying her hands upon a sword so she took her own life by swallowing hot coals instead – a far more horrific method of suicide.[60] The purpose of such lionization is to liken her to her father Cato Uticensis, who disembowelled himself with his bare hands rather than (as he saw it) debase and humiliate himself by asking Caesar for clemency at the conclusion of the civil war in 46 BCE.[61] So in this particular instance, a woman acting in the manner of a man is a positive attribute rather than a negative one. Porcia is praised rather than excoriated.

Plutarch wrote a treatise entitled *On the Bravery of Women* for a female friend of his, a woman named Clea who was one of the priestesses at the Oracle of Delphi, upon the death of their mutual female friend Leontis. He offers the opinion that 'best of all seems the Roman custom, which publicly renders to women, as to men, a fitting commemoration after the end of their life'.[62] Many of the examples that he includes in this work revolve around the actions of women during times of war. For instance, when, early in Rome's history, the Etruscans led by Lars Porsena came to terms with Rome and were provided with ten young men and ten young women as hostages, one of the female hostages, Cloelia, planned and executed a daring escape.[63] She claimed the women needed to bathe, then led her nine companions away from the Etruscan camp and down to the River Tiber. Having managed to procure a horse – presumably one of the Etruscan cavalrymen's – she mounted it and swam it across the river, encouraging the other young women to follow behind her through the water.

When the women returned to Rome, they were simultaneously praised for their bravery and admonished for breaking the terms of the agreement, and were promptly sent back to the Etruscans. Once again ensconced in the Etruscan camp, the women were questioned by Lars Porsena about who the instigator of the prison break had been, but they remained silent, refusing to turn Cloelia in. However, a defiant Cloelia freely admitted her culpability, and Lars Porsena was so impressed with her bravery that he gifted her with a horse, 'because he admired her strength and daring as above that of a woman, [and] deemed her worthy of a gift fitting for a warrior'.[64] Cloelia was subsequently commemorated with an equestrian statue on the Via Sacra, near the Temple of Jupiter Stator, on the north-east side of the Clivus Palatinus. It is the only case in Roman history of a woman being so honoured in the city of Rome, and it was considered so significant a monument that when it was destroyed in one of the fires to which the city centre was prone, it was reconstructed and reinstated.[65]

Even anonymous women lower down the social hierarchy were acclaimed for their martial endeavours *in extremis*, including the weaponization of their own bodies. It seems to have been a common occurrence (or at least a common literary trope) that women cut off their hair and donated the lengthy tresses for use as bow strings and catapult ropes, and these women receive nothing but praise and admiration for their actions.[66] There was reportedly even a temple dedicated to a manifestation of the goddess Venus known as Venus Calva (Venus the Bald) in Rome, dedicated in honour of the women who sacrificed their hair for this purpose during the siege of Rome by the Gauls in 382 BCE.[67] The same is true of women in cities under siege who are recorded as throwing roof tiles and debris at advancing enemy troops – King Pyrrhus of Epirus was famously killed during the Battle of Argos when an elderly woman threw a roof tile at his head, stunning him and knocking him from his horse, and a nearby soldier took advantage of the situation and swiftly decapitated him.[68] So why is Fulvia, not to mention her attempts to ensure the safety of her husband, her children and her property, treated so differently?

CHAPTER 11

FULVIA'S LAST ACT

UNDER NORMAL CIRCUMSTANCES, THE death of an elite Roman matriarch would have been marked by all manner of formal mourning. Had Fulvia died in her own bed in her own home in Rome or Tusculum, her body would have been washed, anointed with scented oils, dressed in her finest silken clothing, garlanded with fragrant flowers and displayed on a couch in the atrium. There would have been a funeral procession through the city to the family tomb – presumably the tomb where Bambalio and the preceding members of the Fulvian clan had been interred. Since human burials were not permitted within the *pomerium*, the sacred boundary of the city of Rome, tombs lined the roads leading into and out of the metropolis. Some aristocratic Republican family tombs still survive, and can be visited today – such as the Tomb of the Scipios, situated between the Via Appia and the Via Latina, in use from the early third century BCE until the early first century CE – and they show how grand and ornate the Fulvian tomb could have been. It would not have been beyond the realms of possibility for Fulvia to have had commissioned, either by herself or by Antony, a tomb of her own, such as the Tomb of Caecilia Metelli further down the Via Appia, built in the latter part of the first century BCE for Fulvia's contemporary, the daughter of the consul of 69 BCE and the daughter-in-law of Crassus, who had died fighting the Parthians at the Battle of Carrhae in 53 BCE (see fig 12).

But Fulvia died alone and, by and large, unattended in Greece. The only members of her family we can say for certain were with her were her three youngest children. Assuming her eldest son, Publius Claudius Pulcher, was with her, the duty of arranging her funerary rites would have fallen to him. He would have been in his late teens at this point, so finally old enough to take control of his patrimony and live independently, but both his paternity and proximity to Antony would have endangered him as much as Fulvia's youngest children's did them, so he may have considered it sensible to leave Rome to Octavian for the time being and accompany his mother into exile. Besides, spending time in Athens and other Greek cities was no hardship for a wealthy young man; rather, it was a rite of passage akin to the later Grand Tour undertaken by British aristocratic youths, or the contemporary gap year. Assuming that Fulvia's only daughter, Claudia, was with her, the duty of preparing the body, or at least directing the household staff to prepare the body and overseeing the process, would have fallen to her. Since Fulvia's ancestral masks had in all likelihood been left locked in their storage cupboards in the atrium of the family home back in Rome, that element at least would have been missing from the funerary procession.

One funerary relief from the Tomb of the Haterii, located on the Via Labicana to the south-east of Rome, shows a wealthy woman lying in state in her atrium as her family mourn around her.[1] This gives us a sense of what Fulvia's laying out would have looked like, augmented by all the luxurious and sumptuous touches that wealth could provide, such as floral garlands, burning torches, fragment incense and gentle flute music.

The funerary procession through the city from the deceased's house to their tomb would have culminated in the deceased being cremated on a pyre outside the tomb, their ashes then collected and deposited

Relief from the Tomb of the Haterii, circa late first century BCE

in a luxurious urn, then placed inside a niche adorned with a plaque inscribed with the deceased's achievements. If Publius was presiding over the proceedings, he would have performed a *laudatio*, an honorific speech in which he would enumerate his mother's virtues and achievements.

There were two stories regarding how women came to be granted the right to a *laudatio*.[2] According to Livy, it was bestowed by the Senate in 390 BCE as a gesture of gratitude for their sacrifice of their jewellery to pay the Gauls during the siege of Rome, in order to avoid having to melt down the sacred gold. Plutarch, however, places the grant slightly earlier, in 395 BCE, in response to matrons making offerings to the Sanctuary at Delphi in the wake of the destruction of the city of Veii. Both explanations emphasize collective rather than individual action. It was not until almost three centuries later, however, in 100 BCE, that the first woman received such a commemoration: her name was Popilia, and she was honoured by her son.[3] After that, it seems to have become customary, and a number of examples of prominent women's *laudationes* are recorded in ancient sources, although these are mentioned because of the men who delivered them rather than the profiles of the women in question: for example, Caesar commemorated his aunt Julia and his wife Cornelia (both nakedly political acts, as these women were connected to Marius, the arch-enemy of the dictator Sulla, and promoting them emphasized Caesar's links with the former and his antipathy towards the latter), while Octavian followed in his great-uncle's footsteps and commemorated his grandmother Julia, Caesar's sister. More routinely, Atticus commemorated his mother Caecilia, who died at the ripe old age of ninety, when he himself was a venerable sixty-seven, at a private rather than a public funeral.[4]

The two examples of this practice of *laudatio* that have survived from this period are the *Laudatio Turiae* and the *Laudatio Murdiae*. Murdia's son hedges his bets by saying 'it is difficult to find new kinds of praise for a woman, since their lives are disturbed by little variation', but this disclaimer would surely not have applied to Fulvia, and to whomever befell the responsibility of delivering her *laudatio*, they would have had plenty of meaty material.[5] If Publius was not present, perhaps Gaius, as the second son, would have done so. Although he would have been around ten years old at the time, this would not necessarily have been too young – Octavian had performed the *laudatio* for his grandmother at the only slightly older age of twelve. Coming from her children, Fulvia's *laudatio* would likely have had more in common with those of the unnamed woman known as Turia, Murdia, and Atticus' mother Caecilia, and emphasized her private qualities rather than her public ones.

It is possible that Fulvia's urn was temporarily interred somewhere local until such a time as her family could return to Italy and arrange a more permanent resting place. Alternatively, like her brother-in-law Appius Claudius Pulcher, Clodius' oldest brother, who had died abroad in Euboea (modern Evia in Greece) in 48 BCE, a tomb could have been built for her locally.[6] Yet if her children had hoped to set up a monument like Caecilia Metella's to honour their mother – who had, after all, for a time been the most powerful and influential woman in the Republic – they were probably disappointed. The deteriorating political situation over the next few years would have made that exceedingly unwise, and even once things settled down following the deaths of Antony and Cleopatra in 30 BCE, under Octavian's regime there was a concerted and sustained effort to minimize the visibility of women, and neutralize the influence they exerted, in Roman society. They may have had to settle for building a more modest tomb on Fulvia's family estate at Tusculum, just as the family of the great general Lucullus had done at his estate nearby. Unfortunately for us, no trace of Fulvia's tomb has so far been found.

And what of Fulvia's will? It is probable that she left the bulk of her vast estate – both what she had inherited from her parents and what she had managed to acquire for herself through fair means as well as foul – to her five children. Since Roman daughters could inherit from their parents just like sons, Fulvia may have divided things equally between her children, just as her peer Murdia did.[7] This would have been fair to Claudia, who would need a dowry were she to embark upon a second marriage, and to Gaius, whose father had been nowhere near as wealthy or powerful as his siblings' fathers and yet was still expected to climb the *cursus honorum* with all the incurred expenses. After all, Fulvia had no idea of the grim fate that was coming for her children in the years following her death, even if the seeds had already been sown by her own actions.

It was not unheard of for Roman husbands to end their marriages without warning upon returning from a lengthy sojourn abroad, for both personal and political reasons. Lucullus, arriving home from the Third Mithridatic War in the East in 66 BCE, promptly divorced his wife Clodia Luculli, one of Clodius and Clodia Metelli's sisters, even though she was the mother of his young daughter.[8] The problems that he had had with her brother Clodius while on campaign, such as Clodius inciting a mutiny against him, were undoubtedly a factor in his decision, although Lucullus preferred to accuse his wife of committing incest with her brother, a charge he would repeat a few years later at Clodius' trial for sacrilege, rather than admitting that a mere pipsqueak had undermined his imperium and suborned his soldiers.[9]

Pompey the Great, arriving home from the East in 62 BCE, divorced his wife of eighteen years Mucia Tertia without explanation, although she was the mother of his only surviving children. While there was some gossip that she had been one of Caesar's conquests, the fact that Pompey immediately entered into an alliance with Caesar and married Caesar's much younger daughter Julia suggests that it was not Mucia who was to blame for the split.[10] Meanwhile Cicero came back to Italy after the end of the civil war between Caesar and Pompey in 47 BCE and divorced his wife of three decades, Terentia. He seems to have been under the impression that she had not administered their property in his absence as well as she might have done, but there are indications he was suffering something akin to a midlife crisis, and the fact that he quickly married Publilia, who was young enough to be his granddaughter, does not help matters.[11] In the latter two cases, the men came in for their fair share of criticism, as divorcing your wife and the mother of your children after a marriage of long duration for spurious reasons was seen as rather distasteful. However, withdrawing your consent to a marriage and issuing a notification of divorce is rather different to abandoning your spouse on their deathbed.

While some Roman poets such as Tibullus had pondered their own mortality and faced the possibility of their own deaths far from their loved ones, his peer Propertius reversed this scenario, and envisaged the ghost of his lover Cynthia haunting him and berating him for his absence from her deathbed and the subsequent funerary rites instead. The embittered spectre, still scorched from her funeral pyre, asks, 'Treacherous one, from whom no girl can expect better, can sleep so soon have power over you?'[12] She is aghast at his dismissal of the love and passion that the couple shared, and proceeds to reprimand him:

No one cried aloud upon my eyes at my passing: I might, had
you called me back, have gained another day. No watchman
rattled his cleft reed for my sake, and a jagged tile gashed my
unprotected head. Besides, who saw you bowed with grief at
my funeral or your suit of mourning warmed with tears? If
it irked you to accompany the cortege beyond the gates, still
you might have bade my bier move more slowly to that point.
Why, ungrateful man, did you not call the winds to fan my
pyre? Why was my funeral fire not perfumed with spice? Was
it then too much to cast hyacinths upon me, no costly gift, and
to hallow my grave with wine from a shattered jar?[13]

Clearly, Propertius had a guilty conscience. But did Antony? So
it would seem, as too little, too late, he came to regret his impulsive
behaviour and consider himself to hold some responsibility for Fulvia's
demise.[14] Some Roman husbands chose to end their lives rather than
live without their beloved wives – the senator Gaius Plautius Numida
stabbed himself to death upon hearing of his wife's demise, while within
living memory Marcus Plautius Hypsaeus had fallen on his sword
beside his wife Orestilla's funerary pyre at Tarentum, leaving his friends
to pick up his corpse and place it on the pyre beside hers, so the pair
could be cremated together – and Antony did indeed mark Fulvia's
death with another, just not his own.[15] Instead, he eased his guilt over
her miserable end by having Manius executed, blaming him for dripping
poison in Fulvia's ear about his extramarital dalliances with Glaphyra
and Cleopatra.[16] That did not prevent him from seeking to leverage his
bereavement in the pursuit of political and military advantage, however,
and this was a tactic that Fulvia would undoubtedly have understood,
having done it herself twelve years previously. He sailed from Greece to
Italy, aiming to land at the port of Brundisium on the Adriatic coast. Yet
upon disembarking his ship, he found himself blockaded by Octavian's
forces. His rival was on the verge of declaring war.[17]

But upon finally coming face to face with Octavian and sitting down
to parlay, with their troops applying a considerable amount of pressure

upon them both, the pair came to an understanding that would come to be known as the Pact of Brundisium. With both Lucius and Fulvia safely out of the way and unable to put forward their versions of events, Antony and Octavian agreed to blame Fulvia for the fiasco of the Perusine War and renew their alliance. Since Antony was now conveniently single again, Octavian suggested he marry his elder sister Octavia, herself recently bereaved after the death of her husband Claudius Marcellus.[18] Octavia's bereavement was so recent that not only was the official mourning period not yet over, but she was actually pregnant with her late husband's child, and consequently the marriage required special dispensation from the Senate.

In one key respect, Antony and Octavia's marriage was the first of its kind. It was not a union between individuals, or even an alliance between two families, as was standard practice for an elite Roman marriage, but rather a coalition on behalf of the entire Roman Republic – in addition to Antony and Octavia, and Octavian, the Senate, the legions and the *plebs* had a vested interest in it and its success.[19] This vicariousness is reflected in a statue of the goddess Concordia (Concord) and its accompanying altar set up later that year, on 12 October, in honour of the Pact of Brundisium in the Italian town of Casinum, by the joint magistrates Marcus Papius and Lucius Matrius.[20]

Just as Antony had minted and issued a series of coins bearing Fulvia's image, so he now minted and issued a series of coins bearing Octavia's, celebrating both the marriage and the alliance that it cemented. On one beautifully ornate silver denarius, Antony is depicted on the obverse face wearing a crown of ivy and enclosed by a wreath of ivy and flowers,

A silver denarius depicting Marcus Antonius and Octavia

presumably a reference to Dionysos, one of his favourite deities. On the reverse face, a bust of Octavia sits upon a container known as a *cista mystica* – a cult object associated with Dionysos – flanked by writhing intertwined snakes.[21]

Little did he know that marrying Octavian's sister would prove to be a major mistake, rendering his personal life political fodder for the next decade, and ultimately leading to his own downfall and death in 30 BCE.

What if Fulvia had not died when she did? Would Antony have been any more successful in his struggle for supremacy with Octavian over the decade that followed?[22] He may not have appreciated it in the spring of 40 BCE, but Fulvia had long been his most significant asset, not just in the city of Rome but also in Italy during his long periods of absence.[23] Fulvia was not merely his close friend Curio's widow but, much more importantly, Clodius' widow. She had continued to wield a significant amount of influence over Clodius' comrades such as Sextus Cloelius, Quintus Fufius Calenus and Titus Plancus Bursa, his many clients, and the Clodiani. She had worked in tandem with his mother Julia to prevent him from being declared a public enemy in 43 BCE. She had travelled around Italy, her and Antony's children in tow, to remind his veterans of where their loyalty should lie. Finally, she had gone to war to protect his interests in 41 BCE, and had Antony's brother Lucius not ultimately worked against her, and Antony's generals with their legions not waited out the conflict, she might have succeeded in neutralizing Octavian for good. Even once the Perusine War had concluded in Octavian's favour in 40 BCE, she was still working behind the scenes to find new alliances for Antony, opening lines of communication with the navies of Sextus Pompey in the Mediterranean Sea around Sicily and Gnaeus Domitius Ahenobarbus in the Ionian Sea. It is clear that after Fulvia's death in 40 BCE, Antony lost the foothold that he had in Rome, and Italy more broadly, and was unable to regain it.

Had Fulvia not died, no doubt she would have continued to work not only on Antony's behalf but, even if he had divorced her over the embarrassing failure of the Perusine War, also on behalf of their children, Antyllus and Iullus, as the two boys were Antony's legal, political and military heirs. She would have been assisted by their older brothers, Publius Claudius Pulcher and Gaius Scribonius Curio, and their older sister, Claudia Pulchra, for whom she could have arranged influential marriage alliances.[24] She would have been able to fend off Octavian's regular challenges to Antony's authority, reminding everyone that Octavian had only defeated Sextus Pompey in 36 BCE because Antony had provided him with the necessary naval support, and intervened to prevent the theft, illegal opening, and damaging reading of Antony's will before the Senate in 32 BCE (and, in fact, had Fulvia been alive and still his wife, the contents of his will would have been very different). She may well have found Antony's continuing relationship with Cleopatra irksome, at the very least, but out of sight, out of mind – and in any case, neither the Queen of Egypt nor her and Antony's children were any threat to Fulvia's pre-eminent position in Rome. In fact, their blood links to two of her own children would only have strengthened her position, and that of the next generation. With Antyllus and Iullus, ably supported by Publius and Gaius, dominant in Rome; Caesar's son Ptolemy XV Caesar and Antony's daughter Cleopatra Selene ruling in Egypt; Antony's sons Alexander Helios (and his bride Iotape of Media) ruling in Armenia, Media and Parthia, and Ptolemy Philadelphus in Syria, Phoenicia and Cilicia; and Antony's older daughter Antonia Prima's descendants ruling in Pontus, the entire ancient Near East would have been under her extended family's control.

By the early 20s BCE, thanks no doubt in part to Fulvia's own activities, it had become more usual and acceptable for women to have a visible public profile, both in Rome and elsewhere around the Empire, and for them to almost literally cement that public profile in people's minds through the commission of buildings and other types of monuments. One example can be found in Pula in Croatia, and is known as the Arch of the Sergii.[25] While today it is a free-standing triumphal arch, when it was built in the 20s BCE, it was set against the Porta Aurea, one of the gates by which people entered or exited the colony, and therefore highly visible. It was paid for by Salvia Postuma with her own money, and it commemorated three members of the Sergii. First and foremost was Salvia's husband, Lucius Sergius Lepidus, who had served as a military tribune in the Twenty-Ninth Legion at the Battle of Actium on 2 September 31 BCE, where Octavian finally defeated Antony and Cleopatra at sea off the coast of Greece, but his father Lucius and uncle Gaius were also mentioned, and statues of the three men would have been set up on the top. No doubt, had she been given the chance, Fulvia would have patronized many cities and towns around the Empire with similar constructions, and we would have more definitive material evidence of her beyond the lead sling bullets of Perusia – perhaps even some inscriptions giving us her own words.

Most importantly and impactfully, had Fulvia lived, since Antony would not have married Octavia in 40 BCE and fathered two daughters by her, the Julio-Claudian dynasty as we know it would not have existed. Octavian would have been left with his sole child Julia and his sister's only son Marcellus, and their short-lived marriage, terminated by Marcellus' early death, was childless. The emperors Caligula, Claudius and Nero, all descended from Antony's daughters by Octavia, would never have been born.

Certainly, some Romans wondered what might have been. In the years after the Battle of Actium, the poet Horace, who had celebrated Cleopatra's defeat and subsequent death in florid writing the moment he heard about it, raised the possibility of a different outcome.[26] He recounted his friend Lollius' penchant for re-enacting the battle, with himself and his brother taking the places of Octavian and Antony in command of their enslaved staff standing in for the *imperators'* respective land and sea forces.[27] A century later, the poet Lucan obliquely alluded to Horace's flight of imaginative fancy in his own work on the earlier civil war between Caesar and Pompey.[28] As much as the propaganda of the Augustan Principate might have liked to present Octavian's victory as inevitable, the outcome of Actium had been far from a foregone conclusion: after all, in advance of the battle, one man trained two ravens to speak, one to say 'Hail Caesar, the victorious commander', the other 'Hail the victorious commander Antony', and then greeted Octavian upon his return from the battle with the appropriate raven, for which Octavian paid him 20,000 sesterces, then laughed heartily when he discovered the ruse.[29] To the victor, the spoils.

CHAPTER 12

FULVIA'S CHILDREN

THE LATE REPUBLIC SAW a dramatic decline in both the number and the size of the families that comprised the senatorial order. While the series of civil wars fought over the course of the period spanning the mid-second century BCE to the mid-first century BCE was undoubtedly the primary cause of this winnowing, it is fair to say that these families were small to start with. Ancient commentators were happy to place the blame squarely on women for this, accusing them of using a range of contraceptive measures to avoid getting pregnant and seeking abortions if those contraceptive measures proved unsuccessful – all in the service of preserving their looks and figures.[1] This was one misogynistic accusation that could definitely not be thrown at Fulvia. She proved to be surprisingly and rather unusually fecund for a senatorial woman, not only bearing each of her three husbands children, but also providing each of them with a male heir to carry on the family line. This was something that, despite having made other marriages, they had previously lacked. In the case of Antony, she provided him with two: an heir and a spare.

Again, unusually for a senatorial woman, all of her children survived to adulthood. They did not, however, lead long lives, and three of the five came to violent ends, all at the hands of Fulvia's enemy Octavian, later known by the name Augustus. Is it fair to describe Fulvia as 'simultaneously ambitious for and destructive to' her brood, as one modern historian has done?[2]

Her only daughter, Claudia, sometimes known as Clodia Pulchra, one of the children from her first marriage to Publius Clodius Pulcher, left only the faintest of footprints in the historical record. After her marriage to Octavian was humiliatingly dissolved and she was sent back home to Fulvia in 41 BCE, we hear nothing more about her.[3] There was nothing inherently shameful about divorce, especially under such circumstances when it was patently clear that Octavian's motivation was entirely political and Claudia herself was not at fault, so there was no reason why she might not have remarried. She still had the cachet of her famous father and powerful stepfather. Perhaps she did remarry, and then lived a happy life in obscurity.

Fulvia's eldest son, Publius Claudius Pulcher (born *circa* 59 BCE), the other child of her first marriage, seems to have started out with such potential. After his near brush with death following his father's murder in 52 BCE, the next reference to him is found in a letter sent by Antony to Cicero around 22 April 44 BCE, soon after the assassination of Julius Caesar. The boy's stepfather writes:

> But I must say that if you wish to take a view in accordance with humanity, wisdom, and a regard for myself, you will surely show yourself indulgent, and you will be willing for P. Claudius, a lad of the highest promise, to think that you refrained from bearing hard upon his father's friends when it lay in your power. Allow it, I beg you, to appear that you were his father's enemy for patriotic reasons, not because you despised the family. We lay aside feuds started on public grounds with greater credit and more readiness than those of arrogance. Further, give me the opportunity to influence the boy here and now and

persuade his impressionable mind to the opinion that quarrels should not be hereditary.[4]

Whether Antony was exaggerating Claudius' talents, and whether or not Cicero succeeded in influencing the boy, is open to interpretation based on what we know about his life and career. (After all, Cicero's mentorship of Caelius did not prevent him from veering off track on multiple occasions and, ultimately, coming to a sticky end after allying himself with Milo and attempting to raise a rebellion against Caesar in 48 BCE.)[5] Cicero's rather obsequious reply certainly indicates that he was open to reconciliation between the two families:

> As for young Clodius, I think it is for you to imbue his impressionable mind, as you say in your letter, with such sentiments as may persuade him that there is no residue of family feud between us... So since in making this request of me you say that you will not use your power in the matter against my wishes, you may if you think proper present the concession to the boy also as coming from me; not that in view of our respective ages I could reasonably envisage any danger from his quarter, nor that a man of my standing need greatly fear any conflict, but in order that we ourselves may be on closer terms than we have been on hitherto.[6]

At some point, Claudius had reverted to the traditional spelling of his family name, no doubt finding it politically expedient to link himself with the imperial family. It has been suggested that when Octavian contracted a marriage with Claudius' younger sister Claudia to firm up his alliance with Antony in 43 BCE, he also contracted a marriage between Claudius and his oldest niece Claudia Marcella Major, the daughter of his sister Octavia and her first husband Gaius Claudius Marcellus.[7] This would have provided Octavian with a much stronger link to the Claudii, and Clodius specifically, allowing him to draw on the popular support that Clodius had always enjoyed – and was, now that his son had reached maturity, being passed on to him and away from Fulvia and Antony. Then, at some point, this marriage was dissolved, and Marcella was married to Agrippa in 28 BCE; and when that marriage was also dissolved in order to allow Agrippa to marry Octavian's daughter Julia in 21 BCE, Marcella was married to Iullus Antonius, Claudius' youngest half-brother. Claudius' tangible link to Clodius and his marital link with Octavian may, in point of fact, be part of the reason why he did not meet the same fate as his three half-brothers; considering that he was the oldest of Fulvia's children, old enough to remember his own father, he may have had less loyalty to Antony than his half-brother Curio, who had only known Antony as a father, and who had gone to Egypt with him and Antyllus.

Claudius certainly climbed the *cursus honorum* in the years after Antony's downfall and death, going all the way to the position of praetor at some point after 31 BCE. He also held an important religious position – that of augur, with responsibility for interpreting signs from the heavens, such as bird flight. However, Valerius Maximus includes him in a list of individuals who disgraced their famous parents, describing him as falling into dissipation and gaining notoriety for his relationship with a sex worker before eating himself to death.[8]

Whatever the true circumstances of his death, his funerary urn has survived and is currently exhibited in the Louvre in the department of Egyptian antiquities.[9]

It is a fascinating object – it is two feet tall, carved from a single piece of calcite alabaster, and was manufactured in Egypt in either the ninth or eighth century BCE for the purpose of serving as a votive

The funerary urn of Publius Claudius Pulcher

offering from the Theban priest Nebneteru, to ensure the pharaoh's continuing health and good fortune. When it was originally dedicated, it probably contained some sort of expensive unguent. Upon the Roman conquest and annexation of Egypt by Octavian in 30 BCE, the Roman enthusiasm for Egypt ensured that many Egyptian antiquities were seized and imported to Rome. The vase was one of these, and was likely purchased by Claudius or a member of his family and reused as a cinerary urn upon his death. In order to serve this new purpose, a lid and two handles were carved from Italian alabaster and fitted to the vase, before a Latin inscription was inscribed onto it: 'Publius Claudius Pulcher, son of Publius, grandson of Appius, great-grandson of Appius. A quaestor, quaesitor, praetor, and augur.'[10] The urn was discovered near the Theatre of Marcellus in 1615, which suggests that the family tomb of the Claudii was located somewhere nearby. This would have been a very impressive funerary urn, redolent of wealth, status and sophistication, as well as being the height of fashion.

Publius Claudius Pulcher seems to have succeeded in fathering two children. His son, also named Publius Claudius Pulcher, likewise climbed the *cursus honorum*, reaching the position of consul in 21 or 22 CE. His daughter Claudia Pulchra made a brilliant marriage to Publius Quinctilius Varus, consul in 13 BCE, but he was killed in Germany in the famous Battle of the Teutoburg Forest, otherwise known as the 'Varian Disaster', in which German forces ambushed and wiped out three legions. Claudia was subsequently caught up in treasonous conspiracies, and prosecuted by Gnaeus Domitius Afer for adultery with a man named Furnius in 25 CE. He also accused her of practising witchcraft and planning to poison the emperor Tiberius. Despite her cousin Agrippina the Elder's attempts to intercede with the emperor on Claudia's behalf, she and Furnius were found guilty and exiled.

Fulvia's second son, Gaius Scribonius Curio, only a baby when his father was killed in Africa, was raised by his stepfather Antony, so it is hardly surprising that he should have taken his side in the civil war between Antony and Octavian and accompanied Antony to Egypt in 31 BCE. But upon Octavian's invasion and Antony's defeat the following year, because Curio refused to beg Octavian's forgiveness, he was amongst those most severely punished and was executed, and thus gained the distinction of being one of the most talked-about casualties of the war.[11] He had only just turned eighteen.[12] Octavian's excuse was that Curio was of military age, so it was appropriate to treat him as an enemy combatant, but the historian Cassius Dio, who is generally positive about Octavian, is critical about this hair-splitting.[13]

Fulvia and Antony's eldest son, Marcus Antonius Antyllus, was also in Egypt with Antony in 30 BCE. As his father's political heir, highlighted on coinage issued by Antony with himself on the obverse face and Antyllus on the reverse, Antyllus was an obvious target.[14] No doubt Octavian looked at Antyllus and saw himself as a young man, determined to avenge his father, and was determined to avoid history repeating itself to his detriment.[15] But in advance of suffering the clean death of an execution, Antyllus was betrayed by his tutor Theodorus, captured by Octavian's soldiers, and despite attempting to claim sanctuary at the altar of the Deified Julius Caesar in Alexandria, brutally murdered. His head was cut off as so many others' had been a decade earlier during the proscriptions ordered by his father.[16] Perhaps he thought that showing obeisance to Caesar would endear him to Octavian and save him. If so, he was wrong. To add insult to injury, Theodorus robbed his decapitated corpse, stealing an amulet that Antyllus wore around his neck. He did not get away with it though: Octavian found out about the theft and had him crucified.

Fulvia's youngest child, her second son by Antony, Iullus (born 42 BCE), was very young when she died and likely had no memory of her. He was raised in his father's house in Rome with Octavia to all intents and purposes his mother, and it was likely a combination of this, and the fact that he spent very little time with his father – who spent most of the decade from 40 to 30 BCE in the East – that saved him from suffering a similar fate to his older half-brother and brother.[17] He presented an opportunity for Octavian to wash away the stain of the blood that executing Curio and Antyllus had left upon his hands, enabling him to present himself as a family man, a *pater familias* presiding over a sprawling household full of the bereaved children of his deceased enemies – a different angle on the traditional Roman virtue of clemency.[18] He had, after all, been named to honour Antony's connection to the Julian family.[19] It may also have pleased Octavian to suborn the affections of Antony's last remaining Roman son.

Iullus was apparently only preceded in Octavian's favour by the sons of his right-hand man Agrippa (also his own grandsons and later adopted sons) and the sons of his wife Livia (his stepsons; one of them, Tiberius, was later his adopted son).[20] Iullus married one of his stepsisters, Octavia's daughter Claudia Marcella Major, in 21 BCE, and it has been suggested that the pair of them are depicted amongst other members of Augustus' household on the north frieze of the Ara Pacis Augustae, the Altar of Augustan Peace, dedicated in 13 BCE and completed in 9 BCE. When Octavia died in 11 BCE, he was one of the pallbearers during her funerary procession.[21]

Iullus studied with the formerly enslaved Lucius Crassicius Pansa, an old friend of his father's, who had started out as a playwright before turning to poetry and became known for his commentary on the famous Latin poet Cinna's popular poem *Zmyrna*.[22] It would appear that Iullus showed rather more talent as a poet than was usual for an elite young Roman, as his poetry was praised by another friend of his father's, the poet Horace, and likened to the Greek poet Pindar's work. In one of his *Odes*, Horace was eagerly anticipating Iullus composing a poem to celebrate Augustus' victories in Gaul and Spain, and the military triumph that would no doubt result:

> You, a poet of larger quill, will celebrate Caesar when, decorated with a well-earned wreath of bay, he drags the fierce Sygambri up the Sacred Hill. The Fates and the gods in their goodness have given nothing greater or better than him to the world, nor will they do so even if the ages return to their original gold. You will celebrate the days of joy, the capital's public holiday, and the Forum bereft of lawsuits in honour of the valiant

Augustus' return which has been granted to our prayers. Then, if I have anything to say that is worth hearing, I shall join in to the best of my ability, singing 'O glorious day, o worthy of all praise!' in my joy at Caesar's return.

And while you take the lead, we shall cry more than once 'Io Triumphe!' The whole city will cry 'Io Triumphe!' and we shall offer incense to the kindly gods. You will discharge your debt with ten bulls and as many cows, I mine with a young calf which, after leaving its mother is now growing up in the lush meadows to fulfil my vows; on its forehead it has a bright crescent like that of the moon as it brings round its third rising; where it has that mark it is snow-white in colour; the rest of it is tawny.[23]

One of Iullus' works, an epic poem comprising twelve books, was dedicated to the Greek hero Diomedes, one of the participants in the Trojan War who was on a par, after Achilles, with Ajax the Great and Agamemnon as one of the greatest warriors amongst the Greeks.[24] After the Trojan War was over, he travelled to Italy and stayed at the court of Daunus, King of the Daunians, marrying his daughter Euippe, before founding a series of cities in Magna Graecia, southern Italy. There may have been a message for Augustus in Iullus' choice of Diomedes for his hero: in Virgil's *Aeneid*, the Italian warrior Turnus travels to Diomedes' kingdom to request his aid in the war against the Trojan interloper and ancestor of the Julio-Claudian dynasty Aeneas, but Diomedes refuses, stating that he no longer wishes to fight Trojans, but to live in peace.[25]

Like his elder half-brother Publius, Iullus climbed the *cursus honorum*. He was honoured with a priesthood, and served as praetor in 13 BCE, consul in 10 BCE and proconsul (governor) of the province of Asia in 7 BCE (although it is rather pointed that he was denied military command and was not permitted to govern a province that required legions).[26] As praetor, he was responsible for throwing celebratory games upon Octavian's return to Rome, including horse races and wild-beast hunts, capped off with a banquet on the Capitoline.[27] Unfortunately, he made the mistake of committing adultery with his foster sister, Augustus' daughter Julia, and becoming caught up in a conspiracy against the emperor in 2 BCE.[28] Velleius Paterculus called the affair 'shameful to narrate and dreadful to recall'.[29] When his transgressions were uncovered, Iullus was forced to commit suicide in an attempt to regain his lost honour.

It is possible that the affair was triggered by Julia's husband Tiberius' prolonged absence from Rome, and her resultant desire for protection for herself and her young family, as she had five children, two of whom, Gaius and Lucius, were Augustus' favoured heirs. It is also possible that Iullus had designs on some sort of regency for himself; certainly, ancient commentators such as Pliny the Elder and Cassius Dio assumed so. Seneca the Younger observed that Augustus had for 'a second time the need to fear a woman in league with an Antony'.[30] However, Iullus was not Julia's only lover. She had been flagrantly unfaithful to her previous husband, Agrippa, as well as Tiberius, and when challenged about the fact that her children all resembled her husbands rather than her lovers, she explained that she was only unfaithful when she was pregnant, so as not to get caught out conceiving a love child. The pithy way that she put it was: 'I take on a passenger only when the ship's hold is full.'[31] Other lovers whose names have been preserved were Quintius Crispinus, Appius Claudius, Sempronius Gracchus and Scipio, none of whom were punished as severely as Iullus.[32]

Iullus had two children. His son, Lucius Antonius (born 20 BCE) – named after his uncle who had once allied himself with Fulvia and fought the Perusine War, since it was no longer permissible to name him after his grandfather – was described by Tacitus as 'the bearer of a great but luckless name'.[33] After his father's death in 2 BCE, he was sent away to Massilia, where he studied law at the famed university, a rival to that of Athens. He died in 25 CE, at the age of forty-five, and he was interred in the tomb of the Octavii, his grandmother Octavia's family.[34] Little is known about Iullus' daughter Iulla Antonia; as is the case with so many Roman women, the only evidence of her existence comes from a reference in an inscription set up by one of her freedmen.[35] And so, in this way, Fulvia's dynasty disappeared from recorded history.

CONCLUSION

FULVIA'S LEGACY

B OTH OCTAVIA, OCTAVIAN'S ELDER sister, and Livia, his third wife, were well acquainted with Fulvia. Since she was at least a decade their senior, they would have witnessed her testing the boundaries and limits of female power and agency during the triumviral period, in ways that they were not yet able to attempt. Fulvia was not alone in this, of course, as her own older peers Servilia, Terentia and Clodia had been doing likewise in different ways for years, and she had certainly learned from them.[1] But Octavia and Livia undoubtedly came to view her as a cautionary tale and an object lesson in what *not* to do as the wife of a triumvir and a pre-eminent woman in Rome.[2] Consequently, they would come to occupy what can be described as 'public but not civic' roles in the Late Republic and Early Principate.[3]

Octavian, for his part, was determined that they should not fall victim to the same powerful forces that had targeted and victimized Fulvia. Since he had been one of the main instigators in the destruction of her reputation, both during her lifetime and after her death, he was

well aware of how one's female relations could be sacrificed on the altar
of political and military expedience, a means of scoring points against
an opponent and gaining the upper hand in any sort of rivalry with no
thought or care for the collateral damage. While Antony was nowhere
near as disrespectful of Livia as Octavian had been of Fulvia, he did still
publicly question Octavian's morals and marital fidelity, accusing him
of divorcing Scribonia because she would not tolerate his affair with
Livia, bedding the wife of a former consul in front of her husband in
his own house, and cutting a swathe through the wives and daughters
of the social elite (unlike Antony himself, who kept his extramarital
affairs to his social inferiors and foreigners, as a Roman gentleman was
supposed to do).[4] The biographer Suetonius quotes from one of the
letters that passed between the pair, where Antony lambasts Octavian
for his hypocrisy:

> What has made such a change in you? Because I am fucking
> the queen? She is my wife. Am I just beginning this, or was it
> nine years ago? What then of you – do you fuck only [Livia]
> Drusilla? Good luck to you if when you read this letter you
> have not been in Tertulla or Terentilla or Rufilla or Salvia
> Titisenia, or all of them. Does it matter where or in whom you
> have your stiff prick?[5]

It was with this in mind that in 35 BCE he awarded Octavia and Livia
the sort of protection that tribunes possessed, rendering their persons
sacrosanct (protected by the gods), and any word or deed against them
illegal. An additional aspect of this honour that is worth noting is that
it permitted statues of the two women to be set up in public spaces, the
first time real-life Roman women had been so treated since Cornelia,
the Mother of the Gracchi, which is why so many marble portraits of
Octavia and Livia have survived into the present to be displayed in
museums.[6] Even so, the amount of portraits of Livia that have survived
far outnumber the amount of portraits of Octavia, due to the fact that
Livia lived forty years longer than her sister-in-law, and was the wife,

mother, grandmother and great-grandmother of emperors, so achieved a consistently higher level of public exposure.[7] This is why we can come face to face with Octavia in a museum sculpture gallery, but not, unfortunately, her predecessor Fulvia.

Just as Octavian set himself up as the polar opposite of Antony, so too did Octavia and Livia set themselves up as the polar opposites of Fulvia. This was a means of allowing the dust to settle – a way of reassuring those more traditional members of society who had been distressed by Fulvia's high profile and alienated by her blatant, frenzied and decidedly unfeminine politicking. Whereas Fulvia had rendered support to Antony by breaking his fragile peace with Octavian and waging war on his behalf, Octavia chose a different path.

First, her marriage marked and in some ways manifested the cessation of hostilities between Antony and Octavian, and was seen as symbolic of the longed-for end of the civil wars. Both poets and prophets celebrated the union and eagerly anticipated the birth of a son who would unite the two men for decades to come. Virgil rhapsodized that 'now a new generation descends from heaven on high. Only do you, pure Lucina, smile on the birth of the child, under whom the iron brood shall at last cease and a golden race spring up throughout the world!'[8] (Unfortunately, like his first wife Antonia Hybrida and unlike Fulvia and Cleopatra, Octavia would only succeed in bearing Antony daughters, Antonia Major and Antonia Minor.)

Second, Octavia took to acting as mediator between her husband and her brother, and persuaded Antony to renew his alliance with Octavian rather than reject him in favour of Sextus Pompey through the Treaty of Tarentum (modern Taranto) in 37 BCE. This recalled the role of the Sabine women in interceding between their Sabine fathers and Roman husbands and preventing war between the two kingdoms, soon after the foundation of Rome in the eighth century BCE.[9] It was not even the first time that Octavia had been placed in this position: her great-uncle Caesar had offered her hand in marriage to Pompey after the death of his daughter Julia, as a means of stabilizing and continuing their political alliance, although Pompey turned the offer down and looked elsewhere for his final wife; and she had also run interference between Caesar and her first husband Gaius Claudius Marcellus, who was Caesar's implacable enemy, especially during Marcellus' consulship in 50 BCE.[10] The Second Triumvirate had technically expired on 1 January 37 BCE, but with the treaty it was renewed for a further five years – with an expiration date of the last day of 33 BCE. Yet we do have to bear in the mind the bias of our sources, who promoted Octavia in order to suppress not only Fulvia, but also Cleopatra.

Livia too worked to avoid outbreaks of hostility, interceding with Octavian and encouraging him to pursue clemency in the manner of Caesar, rather than vengeance in the manner of Antony egged on by Fulvia. When Octavian was fretting about ordering the execution of a man who had been conspiring against him in 4 CE, Livia offered her advice:

> Follow the practice of physicians, who when the usual remedies do not work try just the opposite. So far you have accomplished nothing by severity. Salvidienus was followed by Lepidus, Lepidus by Murena, Murena by Caepio, Caepio by Egnatius, to say nothing of the others whose monstrous daring makes one ashamed. Try now how mercy will work: pardon [Gnaeus Cornelius] Cinna. He has been arrested; now he cannot do you harm, but he can help your reputation.[11]

He did as she advised.

While Octavia occupied the more prominent position of the two during the 30s as the wife of one triumvir and the sister of another (on occasion she would bemoan her invidious position), over time her influence on both waned (Antony divorced her in 32 BCE, but for some years after that she was still highly influential in Rome).[12] A key event here was the death of Marcus Claudius Marcellus, Octavia's only son and Octavian's only male heir related to him by blood, in 23 BCE at the age of nineteen. Early on, he had been marked out and particularly favoured by Octavian, even above his right-hand man and the architect of all his military victories, Agrippa. He had been married to Octavian's only biological child, Julia, at the age of seventeen in 25 BCE, and much was expected of the match. Unfortunately, Marcellus contracted an illness and, despite a course of cutting-edge cold-water treatment by the famous physician Antonius Musa (one of Antony's freedmen), he died at the pleasure resort of Baiae.[13] His ashes were placed in the newly built Mausoleum of Augustus on the Campus Martius in Rome, giving him the dubious honour of being the first member of the imperial family to be interred there.

Despite Marcellus' relative youth and inexperience, numerous Augustan poets commemorated him. Propertius wrote a rather sycophantic poem which placed him on the same level as his illustrious ancestors Caesar and Marcus Claudius Marcellus, who was a hero of the Second Punic War (218–201 BCE).[14] On one notable occasion, Virgil gave a private reading from the sixth book of the *Aeneid* to the imperial family, and part of this included Aeneas' journey through the Underworld, where he encounters the shade of Marcellus. At his mention of her son, and Virgil's reliving of his funeral, Octavia fainted.[15] This suitably dramatic episode has been depicted by many artists, such as Jean-Auguste-Dominique Ingres in his 1812 painting *Tu Marcellus Eris*, or *Virgil Reading the Aeneid before Augustus, Livia, and Octavia* (see fig 13). She subsequently refused to allow Marcellus' name to be mentioned in her presence or looked upon his portrait, rejected all helpful advice and counselling, lived in seclusion, and took to crying, moaning and wearing mourning garb for the rest of her life.

By comparison, Livia's mourning upon the death of her younger son Drusus in 9 BCE at the age of twenty-nine after suffering a riding accident while on campaign in Germania was relatively restrained.[16] In the wake of her journey accompanying his remains from Pavia back to Rome, her witnessing of the public mourning for him, and her depositing of his ashes in the family mausoleum, she remained stoic. Although she grieved her loss, she went to great pains to keep her public expressions of grief to a minimum, enlisting the assistance of the philosopher Arius to help her cope. He advised her to do essentially the opposite of what Octavia had done, and to mention Drusus often and commemorate him with statues and monuments (a number of these still survive today). The elegiac poem *Consolation to Livia*, once attributed to the poet Ovid but now thought to have been written later, during the reign of the emperor Tiberius and after Livia's death, aligns with this advice.[17]

We can contrast these expressions of grief by Octavia and Livia with those of Fulvia upon the death of Clodius – while Octavia may not have weaponized her grief to score political points and enact vengeance, she certainly went past the point at which the Romans considered it appropriate to mourn, leading to speculation that it was less Marcellus she mourned, and more his future as Augustus' heir and the next emperor of Rome – and what that would have brought her as his mother. She forgot herself, and she forgot her place.

But as time went on, while Fulvia provided a multifaceted model for the women of the Julio-Claudian dynasty, the elements of her story that served as a cautionary tale either faded from memory or were ignored, and subsequent generations of imperial women became less careful. Over the course of the next three generations, emperors' daughters and granddaughters Julia the Elder, Julia the Younger, Agrippina the Elder, and wives such as Messalina and Agrippina the Younger behaved in ways that caused them to fall prey to the same criticisms, experience equally dramatic downfalls, and suffer similarly sad and lonely deaths.

While Fulvia's alleged adulteries were only implied by especially unreliable and malicious narrators seeking to score political points against her and her husbands, Julia the Elder and Julia the Younger's adulteries are matters of historical fact. Octavian subsequently referred to his daughter and his granddaughter as two of his three boils, or suppurating sores, and paraphrased Homer's *Iliad* in his wish that he had never married nor fathered a child.[18] The two women brought shame on his household by their flagrant adultery, in direct violation of his morality laws (the *leges Iuliae*), and their intrigues with their lovers skated perilously close to conspiracy and treason, as these were now being conceptualized. In fact, since Julia remained under Octavian's *patria potestas*, interacting with her with a view to corrupting the line of succession was, quite literally, treason (the traditional euphemism for adultery, 'criminal conversation', seems particularly apt in this instance). Both women were exiled to small islands off the coast of Italy as punishment for their transgressions.[19]

Julia the Elder (39 BCE–14 CE) had liaisons all over Rome, with scurrilous gossips delighting in relating that she took particular pleasure in frolicking with her lovers on top of the Rostra in the centre of the Forum, which by that time had been decorated with the prows of Antony's ships sunk by Octavian's navy at the Battle of Actium in 31 BCE, the high point of Octavian's military career and the source of his personal authority, as opposed to that which he had inherited from Caesar. This was a public performance of an entirely different nature from Fulvia's own activities in that specific location in 52 BCE during Milo's trial for Clodius' murder.[20] The poet Ovid, also permanently exiled around this time for what he described as 'a poem and a blunder', may have been involved in the escapades too.[21]

There is some indication that Julia and her lovers were part of a conspiracy against Octavian and Tiberius, since Tiberius had been living away from Julia on Rhodes for several years, leaving her and her sons unprotected and vulnerable. Julia was sent first to a luxury villa on the island of Pandateria (modern Ventotene, one of the Pontine Islands in the Tyrrhenian Sea), where she was accompanied by her mother Scribonia, in 2 BCE, before being transferred back to the mainland six years later, to Rhegium (modern Reggio Calabria), where she lived in slightly less stringent circumstances, allocated an allowance and permitted to go into town, but never allowed to return to Rome.[22] However, once her ex-husband Tiberius ascended to the imperial purple in 14 CE, he rather spitefully reinstituted the harsh conditions of her original exile and may even have had her murdered, or at the very least starved to death. Prior to this, there was at least one plot hatched to release her from captivity, with two men named Lucius

Audasius and Asinius Epicadus seeking to liberate her and her last surviving son Agrippa Postumus, who had also been exiled, and use them against Octavian and his regime.[23]

Vipsania Julia Agrippina, also known as Julia the Younger (19 BCE–29 CE), was even less fortunate than her mother. She was charged with adultery for having an affair with Decimus Junius Silanus, exiled to Tremirus (modern Isole Tremiti/Isole Diomedee, an archipelago off the coast of Apulia in the Adriatic Sea that was used for the internment of political prisoners during the fascist regime of Benito Mussolini in the early to mid-twentieth century) and the child that she was pregnant with was exposed and presumably left to die by order of Octavian.[24] Around the same time, her husband Lucius Aemilius Paullus and his conspirator Plautius Rufus were accused of conspiring against Octavian.[25] Julia the Younger remained in exile on Tremirus for twenty years, finally dying there in 29 CE.

Vipsania Agrippina (*circa* 14 BCE–33 CE), more commonly known as Agrippina the Elder, the granddaughter of Octavian and the wife of Antony's grandson Germanicus – the adopted son and heir presumptive of the emperor Tiberius – joined her husband on campaign along the Rhine in Germania in the period 14–16 CE.[26] Like Fulvia, she presented her children to the legions, and like Fulvia, she involved herself in military manoeuvres.[27] She paraded her young son Gaius, the future emperor Caligula – so nicknamed because of the miniature military costume, complete with boots, *caligae*, that he wore. According to Tacitus, who was using an unfortunately no-longer-extant treatise entitled *History of the German Wars* written by Pliny the Elder, who had himself served with distinction in the army in Germania in the late 40s and into the 50s CE, she prevented the destruction of the bridge over the Rhine at Vetera (modern Xanten in Germany), then stood at the bridgehead, thanking the troops for their service as they flooded over and returned to the safety of their military encampment.[28] He described her as 'a great-hearted woman who assumed the duties of a general throughout those days', as she oversaw the subsequent relief efforts, ensuring destitute soldiers were given blankets and the wounded received dressings.[29] Yet her actions met with considerable censure from Tiberius, and he excoriated her for appearing to court the popularity of the legions so blatantly.[30]

Yet this was not the only occasion upon which Agrippina appears to have sought to emulate Fulvia.[31] Germanicus died suddenly and mysteriously at Antioch in Syria on 10 October 19 CE, apparently bewitched and poisoned by his enemy Gnaeus Calpurnius Piso and his wife Plancina. His body was taken from Epidaphnae to Antioch, and there it was cremated, before his ashes were collected, deposited in an urn and taken on the long journey back to Italy, for interment in the Mausoleum of Augustus on the Campus Martius in Rome. This journey was a popular subject for neoclassical history painters, such as Gavin Hamilton's depiction *Agrippina Landing at Brundisium with the Ashes of Germanicus* (1765–72) (see fig 14).

Just as the common people had been grief-stricken by Clodius' death in 52 BCE, so were they now as word of Germanicus' demise spread through the city. According to Tacitus, all business was cancelled, the shops closed, the courts shut down.[32] Then, according to Suetonius, they rampaged through the city, stoning temples, destroying altars and throwing their own household gods into the streets.[33] When Agrippina's ship docked at the port of Brundisium early in 20 BCE, she disembarked to find herself greeted by a crowd of hundreds, if not thousands, of mourners, with people clambering up onto roofs and the city walls in order to have sight of her.[34] Clad in dark mourning garb and clutching the urn containing Germanicus' ashes, she made her way back along the Via Appia to Rome, and she used the opportunity presented by her visibility to accuse Piso and Plancina of murder, carried out on the orders of Tiberius. The fact that all the literary sources that record Germanicus' death include these accusations, and validate them by presenting them as fact, shows how successful she was in getting across her side of the story.[35]

Tiberius had no choice but to agree to Piso's prosecution for murder, and the trial commenced in December 20 CE. Piso committed suicide, but that did not stop the trial going ahead and his reputation being excoriated posthumously in inscriptions inscribed on bronze that still survive.[36] Plancina was convicted but pardoned after intercession from the empress Livia, a close friend of hers.[37] Just as Agrippina's military intervention had riled Tiberius, so did her judicial intervention. Relations between them became increasingly strained until he had her exiled, imprisoned, tortured, blinded, and finally murdered in 33 CE.

And just as Fulvia had apparently added at least one person to the list of individuals that the members of the Second Triumvirate were planning to proscribe in order to gain possession of their estates, so too did the wives of the emperor Claudius (Antony's grandson, incidentally) apparently seek to augment their own property portfolios by homicide. According to the historian Tacitus, Claudius' third wife Messalina had the consul Decimus Valerius Asiaticus prosecuted in order to gain possession of his beautiful gardens, the famous Horti Luculliani on the Pincian Hill, while his fourth wife Agrippina did likewise with Statilius Taurus and his Horti Tauriani.[38] As discussed previously, there may well have been more to Fulvia's actions than the historical commentators chose to include in their coverage of the events of 42 BCE, and equally there may well have been more to the two empresses' actions than simple greed and avarice. After all, by the middle of the first century CE, the imperial family were in possession of a number of beautiful gardens in and around Rome – including the Horti Agrippinae, the estate of Caligula and Agrippina the Younger's mother on the right bank of the Tiber, as well as the Horti Lamiani and the Horti Maecenatiani on the Esquiline Hill, the latter of which contained the first heated swimming pool in Rome – so neither empress was short of green space.[39]

Asiaticus had been involved in the conspiracy that brought down the emperor Caligula in 41 CE, yet was at the pinnacle of his career in 46 CE, having been elected consul for the second time (a relatively rare honour at this point in Roman history, when the position was monopolized by the emperor and other members of the imperial family), and purchased the Horti Luculliani that same year, immediately undertaking an extensive renovation and restoration.[40] However, very shortly afterwards he was arrested on charges of sexual impropriety and treason, convicted before an imperial tribunal, and forced to commit suicide. Of course, Messalina did not come out and say that acquiring his estate was her motivation. Rather, she claimed that Asiaticus had designs on the throne, and being of Gallic extraction, was plotting mutiny with the Gallic legions and planning to march on Rome to seize the throne from Claudius.[41]

A few years later, Titus Statilius Taurus, elected consul in 44 CE along with Agrippina's second husband Gaius Sallustius Passienus Crispus, owner of the Horti Tauriani on the Esquiline Hill, fell afoul of Agrippina in 53 CE, committing suicide before he could be convicted.[42] While Agrippina's motives were, like Messalina's, attributed to her desire to possess his beautiful gardens, there may have been a more mundane reason: the Horti Tauriani seem to have been located just outside the Porta Maggiore, at the confluence of several aqueducts completed in the period 52–53 CE, thus placing them at the heart of the city's water supply and critical imperial infrastructure. Since the Roman government had the legal right to seize land adjacent to an aqueduct, this may well be what happened here, albeit with the accusation of impiety lodged against Statilius Taurus as a means of saving money.[43]

Neither woman had long to enjoy their ill-gotten gains, however: abandoned by everyone except for her mother, Messalina committed suicide in the very same gardens after her adultery was revealed to Claudius, while Agrippina was brutally murdered by a troop of soldiers unleashed by her ungrateful son Nero (Antony's great-great-grandson), Claudius' successor as emperor. Any thoughts that she had had about wielding influence through her son, as she had done with her husband, were stymied early on in his reign. She was excluded from meetings between the emperor and the Senate and had to resort to listening in from behind a curtain at the back of the room, and on one occasion when Nero was receiving an embassy from the kingdom of Armenia, she was physically intercepted on her way to join him on the dais and swiftly diverted elsewhere.[44] While imperial women could gain influence through proximity to their male relations, this same proximity could make them vulnerable and put them in the firing line.

———— ⚬⚬⚬ ————

Fulvia was not only forgotten by her high-profile female successors, she was also forgotten by the world at large. Unlike other women of this period, represented time and again in dramatic performances on theatrical stages and in glossy period pieces on television and cinema screens, she has not left much of a mark on popular culture. Just as ancient authors, with the benefit of hindsight, presented her as a warm-up act to Cleopatra VII, so too can contemporary recreations of the fall of the Republic tend to marginalize her, if they even bother to include her at all. One obvious reason for this is that it is simply expedient – a matter of streamlining the narrative by reducing the number of characters and the complexity of the political narrative being presented.[45] This goes all the way back to William Shakespeare's *Antony and Cleopatra* (first performed *circa* 1607), with Antony receiving the report of Fulvia's death at Sicyon in Act 1, Scene 2. In the television series *Cleopatra*, released in 1999, Fulvia does not appear as a character, but is at least mentioned in conversation, used as a means of distracting Antony (played by Billy Zane) on his way into the Senate House and thus facilitating the assassination of Caesar (played by Timothy Dalton) on the Ides of March, as a messenger appears and tells Antony that Fulvia requests an immediate audience with him. No explanation is given as to her identity, however, so anyone coming to the series with no knowledge on Roman history would not discern from this throwaway reference that she is Antony's wife – and indeed she is never mentioned again, not even when Antony marries Octavia in 40 BCE.

Yet excluding Fulvia from the narrative of the events of the period 44–40 BCE does render Antony's breach with Octavian somewhat problematic, requiring an alternative explanation for the breakdown of the Second Triumvirate, and often a premature entrance of Cleopatra as a wedge between the two men. It also interferes with the subsequent simplistic presentation of Octavia as the 'good' Roman woman and Cleopatra as the 'bad' Egyptian woman.[46]

HBO's *Rome* television series (2005–2007) takes a slightly different approach, for while Fulvia is excised entirely, her role in the events of the 50s and 40s BCE devolves onto the character of Atia of the Julii, a fictionalized rendering of Atia Balba Caesonia, the mother of Octavian and Octavia, played with gusto by Polly Walker opposite James Purefoy as Antony (see fig 15). She has a lot in common with the portrayal of Fulvia in the ancient literary tradition: she is avaricious, jostling for advantageous position in the local social hierarchy; she is vengeful, becoming enmeshed in vicious feuds when she feels she has been slighted; she is murderous, casually ordering minions to remove permanently people she considers obstacles. While the character is not Antony's wife in this version of events, she is his lover (although she declares her love and proposes marriage to him, he refuses).

The depiction of their relationship throughout the series draws on the tradition of Antony being in thrall to and dominated by the women in his life, and also the 'cruel mistress' character of much Roman love elegy (Catullus' poetry on this subject is even read at one point, an Easter egg for those in the know).[47] Like Fulvia, the historical Atia died in the late 40s, but *Rome* keeps her alive to the bitter end, her final scene presenting her looking wistfully at an effigy of Antony in his death throes displayed during the culmination of Octavian's Triple Triumph in 29 BCE, thereby undercutting the character's victory and rendering it bittersweet.[48]

Outside of television and film, Fulvia has recently appeared as a character in a video game, albeit not one set in Late Republican Rome. *Dante's Inferno*, an action-adventure hack-and-slash game developed by Visceral Studios and published by Electronic Arts in 2010, loosely based on *Inferno*, the first canticle of Dante Alighieri's *Divine Comedy*, in turn loosely based on Aeneas' experiences in the underworld in Virgil's *Aeneid*, has Fulvia make a brief appearance. She is 'Fulvia of Tusculum', one of twenty-seven Damned Souls encountered as the player, as Dante, makes their way through the nine circles of Hell in pursuit of his wife Beatrice. Fulvia can be found in the fourth circle of Hell, the circle of Greed, as one of the enemies the player has to overcome before facing off with the final boss (along with the treacherous Vestal Virgin Tarpeia). The unfortunates residing here are slowly being boiled alive in molten gold, overseen by Pluto, the god of wealth. To have been doomed to the circle of Greed, one must have been guilty of either hoarding or spending excessively during their life. Fulvia is considered the former, and the identifying label and caption that appears onscreen alongside her describes her as 'One time wife of Marc Antony, possessed by an unbearable greed. Called the Greediest Woman in all of Rome, she pursued any opportunity to seize power.'[49]

As a non-playable character, Fulvia is given some dialogue, voiced by Beth Cordingly, and all of this revolves around three themes that are present in the ancient sources that deal with her, the result of an uncritical reading of them. First is her greed: 'Why do I hoard? Why do you squander?' Second is her ambition: 'I won't be married to any man who doesn't have great ambition.' Third, and most extensive, is her enmity against Cicero. She rails against his 'hateful rhetoric', she orders Antony to slaughter his enemies, starting with Cicero, and display his head and hands in the Forum, and declares 'I will publicly stab Cicero's tongue with my hairpins!' However, when apprehended by Dante, she protests that she's simply a harmless woman and denies being involved in politics at all. She is presented as naked, withered and unarmed, and as such is no match for Dante. The player is given the choice of absolving her of her sins in order to attain the Damned achievement and trophy; and if they choose not to absolve her, she is impaled on Dante's sword and immolated.

But even here, Fulvia is a minor character in this game while Antony and Cleopatra play much larger and more memorable roles. By the time the player reaches Fulvia, they will already have encountered, and dispatched, both Antony and Cleopatra in the second circle of Hell, the circle of Lust.[50] Yet for all that this portrayal simply reiterates the broad brushstrokes of the worst of the portrayals of her in the ancient sources, at least Fulvia appears here as a character in her own right, with her own agency, rather than as an appendage.

<p style="text-align: center">~~~</p>

So, when all is said and done, what can we say of Fulvia? She was an exemplary Roman *matrona* by the standards of the Late Republic during which she lived and died: she married three men from ancient patrician and plebeian noble families, succeeding in resurrecting, at least for a little while, her own maternal and paternal families' standing; she bore each of those men their first sons and heirs to continue their family lines; and she was a supportive and loyal wife who did her utmost to preserve her husbands' positions in Rome, not only when they were present in the city or temporarily absent from it, but also, in the case of her first and second husbands, in the wake of their deaths. But she was also an exemplary Roman *matrona* by the standards of the Principate established by her arch-enemy Octavian in his guise as the first emperor Augustus – for all that Augustus sought to revive what he considered to be traditional ways of doing things, especially in respect of women and the ways in which they lived their lives, what he dictated women should do through the *leges Iuliae*, the Julian Laws, he was to all intents and purposes requiring that women behave like Fulvia.[51] He demanded that they marry as soon as was biologically possible, and that women of the senatorial and equestrian orders marry men of equivalent status to themselves – Fulvia did that, when she married her first husband Clodius. He demanded that they remarry within a certain period of time after being divorced or widowed for as long as they were of childbearing age – Fulvia did that too, not once but twice. He demanded that they bear children to replenish the dwindling senatorial and equestrian orders, and offered mothers of three children special legal privileges such as the right to transact legal and economic business without a tutor and to receive bequests and legacies – Fulvia bore five children, and worked tirelessly to manage not only her own property portfolio but also her husbands' and her children's during their minorities. So where did it all go so wrong?

Fulvia's most serious transgression, and the one used against her again and again by her enemies during her lifetime and in the decades and centuries that followed, was her desire to provide for herself and her family, and the ways she sought to make that desire real.[52] Her pursuit of power and influence, wealth and property, was a means of providing security for herself and her children at a time when the society in which she lived was undergoing a slow-motion implosion; old social mores and norms were being violated left, right and centre by both her male and female peers. The Late Antique historian Orosius, drawing on the works of all the earlier writers that we have explored, noted her liminality and summed her up as follows: 'Nobody knows whether in this change from the rank of a consul to that of a king she is to be counted as the last representative of a declining power or the first of a rising power, but certainly she acted in a haughty manner towards those who were placing her in a position to be arrogant.'[53] If we consider what the sources tell us of her career, and we accept that what was written about her was true, or even only partly true, the worst that can be said of her is that she delighted in the death of a man who had gone out of his way to make her life miserable for a decade, and ordered the death of another man with whom she seems to have had some prior dealings.

While I certainly do not condone stabbing one severed head with a hairpin, or setting up another in front of a building as a gruesome warning to would-be resistors, compared to Caesar's war crimes at the Siege of Alesia and subsequent genocide in Gaul, or Crassus' crucifixion of six thousand enslaved people, lining the Via Appia from Rome to Capua, at the conclusion of the Third Servile War – deeds for which both men were feted in antiquity (and in some circles, are still feted today) – this is a minor transgression. For those who would argue that such a comparison is a false equivalency, let us consider the contemporaneous stories of Octavian ordering that an equestrian taking down notes during one of his speeches be stabbed to death for fear of him being a spy, driving the consul-elect Tedius Afer to commit suicide by jumping to his death from a great height for simply criticizing him, and gouging out the eyes of the praetor Quintus Gallius with his bare hands for nothing more than holding some note tablets under his cloak that he mistook as a weapon.[54] And let us consider Pomponia Attica brutally and sadistically torturing a freedman – someone who was no longer an enslaved person who did not exist as a legal entity and who could be mistreated with impunity, but an actual Roman citizen – for betraying the whereabouts of her proscribed family members.[55] Or even, since Fulvia did not actually kill Cicero but simply bore witness to the mistreatment of his corpse, let us consider Fausta looking on from inside the comfort of her carriage while Clodius was stabbed to death in the road, and likely not even flinching as its wheels ground him into the cobbles.

What we must remember is that Fulvia was living at a very different time, and through very different circumstances to us, and we should judge her accordingly. After all, she lived and died a century before the advent of Christianity and the prevailing belief in turning the other cheek and forgiving trespasses. For the Romans of the Late Republic, these laudable actions could have potentially devastating consequences – Caesar's clemency to those who took Pompey's side against him in the civil war meant that they were alive to conspire against him and stab him to death en masse in Pompey's Theatre a few years later. Even Octavian, once he became the undisputed master of the Roman world and the first emperor Augustus, had to think very carefully about when, how and to whom he granted mercy and forgiveness for trespasses against him, and was intransigent against those closest to him when they transgressed.

So why should Fulvia have forgiven those who terrorized her and her children, excused the murder of her first husband, and conspired to murder her third husband? Is it because we expect better, or at least different, behaviour from women than men? This is the heart of it. But the chauvinism, sexism and misogyny meant to subjugate Fulvia had quite the opposite effect. Ironically, these attempts to demonize and marginalize her ultimately succeeded in transforming her into one of the most enigmatic and fascinating women of the Roman Republic.

ACKNOWLEDGEMENTS

J UST AS WITH MY previous book, *Cleopatra's Daughter: Egyptian Princess, Roman Prisoner, African Queen*, my first thank you goes to my agent Doug Young at PEW Literary. He has been Fulvia's champion from the earliest days, when I was pondering what to write next, and he thought she sounded fascinating and intriguing. He has listened patiently to my hare-brained literary schemes and worked hard to make them happen. On that note, I have been treated extremely well by everyone at PEW over the last five years, with special thanks going to Patrick Walsh for publishing industry advice, Margaret Halton for working on selling foreign language rights, and Terry Wong for patiently talking me through all the financial details of various contracts and advances and solving any problems that have arisen.

On the publishing and editorial side, I would like to thank James Nightingale and Clare Drysdale at Atlantic Books and Heather Gold at Yale University Press, and my tireless copy-editor Gemma Wain. Changing both UK and North American publishers at the same time was a stressful process, but I have had nothing but positive experiences with both so far. I would also like to express my gratitude to everyone at my Dutch publisher Omniboek, as they published the first foreign-language translation of *Cleopatra's Daughter*. Fabiënne Eken, Reina Zenden and Rudmer Koopal hosted me for my first book tour and book signing in May 2023, and extended wonderful hospitality in both Amsterdam and Leiden. Then Omniboek snapped up *Fulvia* so quickly after it was announced that it restored my confidence in myself and my writing.

As is ever the case with a trade history book, this book could not have been written without the academic work of others serving as a foundation and an inspiration. I would especially like to thank Celia Schultz, whose academic monograph on Fulvia was published in the early stages of my research and writing this book, and who has been exceedingly generous with her research, sharing articles with me that I did not have access to. My colleagues Catherine Steel, one of the most eminent Republican historians working in UK academia today, and Lisa Hau for general ancient Roman and Hellenistic history brain-picking and brain-storming. Additionally, Mary Beard for being a source of inspiration and encouragement over email.

I would especially like to thank my popular history partner in crime Emma Southon. Like me, she finds Roman women sufficiently interesting as to want to write books about them and share their stories with everyone else, despite facing many academic challenges. She hosted me for my first UK book event at Waterstone's in Belfast in March 2024 (handily falling in Women's History Month), and discussing Roman women with her and answering audience questions on them was a delightful experience – I hope we get to do more of this in the near future.

On a day-to-day basis, thanks to the members of the Trade Writing Chat WhatsApp group, notably Catherine Fletcher, Estelle Paranque, Caroline Dodds Pennock and Joanne Paul, for solidarity and all manner of information about popular history research, writing, and attempting to make a living as a public historian.

I continue to be very lucky in my friends and their willingness to read my work and offer feedback. Thanks to Claire Millington and to Robert Cromarty for being my first and most enthusiastic and engaged readers.

Finally, my family. First and foremost, my mother Susan Draycott for her willingness to bring order to my chaotic household on a weekly basis. Second, my office would not be complete without Magnus walking, rolling and lying all over it, and pestering me for treats and food periodically throughout the day, thereby allowing me to stretch my spine and legs. Third, Oliver Boyce, for always supporting me. And finally, and most importantly, Evie, for whom I work so hard. She is my greatest achievement.

APPENDIX

ANCIENT SOURCES
FOR FULVIA

W E HAVE MORE LITERARY, documentary and archaeological
evidence for Fulvia than we have for almost any other Roman
woman during the Late Republic. Yet there are significant problems
with this plethora of evidence. The first is that none of it was authored
by Fulvia herself: we have no diary entries, no letters, no memoirs, and
as far as we know, we do not have any more tangible items such as any
of her homes or possessions. The second is that the vast majority of this
evidence is negative in the extreme. All but one of the authors writing
about Fulvia during her life or immediately after her death were
enormously hostile towards her (and any other women who attempted
to behave in a similar manner), and later authors took these portrayals
and doubled down on them, adding details that may be true or may
simply be exaggerated falsehoods.

Here we shall briefly survey the sources that I have drawn on in this
biography, in a rough chronological order. My intention here is not
to cover the contents of these sources extensively, but rather to give a

sense of who the authors were, what their thoughts of Fulvia were, and indicate the extent to which they should not be taken for granted as neutral (not to mention accurate accounts).

We can date quite precisely Fulvia's first appearance in the historical record: the esteemed Roman statesman and orator Marcus Tullius Cicero (106-43 BCE) refers to her twice in a speech that he wrote for the purposes of defending his friend Titus Annius Milo, who stood accused of murdering his (and Cicero's) enemy, and Fulvia's first husband, Clodius on 18 January 52 BCE, and was tried several months later, on 8 April 52 BCE. However, Cicero did not actually give this speech: when the time came, he was so intimidated by the atmosphere in the courtroom that he did not perform to his usual exacting standards, and the transcript we have is one that he wrote up later – perhaps what he would have said, or felt he should have said. In point of fact, in a letter Milo wrote to Cicero from his subsequent exile in Massilia (modern Marseilles), which he was very much enjoying, Milo actually thanked Cicero for not giving it, because if he had, he surely would have been acquitted, and would not be living the life of Riley, consuming the fish dishes that were the port city's speciality.

Although Cicero does not name Fulvia, as respectable Roman women tended not to be referred to by name in public utterances and, at this point in time, she was still considered a respectable woman, he makes it clear that he is referring to her. He twice states that on the day of the murder, Clodius was not accompanied by her, and notes how unusual this was as this had 'scarcely ever' been the case before. These statements serve two purposes. The first is as a slight on Clodius' character, for the Romans considered being unable to do without your wife a sign of weakness and lack of emotional self-control, rather than of a normal happy marriage, and other divisive Late Republican politicians such as Lucius Cornelius Sulla and Gnaeus Pompey met with similar accusations for their partiality to their wives, Valeria Messalla and Julia Caesaris, respectively. The second is to imply that there was something suspicious about Clodius' behaviour that day, an attempt to absolve Milo of the charge of premeditated murder because, unlike

Clodius, Milo was accompanied by his wife (who is also not named), and thus would have been unlikely to have been planning to commit a brutal murder while in her company. However, while Cicero provides no further information about Fulvia in this speech, around a century later Quintus Asconius Pedianus wrote a commentary on the events, giving much more detail about Fulvia's behaviour at the time. What must be borne in mind, and something we see recur throughout the ancient literary sources, is that the portrayal of Fulvia is heavily influenced by the author's feelings about her husband. Cicero hated Clodius, the pair had a long and increasingly bitter feud, and not only was he glad that Clodius was dead, but he also wanted posthumous revenge for Clodius' behaviour towards him, and what better way to get it than to see his murderer acquitted? It is interesting that Cicero does not include the same information about Fulvia that Asconius does – who, writing later, was drawing on a range of sources, including the *acta diurna* (daily official notices, a sort of ancient Roman *Daily Gazette*) and the *acta senatus* (minutes of the meetings of the Senate), and whose aim was to set out a complete account of events, rather than one favourable to himself and his agenda that served to sway the audience to his way of thinking, which was what Cicero was aiming for. As we have seen, there is a lot more to the story, and it is fair to say that on this occasion, Fulvia seems to have got the better of Cicero, and no doubt earned his lasting enmity.

We have much more information about the later years of Fulvia's life, when she was married to her third husband, the Roman consul and triumvir Marcus Antonius. His presence and prominence in the ancient sources ensure and facilitate hers, and she is much more visible in the final decade of her life than at any prior point. During this period, Cicero refers to Fulvia on occasion in his correspondence to his best friend Titus Pomponius Atticus, as both men were personally acquainted with her, but it is in his *Philippics* that he really goes to town, and one cannot help thinking that he must have done so with a certain amount of gusto, since this was his opportunity to pay her back for her previous triumph over him. The *Philippics* are a series of fourteen speeches and pamphlets that he composed in the years 44 BCE and 43 BCE, in the wake of the assassination of Gaius Julius Caesar on 15 March 44 BCE, and they are directed against Antony, whom Cicero considered to be an enemy of the Republic, excoriating him for his behaviour following Caesar's death. In five of the fourteen speeches/ pamphlets, Cicero uses details of Fulvia and Antony's marriage to attack Antony's character, just as he had attempted to use details of Fulvia and Clodius' marriage to attack Clodius almost ten years earlier. Some of the speeches were delivered in person, others were written down and disseminated.

And yet, a contemporary of Cicero's named Cornelius Nepos (*circa* 100–24 BCE), an historian and biographer who chose a mixture of Greek, Roman and Carthaginian luminaries as his subjects, and compared and contrasted them, wrote a biography of Atticus, and in it he recounts some of Atticus' dealings with Fulvia in 43 BCE, and it seems that he did not bear the kind of hostility towards her that Cicero did. Since Nepos was well acquainted not only with Cicero and Atticus, but also Fulvia, and was writing very close to the events depicted, the fact that he is our only positive source for Fulvia should give us pause, as should the fact that his work was aimed at ordinary people, rather than the political, social and intellectual elite.

These are the only ancient sources for Fulvia that were written by people who knew her and were circulating during her life or shortly after her death. Subsequent accounts were authored under a regime that sought to vilify Antony and anyone associated with him, and Fulvia was a casualty of this.

Titus Livius (*circa* 64–12 CE), today more commonly known as Livy, a Roman historian writing in the late first century BCE, wrote a history of Rome comprising 142 books, beginning with Romulus and Remus and concluding with the events of the late first century BCE. This magnum opus made him a household name during his lifetime, with one fan apparently travelling from his home in Hispania (modern Spain) to Rome simply to meet him, and he was considered the standard authority on the history of the Roman Republic. Only one-third of the

142 books have survived, but while the parts of the work that deal with Fulvia are amongst those that have not survived, summaries of these books have, and they indicate that he discussed her involvement in the Perusian War of 41–40 BCE. Considering that he was writing during the reign of the emperor Augustus, it is not surprising that he was critical of Fulvia's participation in military action against him.

Marcus Velleius Paterculus (19 BCE–31 CE), a Roman historian writing in the early first century CE during the reign of Augustus' successor the emperor Tiberius, is one of the earliest surviving historical sources, and the only continuous surviving historical source, for the period from the assassination of Caesar in 44 BCE until the death of Augustus in 14 CE. He served in the legions commanded by Augustus' adopted sons Gaius and Tiberius, placing him very close to the imperial family, and offering an explanation as to his clear impartiality when it comes to Antony and, by implication, Fulvia. He mentions her twice in his discussion of the Perusian War, casting her as something of a woman warrior. Unlike Livy, he was not particularly successful or widely read in antiquity.

Mentioned above, Asconius (9 BCE–76 CE) was an historian writing in the middle of the first century CE who wrote a set of commentaries on Cicero's speeches for the benefit of his two sons in the period 54–57 CE – guidance for them for if/when they chose to embark upon a public career. Through these, he provides us with a considerable amount of not only historical but also political and social context for the events that took place in the early part of 52 BCE, from the death of Clodius to the trial of Milo. He had access to senatorial records for his research, and also used the work of earlier historians and poets, meaning that he was not solely reliant upon Cicero for his account.

The satirical poet Marcus Valerius Martialis (38–41 CE to 101–104 CE), today more commonly known as Martial, active in the second half of the first century CE, quotes a crude and crass epigram about Fulvia that he attributes to Octavian, the future emperor Augustus, himself, supposedly written around the time of the Perusian War and directly referencing the conflict. Assuming that Martial's attribution of the epigram is correct, it allows us an insight into Octavian and Fulvia's relationship during the two-year period that he was married to her daughter Claudia Pulcher, and the interpersonal dynamics between Octavian, Fulvia, Antony, and several other significant historical figures of this period.

The most detailed ancient source for Fulvia is Lucius Mestrius Plutarchus (*circa* 45–125 CE), today more commonly known as Plutarch, who was a polyglot writing in the late first and early second centuries CE and produced a series of biographies known as the *Parallel Lives*, which pair one Greek and one Roman historical figure that Plutarch considered to have specific virtues and vices in common. He wrote a biography of Antony that sought to explain his failures as resulting from his moral flaws and failings – and his relationships with women, particularly strong women, are considered to be one of these. From Plutarch's *Antony* we get insights into Fulvia's character, and the nature and inner workings of her and Antony's marriage across the 40s BCE. Plutarch had the advantage over many of his contemporaries, because his grandfather was actually acquainted with Antony, and so he had access to first-hand information about his life and relationships.

Plutarch's younger contemporary, Gaius Suetonius Tranquillus (*circa* 69–121 CE), today more commonly known as Suetonius, also wrote a series of biographies that have survived, and this series focuses on the first twelve Roman emperors. In the reign of the emperor Hadrian, he served as the emperor's secretary, so had access to the imperial archives, which enabled him to read and quote extracts from correspondence between Antony and Octavian. In his biography of Augustus, Suetonius provides details of the emperor's fraught relationship with Fulvia. In another work that focuses on public speakers, Suetonius includes an anecdote from the orator Sextus Clodius, a friend of Antony's, that provides us with our only physical description of Fulvia.

The historians of the second and third centuries CE, almost two and a half centuries removed from the events that they recount, follow their predecessors in depicting Fulvia in a negative manner, although in an almost comically exaggerated fashion. Lucius Annaeus Florus (known as Florus, *floruit* 130s–140s CE), Appianus Alexandrinus (known as Appian, *circa* 85–95 CE–165 CE), and Cassius Dio (*circa* 164–after 229 CE) provide wonderful details and, in places, wonderfully detailed accounts, but these do need to be taken with a pinch of salt.

More helpful in some respects are the documentary and archaeological evidence for Fulvia. Coins that are thought to depict her in the guise of Nike or Victoria, the Greek and Roman goddesses of victory respectively, were issued in gold, silver and bronze in Rome, Lugdunum (modern Lyon), and Eumeneia in Phrygia (near modern Işıklı in Turkey), a city that was briefly renamed Fulvia in her honour in the period 43–40 BCE. Assuming that this identification is correct, this would make her the first living Roman woman, as opposed to goddesses or deceased mythological or historical figures, to be depicted on a Roman coin. A marble portrait bust that resembles the coin portraits has been proposed as a possible portrait of her.

Finally, several lead sling bullets, which the Romans referred to as *glandes*, have been recovered from archaeological excavations around the city of Perusia (modern Perugia), and due to their inscriptions have been dated precisely to the siege of Perusia that took place over the course of the Perusian War. Many of these are inscribed with messages that relate to Fulvia and her activities.

BIBLIOGRAPHY

Abbreviations

AE – *L'Année épigraphique*

ANRW – *Aufstieg und Niedergang der römischen Welt*

CIL – *Corpus Inscriptionum Latinarum*

ILLRP – *Inscriptiones latinae liberae rei publicae*

ILS – *Inscriptiones Latinae Selectae*

I. Métr. – *Inscriptions métriques de l'Égypte gréco-romaine: recherches sur la poésie épigrammatique des Grecs en Égypte*

Inscr. Ital. – *Inscriptiones Italiae*

RPC – Roman Provincial Coinage

RRC – Roman Republican Coinage

Tab. Vindol. – Vindolanda Tablets

Ancient Sources

All translations of ancient Greek and Latin sources are taken from the Loeb Classical Library unless otherwise stated.

Asconius, *Commentary on Cicero's Pro Milone*

Asconius, *Commentary on Cicero's Pro Scauro*

Festus, *Lexicon*

Orosius, *History Against the Pagans*

Servius, *Commentary on Virgil's Aeneid*

Servius, *Commentary on Virgil's Bucolics*

Sextus Aurelius Victor, *Illustrious Men*

Soranus, *Gynaecology*
Tertullian, *On Monogamy*

Modern Scholarship

Alexander, D. A. (2011), 'Marc Antony's Assault of Publius Clodius: Fact or Ciceronian Fiction?', in A. Mackay (ed.), *ASCS 32 Selected Proceedings*, pp. 1–8.

Arkenberg, J. S. (1993), 'Licinii Murenae, Terentii Varrones, and Varrones Murenae: I. A Prosopographical Study of Three Roman Families', *Historia*, 42/3, pp. 326–51.

Augustakis, A. (2008) 'Women's Politics in the Streets of Rome', in M. S. Cyrino (ed.), *Rome, Season One: History Makes Television*, Malden: Wiley-Blackwell, pp. 117–29.

Austin, L. (1946), 'The Caerellia of Cicero's Correspondence', *Classical Journal*, 41/7, pp. 305–9.

Babcock, C. L. (1965), 'The Early Career of Fulvia', *American Journal of Philology*, 86/1, pp. 1–32.

Barrett, A. A. (2001), *Agrippina: Sex, Power, and Politics in the Early Empire*, London: Routledge.

Barrett, A. A. (2002), *Livia: First Lady of Imperial Rome*, New Haven: Yale University Press.

Barrett, A. A. (2005), 'Aulus Caecina Severus and the Military Woman', *Historia*, 54/3, pp. 301–14.

Baumann, R. A. (1992), *Women and Politics in Ancient Rome*, London: Routledge.

Beard, M. (2007), *The Roman Triumph*, Cambridge: Harvard University Press.

Beard, M. (2018), *Women & Power*, London: Profile Books.

Boatwright, M. (2011), 'Women and Gender in the Forum Romanum', *Transactions and Proceedings of the American Philological Association*, 141/1, pp. 105–41.

Bradley, K. R. (1987), 'Dislocation in the Roman Family', *Historical Reflections*, 14, pp. 33–62.

Brennan, T. C. (2012), 'Perceptions of Women's Power in the Late Republic: Terentia, Fulvia, and the Generation of 63 BCE', in S. L. James and S. Dillon (eds), *A Companion to Women in the Ancient World*, Malden: Wiley Blackwell, pp. 354–66.

Broughton, T. R. S. (1951), *The Magistrates of the Roman Republic*, 2 vols, New York: American Philological Association.

Butrica, J. L. (2002), 'Clodius the Pulcher in Catullus and Cicero', *Classical Quarterly*, 52/2, pp. 507–16.

Caldwell, L. (2015), *Roman Girlhood and the Fashioning of Femininity*, Cambridge: Cambridge University Press.

Campanile, D. (2017), 'The Patrician, the General and the Emperor in Women's Clothing', in D. Campanile, F. Carlà-Uhink and M. Facella (eds), *Transantiquity: Cross-Dressing and Transgender Dynamics in the Ancient World*, London: Routledge, pp. 52–64.

Cargill-Martin, H. (2023), *Messalina: A Story of Empire, Slander and Adultery*, London: Head of Zeus.

Cerutti, S. M. (1997), 'The Location of the Houses of Cicero and Clodius and the Porticus Catuli on the Palatine Hill in Rome', *American Journal of Philology*, 118/3, pp. 417–26.

Charlesworth, M. P. (1933), 'Some Fragments of the Propaganda of Mark Antony', *Classical Quarterly* 27/3/4, pp. 172–7.

Claridge, A. (2010), *Rome: An Archaeological Guide*, Oxford: Oxford University Press.

Cluett, R. G. (1998), 'Roman Women and Triumviral Politics, 43–37 BC', *Echos du monde Classique: Classical Views*, 42, pp. 67–84.

Coarelli, F. (2007), *Rome and Environs: An Archaeological Guide*, Berkeley: University of California Press.

Cohen, S. (2008), 'Augustus, Julia and the Development of Exile "Ad Insulam"', *Classical Quarterly*, 58/1, pp. 206–17.

Cokayne, K. (2003), *Experiencing Old Age in Ancient Rome*, London: Routledge.

Cooley, A. E. (2023), *The Senatus Consultum de Cn. Pisone Patre: Text, Translation and Commentary*, Cambridge: Cambridge University Press.

Cooper, K. (2007), 'Closely Watched Households: Visibility, Exposure and Private Power in the Roman "Domus"', *Past & Present*, 197, pp. 3–33.

Cowan, R. (2018), 'Sideshadowing Actium: Counterfactual History in Lollius' *Naumachia* (Horace, *Epistles* 1.18)', *Antichthon*, 52, pp. 90–116.

Culham, P. (2014), 'Women in the Roman Republic', in H. Flower (ed.) *The Cambridge Companion to the Roman Republic*, Cambridge: Cambridge University Press, pp. 127–48.

Cyrino, M. S. (2008), 'Atia and the Erotics of Authority', in M. S. Cyrino (ed.) *Rome, Season One: History Makes Television*, Malden: Wiley-Blackwell, pp. 130–40.

Dalby, A. (2000), *Empire of Pleasures: Luxury and Indulgence in the Roman World*, London: Routledge.

Damon, C. (1992), 'Sex. Cloelius, Scriba', *Harvard Studies in Philology*, 94, pp. 227–50.

Delia, D. (1991), 'Fulvia Reconsidered', in S. B. Pomeroy (ed.), *Women's History and Ancient History*, Chapel Hill: University of North Carolina Press, pp. 197–217.

Dixon, S. (1986), 'Family Finances: Terentia and Tullia', in B. Rawson (ed.), *The Family in Ancient Rome: New Perspectives*, Ithaca: Croom Helm.

Dixon, S. (2013), *The Roman Mother*, London: Routledge.

Epstein, D. F. (1987), *Personal Enmity in Roman Politics 218–43 BC*, London: Croom Helm.

Erker, D. S. (2009), 'Women's Tears in Ancient Roman Ritual', in T. Fögen (ed.), *Tears in the Graeco-Roman World*, Berlin: De Gruyter, pp. 135–60.

Evans Grubbs, J. (2019), 'Singles, Sex and Status in the Augustan Marriage Legislation', in S. R. Hübner and C. Laes (eds), *The Single Life in the Roman and Later Roman World*, Cambridge: Cambridge University Press, pp. 105–24.

Fabre-Serris, J. (2022), 'Literary Models and Social Challenges: Marital Love According to Ovid in the *Tristia* and *Epistulae Ex*

Ponto', in C.-E. Centlivres Challet (ed.), *Married Life in Greco-Roman Antiquity*, London: Routledge, pp. 76–89.

Fagan, G. G. (2011), 'Violence in Roman Social Relations', in M. Peachin (ed.), *The Oxford Handbook of Social Relations in the Roman World*, Oxford: Oxford University Press, pp. 467–95.

Favro, D. and C. Johanson (2010), 'Death in Motion: Funeral Processions in the Roman Forum', *Journal of the Society of Architectural Historians*, 69/1, pp. 12–37.

Fischer, R. A. (1999), *Fulvia und Octavia: Die beiden Ehefrauen des Marcus Antonius in den Politischen Kämpfen der Umbruchszeit zwischen Republik und Principat*, Berlin: Logos.

Flaig, E. (2022), 'The Year 52 BCE', in V. Arena (ed.), *A Companion to the Political Culture of the Roman Republic*, Malden: Wiley Blackwell, pp. 568–82.

Flory, M. B. (1993), 'Livia and the History of Public Honorific Statues for Women in Rome', *Transactions of the American Philological Association*, 123, pp. 287–308.

Foubert, L. (2016a), 'Crowded and Emptied Houses as Status Markers of Aristocratic Women in Rome: The Literary Commonplace of the *domus frequentata*', *Eugesta*, 6, pp. 129–50.

Foubert, L. (2016b), 'The Lure of an Exotic Destination: The Politics of Women's Travels in the Early Roman Empire', *Hermes*, 144/4, pp. 462–87.

Freyd, J. J. (1997), 'Violations of Power, Adaptive Blindness, and Betrayal Trauma Theory', *Feminism & Psychology*, 7/1, pp. 22–32.

Frier, B. W. (1994), 'Natural Fertility and Family Limitation in Roman Marriage', *Classical Philology*, 89/4, pp. 318–33.

Gabba, E. (1971), 'The Perusine War and Triumviral Italy', *Harvard Studies in Classical Philology*, 75, pp. 139–60.

Garland, A. (1992), 'Cicero's "Familia Urbana"', *Greece & Rome*, 39/2, pp. 163–72.

Geiger, J. (1980), 'An Overlooked Item in the War of Propaganda between Octavian and Antony', *Historia*, 29, pp. 112–14.

Gladhill, B. (2018), 'Women from the Rostra: Fulvia and the
    Pro Milone', in C. Gray (ed.), *Reading Republican Oratory:
    Reconstructions, Contexts, Receptions*, Oxford: Oxford University
    Press, pp. 297–308.

Goldberg, C. (2015–16), 'Decimation in the Roman Republic',
    Classical Journal, 111/2, pp. 141–64.

Graf, F. (1984), 'Women, War, and Warlike Divinities', *Zeitschrift für
    Papyrologie und Epigraphik*, 55, pp. 245–54.

Grant, R. (2023), 'A Massive Archive Tells the Story of Early
    African American Photographers', *Smithsonian Magazine*,
    https://www.smithsonianmag.com/smithsonian-institution/
    massive-archive-tells-story-early-african-american-photogra-
    phers-180982337/.

Gray-Fow, M. J. G. (1988), 'The Wicked Stepmother in Roman
    Literature and History: An Evaluation', *Latomus*, 47/4, pp. 741–57.

Griffin, J. (1985), *Latin Poets and Roman Life*, Chapel Hill: University
    of North Carolina Press.

Haley, S. (1985), 'The Five Wives of Pompey the Great', *Greece &
    Rome*, 32/1, pp. 49–59.

Hallett, J. (1977), 'Perusinae glandes and the Changing Image of
    Augustus', *American Journal of Ancient History*, 2, pp. 151–77.

Hallett, J. (2002), 'Women Writing in Rome and Cornelia, Mother
    of the Gracchi', in L. Churchill et al. (eds), *Women Writing Latin:
    Women Writing Latin in Roman Antiquity, Late Antiquity, and the
    Early Christian Era*, London: Routledge, pp. 13–24.

Hallett, J. (2002), 'The Fragment of Martial's Sulpicia', in L. Churchill
    et al. (eds), *Women Writing Latin: Women Writing Latin in Roman
    Antiquity, Late Antiquity, and the Early Christian Era*, London:
    Routledge, pp. 85–91.

Hallett, J. (2006), 'Fulvia, Mother of Iullus Antonius', *Helios*, 33/2,
    pp. 149–64.

Hallett, J. (2015), 'Fulvia: The Representation of an Elite Roman
    Woman Warrior', in J. Fabre-Serris and A. Keith (eds), *Women

and War in Antiquity, Baltimore: Johns Hopkins University Press, pp. 247–65.

Hallet, J. P. (2018), 'Oratorum Romanarum Fragmenta Liberae Rei Publicae: The Letter of Cornelia, *Mater Gracchorum*, and the Speeches of Her Father and Son', in C. Gray (ed.) *Reading Republican Oratory: Reconstructions, Contexts, Receptions*, Oxford: Oxford University Press, pp. 309–18.

Harders, A.-C. (2009), 'An Imperial Family Man: Augustus as Surrogate Father to Marcus Antonius' Children', in S. R. Hübner and D. M. Ratzan (eds), *Growing Up Fatherless in Antiquity*, Cambridge: Cambridge University Press, pp. 217–40.

Harders, A.-C. (2019), 'Mark Antony and the Women at his Side', in A. Bielman Sanchez (ed.), *Power Couples in Antiquity: Transversal Perspectives*, London: Routledge, pp. 116–35.

Harrisson, J. (2015), 'Antony and Atia: Tragic Romance in *Rome*', in M. S. Cyrino (ed.), *Rome Season Two: Trial and Triumph*, Edinburgh: Edinburgh University Press, pp. 155–68.

Hayne, L. (1978), 'The Political Astuteness of the Antonii', *L'Antiquité Classique*, 47/1, pp. 96–105.

Helbig, W. (1889), 'Osservazioni sopra i Ritratti di Fulvia e di Ottavia', *Monumenti Antichi*, 1, pp. 573–90.

Hemelrijk, E. A. (1987), 'Women's Demonstrations in Ancient Rome', in J. Blok and P. Mason (eds), *Sexual Asymmetry: Studies in Ancient Society*, Amsterdam: J. C. Gieben, pp. 217–40.

Hemelrijk, E. A. (1999), *Matrona Docta: Educated Women in the Roman Elite from Cornelia to Julia Domna*, London: Routledge.

Hemelrijk, E. A. (2004), 'Masculinity and Femininity in the "Laudatio Turiae"', *Classical Quarterly* 2/54.1, pp. 185–97.

Hemelrijk, E., and G. Woolf (eds) (2013), *Women and the Roman City in the Latin West*, Leiden: Brill.

Hersch, K. K. (2010), *The Roman Wedding: Ritual and Meaning in Antiquity*, Cambridge: Cambridge University Press.

Hillard, T. W. (1989), 'Republican Politics, Women and the Evidence', *Helios*, 16, pp. 165–82.

Hillard, T. W. (2021), 'Reading Catullus 113 as the Vilification of Pompey's Ex-Wife Mucia', *Antichthon*, 55, pp. 74–93.

Hölkeskamp, K-J. (2014), 'Under Roman Roofs: Family, House, and Household', in H. Flower (ed.), *The Cambridge Companion to the Roman Republic*, Cambridge: Cambridge University Press, pp. 101–26.

Hopwood, B. (2019), 'The Good Wife: Fate, Fortune, and *Familia* in Augustan Rome', in J. Osgood, K. Morrell, and K. Welch (eds), *The Alternative Augustan Age*, Oxford: Oxford University Press, pp. 63–77.

Huzar, E. G. (1982), 'The Literary Efforts of Mark Antony', *ANRW*, 11.30.1, Berlin.

Huzar, E. G. (1985–6), 'Mark Antony: Marriages vs. Careers', *Classical Journal*, 81/2, pp. 97–111.

Ige, S. (2003), 'Rhetoric and the Feminine Character: Cicero's Portrayal of Sassia, Clodia and Fulvia', *Akroterion*, 48, pp. 45–57.

Jeppesen-Wigelsworth, A. (2013), 'Political Bedfellows: Tullia, Dolabella, and Caelius', *Arethusa*, 46/1, pp. 65–85.

Kajava, M. (1989), 'Cornelia Africani f. Gracchorum', *Arctos*, 23, pp. 119–32.

Keith, A. (2011), 'Lycoris Galli/Volumnia Cytheris: A Greek Courtesan in Rome', *Eugesta*, 1, pp. 23–53.

Keith, A. (2018), 'Historical Roman Courtesans', in R. Berg and R. Neudecker (eds), *The Roman Courtesan: Archaeological Reflections of a Literary Topos*, Rome: Acta Instituti Roman Finlandiae, pp. 73–86.

Kelly, R. (2014), *Mark Antony and Popular Culture: Masculinity and the Construction of an Icon*, London: I.B. Taurus.

Koortbojian, M. (2006), 'The Freedman's Voice: The Funerary Monument of Aurelius Hermia and Aurelia Philematio', in E. D'Ambra and G. P. R. Métraux (eds), *The Art of Citizens, Soldiers and Freedmen in the Roman World*, Oxford: Oxford University Press, pp. 91–9.

Laes, C. (2013), 'Silent History? Speech Impairment in Roman
Antiquity', in C. Laes, C. F. Goodey and M. L. Rose (eds),
Disabilities in Ancient Rome: Disparate Bodies a Capite ad Calcem,
Leiden: Brill, pp. 145–80.

La Follette, L. (1994), 'The Costume of the Roman Bride', in
J. L. Sebesta and L. Bonfante (eds), *The World of Roman Costume*,
Madison: University of Wisconsin Press, pp. 54–64.

Lange, C. H. (2014), 'The Logic of Violence in Roman Civil War',
Hermathena, 196/197, pp. 69–98.

Lange, C. H. (2015), 'Augustus' Triumphal and Triumph-like
Returns', in I. Ostenberg, S. Malmberg and J. Bjørnebye (eds), *The
Moving City: Processions, Passages and Promenades in Ancient Rome*,
London: Bloomsbury, pp. 133–43.

Langlands, R. (2006), *Sexual Morality in Ancient Rome*, Cambridge:
Cambridge University Press.

Leach, E. W. (2007), 'Claudia Quinta (Pro Caelio 34) and an Altar to
Magna Mater', *Dictynna*, 4, pp. 1–12.

Levick, B. (1983), 'The *Senatus Consultum* from Larinum', *Journal of
Roman Studies*, 73, pp. 97–115.

Lindsay, H. (2004), 'The "Laudatio Murdiae": Its Content and
Significance', *Latomus*, 63, pp. 88–97.

Lintott, A. W. (1974), 'Cicero and Milo', *Journal of Roman Studies*, 64,
pp. 62–78.

Lintott, A. W. (1999), *Violence in Republican Rome*, Oxford: Oxford
University Press.

Lintott, A. W. (2009), 'The Assassination', in M. Griffin (ed.), *A
Companion to Julius Caesar*, Malde: Wiley-Blackwell, pp. 72–82.

Logghe, L. (2016), 'The Gentleman Was Not for Turning', *Latomus*,
75/2, pp. 353–77.

Loman, P. (2004), 'No Woman No War: Women's Participation in
Ancient Greek Warfare', *Greece & Rome*, 51/1, pp. 34–54.

Marshall, A. J. (1990), 'Roman Ladies on Trial: The Case of Maesia of
Sentinum', *Phoenix* 44/1, pp. 46–59.

Marshall, B. A. (1985), *A Historical Commentary on Asconius*, Columbia: University of Missouri Press.

Mayor, A. (2014), *The Amazons: Lives and Legends of Warrior Women across the Ancient World*, Rutgers: Princeton University Press.

McCracken, G. (1935), 'Cicero's Tusculan Villa', *Classical Journal*, 30/5, pp. 261–77.

McCracken, G. (1942), 'The Villa and Tomb of Lucullus at Tusculum', *American Journal of Archaeology*, 46/3, pp. 325–40.

McHugh, M. R. (2012), 'Ferox Femina Agrippina Major in Tacitus's Annales', *Helios*, 39/1.

Melchior, A. (2008), 'Twinned Fortunes and the Publication of Cicero's Pro Milone', *Classical Philology*, 103/3, pp. 282–97.

Millar, F. (1988). 'Cornelius Nepos, "Atticus" and the Roman Revolution', *Greece & Rome*, 35/1, pp. 40–55.

Milnor, K. (2011), 'Women in Roman Society', in M. Peachin (ed.), *The Oxford Handbook of Social Relations in the Roman World*, Oxford: Oxford University Press, pp. 609–22.

Moore, K. (2020), 'Octavia Minor and Patronage', in E. D. Carney and S. Müller (eds), *The Routledge Companion to Women and Monarchy in the Ancient Mediterranean World*, London: Routledge, pp. 375–87.

Morello, R. (2008), '*Segregem eam efficit*: Vergil's Camilla and the Scholiasts', in S. Casali and F. Stok (eds), *Servio: Stratificazioni esegetiche e modelli culturali*, Brussells, pp. 38–57.

Morgan, H. J., and M. B. Wallace (1972), 'Appius Claudius and the Hollows of Euboia', *Hesperia*, 41/1, pp. 128–40.

Ober, J. (2001), 'Not by a Nose: The Triumph of Antony and Cleopatra at Actium', in R. Cowley (ed.), *What If 2: Eminent Historians Imagine What Might Have Been*, New York: G. P. Putnam, pp. 23–47.

Ogden, D. (2021), *The Strix-Witch*, Cambridge: Cambridge University Press.

Osgood, J. (2014), *Turia: A Roman Woman's Civil War*, Oxford: Oxford University Press.

Östenberg, I. (2009), *Staging the World: Spoils, Captives, and Representations in the Roman Triumphal Procession*, Oxford: Oxford University Press.

Pelling, C. (1988), *Life of Antony*, Cambridge: Cambridge University Press.

Pepe, C. (2018), 'Fragments of Epideitic Oratory: The Exemplary Case of the *Laudatio Funebris* for Women', in C. Gray (ed.), *Reading Republican Oratory: Reconstructions, Contexts, Receptions*, Oxford: Oxford University Press, pp. 281–96.

Philips, J. E. (1978), 'Roman Mothers and the Lives of Their Adult Daughters', *Helios*, 6.

Plant, I. M. (2004), *Women Writers of Ancient Greece and Rome*, Norman: University of Oklahoma Press.

Pyy, E. (2020), *Women and War in Roman Epic*, Leiden: Brill.

Ramsay, J. T. (2001), 'Did Mark Antony Contemplate an Alliance with His Political Enemies in July 44 BCE?' *Classical Philology*, 96/3, pp. 253–68.

Rawson, B. (1974), 'Roman Concubinage and Other De Facto Marriages', *Transactions of the American Philological Association*, 104, pp. 279–305.

Rawson, B. (2005), 'Circulation of Staff between Roman Households', *Zeitschrift für Papyrologie und Epigraphik*, 151, pp. 223–4.

Reubel, J. S. (1979), 'The Trial of Milo in 52 BC: A Chronological Study', *Transactions of the American Philological Association*, 109, pp. 231–49.

Richardson Jr, L. (1992), *A New Topographical Dictionary of Ancient Rome*, Baltimore and London: Johns Hopkins University Press.

Richlin, A. (2014), *Arguments with Silence: Writing the History of Roman Women*, Ann Arbor: University of Michigan Press.

Riggsby, A. M. (2002). 'Clodius/Claudius', *Historia*, 51/1, pp. 117–23.

Roddaz, J. M. (1988), 'Lucius Antonius', *Historia*, 37, pp. 317–46.

Roller, D. W. (2017), *Cleopatra's Daughter and Other Royal Women of the Augustan Era*, Oxford: Oxford University Press.

Roller, M. (2003), 'Horizontal Women: Posture and Sex in the Roman Convivium', *American Journal of Philology*, 124/3, pp. 377–422.

Roller, M. (2018), *Models from the Past in Roman Culture: A World of Exempla*, Cambridge: Cambridge University Press.

Rollinger, C. (2023), 'The Dynamics of Shame: Elite Poverty in Late Republican and Early Imperial Discourse', in F Carlà-Uhink, L. Cecchet and C. Machado (eds), *Poverty in Ancient Greece and Rome: Realities and Discourses*, London: Routledge, pp. 144–65.

Root, M. V. (1920), 'A Visit to Cicero's Tusculum', *Classical Journal*, 16/1, pp. 34–41.

Russell, B. F. (1998), 'The Emasculation of Antony: The Construction of Gender in Plutarch's Life of Antony', *Helios*, 25/2: pp. 121–37.

Russell, A. (2016), 'Why Did Clodius Shut the Shops? The Rhetoric of Mobilizing a Crowd in the Late Republic', *Historia*, 65/2, pp. 186–210.

Saller, R. P. (1980), 'Anecdotes as Historical Evidence for the Principate', *Greece & Rome*, 27/1, pp. 69–83.

Saller, R. P. (1984), '"Familia, Domus", and the Roman Conception of Family', *Phoenix* 38/4, pp. 336–55.

Saller, R. P. (1987), 'Men's Age at Marriage and Its Consequences in the Roman Family', *Classical Philology*, 82/1, pp. 21–34.

Saller, R. P. (1999), 'Pater Familias, Mater Familias, and the Gendered Semantics of the Roman Household', *Classical Philology*, 94/2, pp. 182–97.

Scheidel, W. (2007), 'Roman Funerary Commemoration and the Age at First Marriage', *Classical Philology*, 102/4, pp. 389–402.

Schultz, C. E. (2006), *Women's Religious Activity in the Roman Republic*, Chapel Hill: University of North Carolina Press.

Schultz, C. E. (2021), *Fulvia: Playing for Power at the End of the Roman Republic*, Oxford: Oxford University Press.

Schultz, C. E. (2022), 'Antyllus and His Friends: Children in Triumviral Politics', *Historia*, 71, pp. 312–36.

Schultz, C. E. (2023), 'A Re-evaluation of the So-called Fulvia Coinage', *Historia*, 72, pp. 58–85.

Schultze, C. (2007), 'Making a Spectacle of Oneself: Pliny on Curio's Theatre', *Bulletin of the Institute of Classical Studies*, 100, pp. 127–45.

Scott, K. (1929), 'Octavian's Propaganda and Antony's *De Sua Ebrietate*', *Classical Philology* 24/2, pp. 133–41.

Scott, K. (1933), 'The Political Propaganda of 44–33 bc', *Memoirs of the American Academy in Rome*, 11, pp. 1–49.

Seager, R. (2014), 'The (Re/de)construction of Clodius in Cicero's Speeches', *Classical Quarterly*, 64/1, pp. 226–40.

Sebesta, J. L. (1994), 'Symbolism in the Costume of the Roman Woman', in J. L. Sebesta and L. Bonfante (eds), *The World of Roman Costume*, Madison: University of Wisconsin Press, pp. 46–53.

Sharrock, A. (2020), 'The Roman Mother-in-Law', in A. Sharrock and A. Keith (eds) *Maternal Conceptions in Classical Literature*, Toronto: University of Toronto Press, pp. 140–66.

Sick, D. H. (1999), 'Ummidia Quadratilla: Cagey Business Woman or Lazy Pantomime Watcher?', *Classical Antiquity*, 18/2, pp. 330–48.

Skinner, M. B. (1983), 'Clodia Metelli', *Transactions of the American Philological Association* 113, pp. 273–87.

Skinner, M. B. (2011), *Clodia Metelli: The Tribune's Sister*, Oxford: Oxford University Press.

Smith, C., and A. Powell (2008), *The Lost Memoirs of Augustus and the Development of Roman Autobiography*, Swansea: University of Wales Press.

Southon, E. (2023), *A History of the Roman Empire in 21 Women*, London: Oneworld.

Southon, E. (2024), *Agrippina the Elder*, New Haven: Yale University Press.

Stevenson, J. (2005), *Women Latin Poets: Language, Gender, and Authority from Antiquity to the Eighteenth Century*, Oxford: Oxford University Press.

Stevenson, T. (2011), 'Women of Early Rome as "Exempla" in Livy, "Ad Urbe Condita", Book 1', *Classical World*, 104/2, pp. 175–89.

Sumi, G. S. (1997), 'Power and Ritual: The Crowd at Clodius' Funeral', *Historia*, 46, pp. 80–102.

Syme, R. (1939, reissued 2002), *Roman Revolution*, Oxford: Oxford University Press.

Syme, R. (1986), *The Augustan Aristocracy*, Oxford: Clarendon Press.

Tatum, W. J. (1992), 'The Poverty of the Claudii Pulchri: Varro, De Re Rustica 3.6.1-2', *Classical Quarterly*, 42/1, pp. 190–200.

Tatum, W. J. (1999), *The Patrician Tribune: Publius Clodius Pulcher*, Chapel Hill and London: University of North Carolina Press.

Taylor, L. R. (1942), 'Caesar's Colleagues in the Pontifical College', *American Journal of Philology*, 63, pp. 385–412.

Traina, G. (2001), 'Lycoris the Mime', in A. Fraschetti (ed.), *Roman Women*, Chicago: University of Chicago Press, pp. 82–99.

Treggiari, S. (1975a), 'Jobs in the Household of Livia', *Papers of the British School at Rome*, 43, pp. 48–77.

Treggiari, S. (1975b), 'Family Life Amongst the Staff of the Volusii', *Transactions of the American Philological Association*, 105, pp. 393–401.

Treggiari, S. (2007), *Terentia, Tullia, and Publilia: The Women of Cicero's Family*, London: Routledge.

Treggiari, S. (2019), *Servilia and her Family*, Oxford: Oxford University Press.

Vio, F. R. (2013), *Fulvia. Una matrona tra i 'signori della guerra'*, Naples: EdiSES.

Vio, F. R. (2022), '*Matronae* and Politics in Republican Rome', in V. Arena and J. Prag (eds), *A Companion to the Political Culture of the Roman Republic*, Malden: Wiley Blackwell, pp. 362–73.

Virlouvet, C. (2001), 'Fulvia: The Woman of Passion', in A. Fraschetti (ed.), *Roman Women*, Chicago: University of Chicago Press, pp. 66–80.

Watkins, T. H. (2019), *L. Munatius Plancus: Serving and Surviving in the Roman Revolution*, London: Routledge.

Watson, P. A. (1995), *Ancient Stepmothers: Myth, Misogyny and Reality*, Leiden: Brill.

Webb, L. (2015), 'Shame Transfigured: Slut-shaming from Rome to Cyberspace', *First Monday*, 20/4.

Webb, L. (2022), 'Female Interventions in Politics in the libera res publica: Structures and Practices', in R. M. Frolov and C. Burden-Strevens (eds), *Leadership and Initiative in Late Republican and Early Imperial Rome*, Leiden: Brill, pp. 147–84.

Webb, L. (2023), 'Impoverished Senatorial Women in Mid-Republican Rome: *Opima Gloria* and *Felix Paupertas*?', in F. Carlà-Uhink, L. Cecchet and C. Machado (eds), *Poverty in Ancient Greece and Rome: Realities and Discourses*, London: Routledge, pp. 117–43.

Weigel, R. D. (1992), *Lepidus: The Tarnished Triumvir*, London: Routledge.

Welch, K. (1995), 'Antony, Fulvia, and the Ghost of Clodius in 47 BC', *Greece & Rome* 42/2, pp. 182–201.

Welch, K. (1996), 'T. Pomponius Atticus: A Banker in Politics?', *Historia* 45/4, pp. 450–71.

Welch, K. (2012), *Magnus Pius: Sextus Pompeius and the Transformation of the Roman Republic*, Swansea: Classical Press of Wales.

Welch, T. (2012), 'Perspectives On and Of Livy's Tarpeia', *EuGeStA: Journal on Gender Studies in Antiquity*, 2.

Welch, T. (2015), *Tarpeia: Workings of a Roman Myth*, Columbus: Ohio State University Press.

Wiseman, T. P. (1970), 'Pulcher Claudius', *Harvard Studies in Classical Philology*, 74, pp. 207–21.

Wood, S. E. (1998), *Imperial Women: A Study in Public Images, 40 BC–AD*, Leiden: Brill.

Woodhull, M. L. (2004), 'Matronly Patrons in the Early Roman Empire: The Case of Salvia Postuma', in F. McHardy and E. Marshall (eds), *Women's Influence on Classical Civilisation*, London: Routledge, pp. 75–91.

Wright, A. (2001), 'The Death of Cicero. Forming a Tradition: The Contamination of History', *Historia*, 50/4, pp. 436–52.

Xinyue, B. (2017), '*Imperatrix* and *bellatrix*: Cicero's Clodia and Virgil's Camilla', in D. Campanile, F. Carlà-Uhink and M. Facella (eds), *Transantiquity: Cross-Dressing and Transgender Dynamics in the Ancient World*, London: Routledge, pp. 164–77.

ENDNOTES

Introduction

1 Macrobius, *Saturnalia* 1.13.17.
2 Cassius Dio, *Roman History* 40.47.1–4.
3 Ogden (2021).
4 Julius Obsequens, *A Book of Prodigies After the 505th Year of Rome* 63.
5 Cicero, *In Defense of Milo* 28; Asconius 31.
6 Cicero, *In Defence of Milo* 55. As an indication of Milo's political connections and sympathies, his wife Fausta Cornelia was the daughter of the deceased dictator Sulla, a leader of the *optimates*, whereas Clodius was more in line with the *populares*. In a nutshell, the *optimates* saw themselves as conservative, traditional and the guardians of the status quo, while the *populares* saw themselves as somewhat more progressive, and representing the Roman people.
7 Asconius 31.
8 Asconius 32; Cassius Dio, *Roman History* 40.48.2.
9 Cicero, *In Defence of Milo* 17; Asconius 55.
10 Erker (2009) 145–6.
11 On the nature and composition of the crowds that gathered at Clodius' funeral, see Sumi (1997).
12 Favro and Johanson (2010).
13 Cicero, *In Defence of Milo* 33. For Sextus Cloelius' role in Clodius' affairs, see Damon (1992).
14 Plutarch, *Tiberius and Gaius Gracchus* 13. See Sumi (1997) 81 for discussion.
15 Dionysius of Halicarnassus, *Roman Antiquities* 1.87.2.
16 Pliny the Elder, *Natural History* 35.22, 34.21.
17 Somewhat ironically, it was rebuilt by Fausta Cornelia's twin brother Faustus Cornelius Sulla, and subsequently known as the Curia

Cornelia (Cicero, *On Endings* 5.2 complained that it looked poky despite technically having been enlarged during the rebuilding). This manifestation of the building would not last long, however, as the Senate voted that it should be rebuilt in 44 BCE so as to remove the name of Sulla from it (Cassius Dio, *Roman History* 44.5.2, 45.17.8), and this manifestation, known as the Curia Julia, was started by Caesar and completed by Octavian in 29 BCE.

18 See, for example, the work of the Everyday Sexism Project (https://everydaysexism.com/), which exists to catalogue instances of sexism experienced on a day-to-day basis, or the End Violence Against Women Coalition (https://www.endviolenceagainstwomen.org.uk/), a group of feminist organizations and experts from across the UK, working to end violence against women and girls in all its forms.

19 Cicero, *Philippics* 6.4; 13.18.

20 Velleius Paterculus, *Compendium of Roman History* 2.74.2; Plutarch, *Antony* 10.3.

21 See Skinner (1983) for 'the Clodia myth'.

22 Freyd (1997) 29–30.

23 Plutarch, *Antony* 10.3.

24 Plant (2004) 106–11.

25 Hemelrijk (1999) 186–8.

26 Tacitus, *Annals* 4.53; Pliny the Elder, *Natural History* 7.46. For discussion, see Southon (2024).

27 For the question of how far we can trust anecdotes as sources in this period, see Saller (1980).

28 While Fulvia has been a popular topic for postgraduate research dissertations over the last two decades, such as Weir (2007) and Wotring (2017), the first academic monograph dedicated to her written in English was Schultz (2021), a carefully measured and balanced account. An earlier work, Fischer (1999), was published in German, and another, Rohr Vio (2013), in Italian.

29 Baumann (1992) 83–9; conversely, Delia (1991).

30 Helbig (1889).

31 Osgood (2014); Hemelrijk (2004).

32 The modern identification of the woman as Turia, and her husband as Quintus Lucretius Vespillo, rests upon the similarity between the account of their experiences during the proscriptions of 43 BCE

given in the inscription, and the account of that couple's experiences during the proscriptions of 43 BCE given in several historical sources, but the accounts are by no means identical.

33 *CIL* VI 41062.30.

1 Fulvia's World

1 The senatorial and equestrian elite were the richest and, consequently, most powerful members of ancient Roman society, required to be in possession of at least one million sesterces and 400,000 sesterces of land (in addition to other types of wealth and property) respectively. In the monarchic, Early and Middle Republican periods, the equestrians had been the officer class of the cavalry of the Roman legions (hence them sometimes being referred to as knights), but by the Late Republic, the difference between the two groups was more a matter of politics (senators' sons and other male descendants were equestrians until they began to climb the *cursus honorum* and were elected to membership of the Senate) and economics (the equestrians were permitted more latitude with how they earned their money, such as through commercial ventures, than senators, for whom such things were considered beneath their dignity) than anything else.

2 Valerius Maximus, *Memorable Deeds and Sayings* 3.8.6, 9.7.1–2, 9.15.1.

3 Plutarch, *Lucullus* 6.3.

4 Macrobius, *Saturnalia* 3.13.11.

5 Aulus Gellius, *Attic Nights* 10.15.26–30.

6 Cicero, *In Defence of Balbus* 55. See Schultz (2006) 75–6 for discussion.

7 Tertullian, *On Monogamy* 17.3–4.

8 Cicero, *On the Responses of the Haruspices* 37; Plutarch, *Caesar* 9–10.

9 Cicero, *In Defence of Caelius* 34.

10 Cicero, *In Defence of Fonteius* 46–7; Cicero, *In Defence of Murena* 73.

11 Plutarch, *Crassus* 1.2.

12 Livy, *History of Rome* 4.44.11–12.

13 Seneca the Elder, *Controversiae* 6.8.

14 Cicero, *On Divination* 1.99; Julius Obsequens, *A Book of Prodigies* 55.

15 Plutarch, *Cicero* 20.1–3.
16 *CIL* VI 30899 = *ILS* 3423 = *ILLRP* 126 (trans. Schultz).
17 *CIL* X 292 = *ILS* 5430 = *ILLRP* 574 (trans. Schultz).
18 *CIL* I² 3025 = *AE* 1973.127 (trans. Schultz).
19 Hyginus, *Fables* 254.
20 National Archaeological Museum of Naples inv. 115398.
21 Valerius Maximus, *Memorable Doings and Sayings* 5.4.7; Pliny the Elder, *Natural History* 7.121.
22 *I. Métr.* 83.
23 Webb (2022).
24 *CIL* VI 1300A; Catullus 38, 55.
25 Stevenson (2005).
26 Catullus 35.15–16.
27 Sulpicia 8.15–20 (Tibullus, *Elegies* 3.8.15–20).
28 On Sulpicius, see Quintilian, *The Orator's Education* 10.5.4. Sulpicia 16.5–6 (Tibullus, *Elegies* 3.16.5–6).
29 *AE* 1928.73. Female readers are very rare, with only four other epitaphs of lectrices surviving, and would likely have been found only in the wealthiest homes, where women were in need of them.
30 Pliny the Elder, *Natural History* 35.147–8.
31 National Archaeological Museum of Naples inv. 9017, 9018.
32 Cicero, *Letters to Atticus* 5.1 (Shackleton Bailey 94).
33 Cicero, *Letters to Atticus* 5.1.

2 Fulvia's Family

1 *Tab. Vindol.*, 291; British Museum inv. 1986,1001.64.
2 Cicero, *In Defence of Plancius* 8.19.
3 Ovid, *Fasti* 3.91, 4.71; Propertius, *Elegies* 2.32.4; Silius Italicus 12.535; Horace, *Epodes* 1.30, *Odes* 3.29.8.
4 Strabo, *Geography* 5.3.12.
5 Coarelli (2007) 514–17.
6 McCracken (1942).
7 Cicero, *Letters to Atticus* 1.4.2 (Shackleton Bailey 9). See McCracken (1935) and Root (1920) for discussion.

8   See McCracken (1942) for discussion.

9   Virlouvet (2001) 66.

10 Laes (2013), although Bambalio is excluded from his catalogue.

11 Cicero, *Philippics* 3.16.

12 Pliny the Elder, *Natural History* 3.19.129; Cicero, *Philippics* 3.16.

13 Although it would not actually be made illegal until 19 CE – see the *Senatus Consultum* from Larinum, a bronze tablet inscribed with text setting out the restrictions, Levick (1983).

14 Cicero, *Academy* 2.89.

15 Valerius Maximus, *Memorable Deeds and Sayings* 7.8.1.

16 If so, this would make Fulvia first cousin to Decimus Junius Brutus Albinus, one of the ringleaders of the conspiracy to assassinate Caesar – more on him and this later.

17 Sallust, *The War with Catiline* 25. Hemelrijk (1999) 84.

18 Plutarch, *Pompey* 55.1–2. Hemelrijk (1999) 78.

19 Metropolitan Museum of Art inv. 03.14.5.

20 Sallust, *The War with Catiline* 25.3.

21 Sallust, *The War with Catiline* 25.1.

22 Cicero, *In Defence of Murena*, 73; Cicero, *On His House* 134. Taylor (1942); Arkenberg (1993) 342–3.

23 Livy, *From the Founding of the City* 1.7.12; there was an ancient bronze portrait of one of Natta's ancient ancestors on the Capitoline Hill that was once struck by lightning – Cicero, *On Divination* 1.12, 2.20–1.

24 Suetonius, *Caesar* 83.2. Taylor (1942) 397. Decimus Brutus was also one of Caesar's heirs, albeit a secondary heir after the three young male relatives.

25 Arkenberg (1993) 334–5; Virlouvet (2001) 67.

26 Pliny the Elder, *Natural History* 10.23.45.

27 Livy, *From the Founding of the City* 8.14.2; Cicero, *On the Nature of the Gods* 1.29.83. Arkenberg (1993) 341–2.

28 Pliny the Elder, *Natural History* 33.16.53.

29 Cicero, *In Defence of Murena* 86–7.

30 Cicero, *In Defence of Murena* 14.

31 Cicero, *In Defence of Murena* 73.

32 Cicero, *Letters to Atticus* 2.1.5 (Shackleton Bailey 21).

33 It is worth noting that the Latin language has an extensive vocabulary when it comes to referring to the members of extended family and kinship networks, with clear differentiation made between the maternal and paternal lines, demonstrating that family ties well beyond the equivalent of our modern nuclear family were considered crucial.

3 Fulvia's Childhood

1   Pliny the Elder, *Natural History* 7.6.41–2.
2   Macrobius, *Saturnalia* 1.16.36.
3   Plutarch, *Roman Questions* 102 (*Moralia* 288C–E).
4   See, for example, the famous diatribe of the sophist philosopher Favorinus on the subject, Aulus Gellius, *Attic Nights* 12.1.
5   Soranus, *Gynaecology* 2.19–20 – wet nurse employment contracts that have survived from Roman Egypt confirm these stringent stipulations were put into practice even lower down the social scale.
6   See Treggiari (1975) for discussion of the epigraphic evidence for the presence of midwives, wet nurses and other childcare staff, both enslaved and formerly enslaved, in elite Roman households.
7   Soranus, *Gynaecology* 2.14–15, 2.31–5.
8   Hallett (2015) 261.
9   Catullus 86.1–2. Translation provided by Robert Cromarty.
10 Suetonius, *On Rhetoricians* 5.
11 My thanks to Dr Claire Millington for this information.
12 Tacitus, *Dialogues* 28.4–6; see also Cicero, *Brutus*, 104. See also Caldwell (2015) 15–44.
13 Musonius Rufus, *On Why Daughters Should Receive the Same Education as Sons*. See also Engel (2000).
14 Cicero, *Letters to Atticus* 12.33 (Shackleton Bailey 269). Atticus was renowned for his many literate and highly educated slaves and freedmen.
15 Suetonius, *Grammarians* 16.
16 Plutarch, *Table Talk* 9.1.3 (*Moralia* 737B).
17 Strabo, *Geography* 14.1.48.

18 Rawson (2005).

19 Cicero, *On Oratory* 3.12.45.

20 Quintilian, *The Orator's Education* 1.1.6.

21 Cicero, *Brutus* 211.

22 Cicero, *Brutus* 211.

23 Plutarch, *Lucullus* 19.7; Plutarch, *Sulla* 26.1–2.

24 Dixon (2013) 223.

25 Langlands (2006).

26 Valerius Maximus, *Memorable Deeds and Sayings* 8.3.

27 Valerius Maximus, *Memorable Deeds and Sayings* 8.3.1–2. Marshall (1990).

28 Pliny the Younger, *Letters* 5.16.1–8. For Minicia Marcella's epitaph, see *ILS* 1030.

29 Saller (1987); Scheidel (2007).

30 Jeppesen-Wigelsworth (2013).

31 Cicero, *Letters to Atticus* 13.21a.4 (Shackleton Bailey 327). Treggiari (2007) 20.

32 Pliny the Elder, *Natural History* 33.4.12.

33 Mayor (2014) 32–3.

34 Hersch (2010).

35 Literally, *manus* means 'hand', so this is figuratively about the power that the hand wields.

36 Culham (2014) 138.

37 Treggiari (2007) 34; Dixon (1986) 95–6. On the Argiletum, see Dalby (2000) 215.

38 Metropolitan Museum of Art inv. 20.49.2–12.

39 Hopwood (2019) 67.

40 See, for example, the marble sarcophagus of Crepereia Tryphaena and its contents, currently on display in the Centrale Montemartini museum in Rome: https://www.centralemontemartini.org/en/percorso/crepereia-tryphaena.

41 La Follette (1994).

42 Pliny the Elder, *Natural History* 10.74.148.

43 Ibid. 21.22.46; Festus 79.23 L, 82.6 L.

44 Festus 56.1 L.

45 Catullus 61.6–7.

46 For an experimental archaeological reconstruction of the hairstyle and costume of the Roman bride, see the work of hair archaeologist Janet Stephens: https://youtu.be/jekmhubglro (accessed July 2023).

47 Seneca the Elder, *Controversiae* 6.8.

48 Martial, *Epigrams* 10.35, see also 10.38.

49 Sulpicia II is quoted by Probus. For discussion, see Hallett (2002).

4 The Ideal Roman Woman?

1 Stevenson (2011) surveys these, and other early exemplars.

2 Livy, *From the Founding of the City* 1.57–60; Dionysius of Halicarnassus, *Roman Antiquities* 4.64–71; see also the slightly earlier Diodorus Siculus, *Historical Library* 10.20–1. Contemporary historians do not tend to take these seriously, seeing it as a form of narrative paralleling those detailing the downfall of other tyrants, such as the Pisistratids of Athens in 508 BCE. Ovid, *Fasti* 2. 741–852 is a poetic reinterpretation.

3 Livy, *From the Founding of the City* 3.44–8; there is an account of a similar episode, although the participants are not named, in a slightly earlier work, Diodorus Siculus, *History Library* 12.24.2–4.

4 Plautus, *Weevil* 470–85 is a famous description of all the disreputable characters to be found in the Forum, and he states that the shrine of Venus Cloacina is where you would go if you wanted to find a liar and a braggart. For the shrine of Venus Cloacina, see Richardson Jr (1992) 92.

5 Livy, *From the Founding of the City* 29.14; Ovid, *Fasti* 4.305–48. Vio (2022) 364–5.

6 Ovid, *Fasti* 4.319–24.

7 Valerius Maximus, *Memorable Deeds and Sayings* 1.8.11; Tacitus, *Annals* 4.64.

8 Livy, *From the Founding of the City* 1.11; Dionysius of Halicarnassus, *Roman Antiquities* 2.38–40. For discussion, see Welch (2012), (2015).

9 Plutarch, *Numa* 13.2.

10 Propertius, *Elegies* 4.4.

11 Dionysius of Halicarnassus, *Roman Antiquities* 3.69.4; Plutarch, *Romulus* 18.1; Varro, *On the Latin Language* 5.41.

12 British Museum inv. 1902,0503.98; British Museum inv. 2002,0102. 4945. It was perhaps the appearance of this coin that inspired Propertius' aetiological elegy on Tarpeia, cited above.

13 Leach (2007).

14 *CIL* VI 492.

15 Martial, *Epigrams* 11.104.21–2 – Lais was a stereotypical prostitute's stage name, after the famous courtesans Lais of Corinth and Lais of Hycarra about whom many salacious anecdotes have survived.

16 *CIL* VI 15346.

17 Metropolitan Museum of Art inv. 37.129a, b.

18 Aulus Gellius, *Attic Nights* 10.23.4–5.

19 Cicero, *Letters to Atticus* 12.51.3 (Shackleton Bailey 293). See Austin (1946) for Cicero's relationship with Caerellia and evidence of their correspondence.

20 Cassius Dio, *Roman History* 46.18.4.

21 For the most detailed and up-to-date study of Clodia, see Skinner (2011), previously (1983).

22 This is still a feature of contemporary political discourse – consider the recent accusations that the British prime minister Boris Johnson was enacting the political agenda of his wife, Carrie Johnson, in his support for the environment, animal rights and LGBTQ+ rights against the prevailing Conservative Party platform, as well as her supposed role in the hiring and firing of numerous Downing Street personnel, and references to her as 'Lady Macbeth' and 'Carrie Antoinette'.

5 Fulvia as a Wife

1 Cicero, *Letters to Atticus* 1.16.10 (Shackleton Bailey 16). See also Butrica (2002).

2 Campanile (2017) 53–6.

3 Cicero, *Letters to Atticus* 1.16.1–11 (Shackleton Bailey 16).

4 Juvenal, *Satires* 6.336–41. See also Juvenal, *Satires* 2.27, where Juvenal states that Clodius was a famous adulterer.

5 Schultze (2021) 34.

6 Cicero, *Clodius and Curio* fragment 6a and 6b.

7 For an overview, see Skinner (2011).

8 *ILS* 54.

9 Suetonius, *Tiberius* 1.2.

10 Livy, *From the Founding of the City* 2.27.1.

11 Varro, *On Agriculture* 3.16.1–2. For discussion, see Tatum (1992).

12 Hersch (2010) 135.

13 Pliny the Elder, *Natural History* 16.30.75, 16.38–48.

14 Pliny the Elder, *Natural History* 16.60.139; Servius, *Commentary on Virgil's Aeneid* 6.216.

15 Festus 282, 283L.

16 Catullus, *Poems* 61.82–6.

17 Metropolitan Museum of Art inv. 53.11.5. Festus 282.16 L.

18 Pliny the Elder, *Natural History* 28.37.135; Plutarch, *Roman Questions* 31 (*Moralia* 271F).

19 Servius, *Commentary on Vergil's Eclogues* 8.29.

20 Plautus, *The Casket* 816–17.

21 Catullus, *Poems* 64.303–6; Lucan, *Civil War* 2.356.

22 Metropolitan Museum of Art inv. 17.190.2076.

23 Catullus, *Poems* 79.

24 Frier (1994).

25 Tatum (1999) 40.

26 Southon (2023) 100.

27 On the Temple of the Nymphs, see Cicero, *In Defence of Caelius* 78, *In Defence of Milo* 73, *Paradoxa* 4.31, *Response of the Haruspices* 57–8. On Clodius' unsavoury property acquisitions, see Cicero, *In Defence of Milo* 74–5.

28 Cerutti (1997).

29 Velleius Paterculus, *Compendium of Roman History* 2.14.3. For discussion, see Cooper (2007).

30 Vitruvius, *On Architecture* 6.5.2.

31 Martial, *Epigrams* 13.32.

32 Cicero, *In Defence of Sextus Roscius of Ameria* 134.

33 Cicero, *On His House* 115–16.

34 Pliny the Elder, *Natural History* 36.23.103. For perspective, it has been estimated that the daily wage of a Roman labourer was three sesterces, so their yearly wage would be 1,095 sesterces, and thus it would have taken an ordinary Roman 13,516 years to save up the money necessary to buy Clodius' house.

35 Pliny the Elder, *Natural History* 36.2.6–7.

36 Claridge (2010) 117–18.

37 Garland (1992).

38 Treggiari (1975b).

39 Plutarch, *Advice to Bride and Groom* (*Moralia* 138–46)

40 Plutarch, *Pompey* 48.5.

41 Pliny the Elder, *Natural History* 36.23.103.

42 Apuleius, *Apology* 10.3; see also Ovid, *Tristia* 2.1.437–8.

43 Skinner (2011).

44 Cicero, *In Defence of Milo* 28, 55.

45 Foubert (2016). There are two inscriptions from Rome which commemorate servile entertainers owned by a woman named Fulvia, who may be our Fulvia; there are likewise two owned by a woman named Clodia, who may be one of her sisters-in-law. See Sick (1999) for discussion.

46 Quintus Tullius Cicero, *Handbook of Electioneering* 10.

6 The First Tribune

1 Plutarch, *Lucullus* 34.2; Cassius Dio, *Roman History* 36.14.4.

2 Plutarch, *Lucullus* 38.1; Plutarch, *Cicero* 29.3–4.

3 Cicero, *Letters to Atticus* 2.9 (Shackleton Bailey 29).

4 Russell (2016).

5 Cassius Dio, *Roman History* 37.42.

6 Cicero, *Against Piso* 11, 26; Cicero, *On His House* 62.

7 Cicero, *On His House* 115–16.

8 Cicero, *On His House* 118, 139.

9 Cicero, *On His House* 25, 83. For discussion, see Skinner (2011) 67.

10 Cicero, *Letters to Quintus* 2.3.1 (Shackleton Bailey 7).

11 Cicero, *Letters to Quintus* 2.3.2 (Shackleton Bailey 7).

12 Cassius Dio, *Roman History* 39.20.1–2.
13 Cicero, *Letters to Quintus* 2.5.4 (Shackleton Bailey 9).
14 Cassius Dio, *Roman History* 39.61.1–2.
15 Cassius Dio, *Roman History* 40.17.1.
16 Fagan (2011).
17 Varro, *On Agriculture* 1.69.2–3.
18 Cicero, *In Defence of Milo* 40; Cicero, *Philippics* 2.21. For discussion, see Alexander (2011), who sees Cicero as deliberately misrepresenting the altercation.
19 Asconius 31.
20 Flaig (2022) 573–4.
21 Richlin (2014) 282.
22 Publilius Syrus, *Maxims* 384.
23 Erker (2009).
24 Cassius Dio, *Roman History* 39.64.
25 Cicero, *Letters to Atticus* 4.3.3; Richardson Jr (1992) 131–2.
26 Cicero, *In Defence of Milo* 64.
27 Richardson Jr (1992) 235.
28 Plutarch, *Roman Questions* 23.
29 Asconius 43.
30 Appian, *Civil War* 2.22–3.
31 The immense substructures of this villa survived long after antiquity, and were illustrated by Giovanni Battista Piranesi in an etching in 1762.
32 Asconius 34.
33 Seneca the Younger, *Epistles* 63.13.
34 Sebesta (1994) 50.
35 Gladhill (2018) 301.
36 Lintott (1970) 71.
37 For the chronology of events, see Ruebel (1979).
38 Asconius 37.
39 Asconius 40.
40 Asconius 40.
41 Gladhill (2018) 300.
42 Gladhill (2018) 302.
43 Asconius 40.

44 Asconius 54–5.
45 Welch (1995).

7 The Second Tribune

1   Tertullian, *On Monogamy* 17.
2   Valerius Maximus, *Memorable Deeds and Sayings* 4.4.*praef.*
3   Plutarch, *Life of Tiberius* 1.4–5.
4   Plutarch, *Life of Gaius* 4.3.
5   Pliny the Elder, *Natural History* 36.4.15–16.
6   Pliny the Elder, *Natural History* 34.14.31. On the statue, see Kajava (1989).
7   *CIL* VI 10043; Capitoline Museums inv. NCE 2925.
8   Cornelia 1; Cicero, *Brutus* 211. For discussion, see Hallett (2018).
9   Plutarch, *Life of Gaius* 4.2, 13.2.
10 Cornelia 1.
11 Asconius 19.
12 Baumann (1992) 78–80.
13 Cicero, *Letters to Friends* 5.2.6–7 (Shackleton Bailey 2).
14 Plutarch, *Pompey* 42.7; Suetonius, *Caesar* 50.1. See Hillard (2021) for discussion of one of Catullus' poems that may also refer to this.
15 Suetonius, *Caesar* 50.1. Haley (1985) 53.
16 Haley (1985) 57.
17 Cicero, *In Defence of Caelius* 48–50, 18.
18 Webb (2015).
19 Plutarch, *Sulla* 35.3–5.
20 Cicero, *Letters to Atticus* 1.14.5 (Shackleton Bailey 14).
21 Cicero, *Letters to Atticus* 2.18.1 (Shackleton Bailey 38), 2.19.3 (Shackleton Bailey 39).
22 Cicero, *Letters to Atticus* 2.24.2 (Shackleton Bailey 44).
23 Velleius Paterculus, *Compendium of Roman History* 2.48.3–4.
24 Cicero, *Letters to Friends* 8.4.2 (Shackleton Bailey 81).
25 Cicero, *Letters to Friends* 8.2.1 (Shackleton Bailey 78) mentions Curio's theatre, so we know that it existed, but it does not go into details about its construction. See Schultze (2007) for discussion.

26 Cicero, *Letters to Friends* 8.8.10 (Shackleton Bailey 84), 8.9.3 (Shackleton Bailey 82).

27 Pliny the Elder, *Natural History* 36.116–20; Cicero, *Letters to Friends* 2.2 (Shackleton Bailey 46).

28 Cicero, *Letters to Friends* 2.3 (Shackleton Bailey 47).

29 Cicero, *Letters to Atticus* 9.15.1 (Shackleton Bailey 183), 10.4.7 (Shackleton Bailey 195).

30 Logghe (2016).

31 Logghe (2016) 374.

32 Cicero, *Philippics* 2.4, 2.44, 2.45.

33 Velleius Paterculus, *Compendium of Roman History* 2.48.3.

34 Propertius, *Elegies* 4.3.3–4.

35 Propertius, *Elegies* 4.3.11–12.

36 Ovid, *Tristia* 1.3.17–24.

37 Propertius, *Elegies* 4.3.13–16.

38 Tibullus, *Elegies* 1.1.75.

39 Tibullus, *Elegies* 1.3.5–9.

40 Ultimately, Juba I would be defeated at the Battle of Thapsus and take his own life as part of a suicide pact involving single combat with the Roman general Marcus Petreius in 46 BCE, leaving Caesar free to seize his kingdom and convert it into the Roman province of Africa Nova, but that was probably cold comfort as far as Fulvia was concerned.

41 Haley (1985) 58.

42 Plutarch, *Crassus* 33.2–4.

43 Cassius Dio, *Roman History* 40.27.3.

44 Lucan, *Civil War* 9.55–72.

45 Valerius Maximus, *Memorable Deeds and Sayings* 4.6.4–5.

46 Publilius Syrus, *Maxims* 260.

47 Plutarch, *Life of Antony* 2.3–4.

48 Cicero, *Philippics* 2.44–6. Campanile (2017) 56–9.

49 Plutarch, *Crassus* 1.1.

50 Plutarch, *Cato the Younger* 25.3.

51 Lucian, *Civil War* 2.326–71.

52 Asconius 19–20.

53 Cicero, *Philippics* 2.11.

8 The Third Tribune

1 The *Philippics* are so-called because he likened them to the ancient Athenian orator Demosthenes' speeches against King Philip II of Macedon.

2 Pliny the Elder, *Natural History* 14.28.148. For discussion, see Huzar (1982); Geiger (1980); Charlesworth (1933) 172; Scott (1929).

3 Plutarch, *Antony* 1.2–3.

4 Cicero, *Philippics* 2.4, 2.42, 2.44.

5 Plutarch, *Antony* 2.3–4.

6 Cicero, *Philippics* 2.3, 3.16–17, 13.23 and *Letters to Atticus* 16.11.1 (Shackleton Bailey 420). See also Huzar (1985–1986) 97–98.

7 Cicero, *Philippics* 2.20, 2.58; Servius, *Commentary on Virgil's Bucolics* 10.1.6. See also Keith (2011), (2018).

8 Sextus Aurelius Victor, *Illustrious Men* 82.2. Traini (2001) 82.

9 Cicero, *Letters to Friends* 9.26.2 (Shackleton Bailey 197).

10 Cicero, *Philippics* 2.58.

11 Cicero, *Against Verres* 2.1.120.

12 Cicero, *Letters to Atticus* 10.10.5 (Shackleton Bailey 201).

13 Suetonius, *Caesar* 50, 52; Plutarch, *Caesar* 49.

14 Suetonius, *Caesar* 49.4, 51.

15 Cicero, *Letters to Friends* 14.16 (Shackleton Bailey 163).

16 Bradley (1987) 42–5.

17 Gray-Fow (1988); Watson (1995).

18 Propertius, *Elegies* 4.11.85–92.

19 British Museum inv. 1867,0101.606. See also *RRC* 541/2.

20 Suetonius, *Augustus* 63.2. For discussion, see Schultz (2022) 322.

21 Plutarch, *Antony* 28.4–7.

22 Cassius Dio, *Roman History* 53.27.5 – after Antony's death in 30 BCE, this house would be seized and bestowed jointly upon Octavian's henchmen Agrippa and Messalla, who divided it up between themselves, although neither got to enjoy it for long: it burned down shortly afterwards, in 25 BCE.

23 Richardson Jr (1992) 114.

24 Cicero, *Philippics* 2.6–6.

25 Servius, *Commentary on Virgil's Aeneid* 8.361.

26 Richardson Jr (1992) 201.

27 Suetonius, *Grammarians* 15.1.

28 Velleius Paterculus, *Compendium of Roman History* 2.77.1–2; Cassius Dio, *Roman History* 48.38; Florus, *Epitome of Roman History* 2.18.4–5.

29 Suetonius, *Tiberius* 15.1.

30 Cicero, *On the Responses of the Haruspices* 49. See also Cerutti (1997).

31 For a general overview of the assassination, see Lintott (2009).

32 Appian, *Civil War* 2.114; Plutarch, *Brutus* 17.2.

33 Cicero, *Letters to Atticus* 14.21.3 (Shackleton Bailey 375).

34 Cicero, *Letters to Atticus* 14.12.1 (Shackleton Bailey 366); Cicero, *Letters to Friends* 10.28.1 (Shackleton Bailey 364).

35 Schultz (2022) 317.

36 Cicero, *Philippics* 1.2.

37 Cicero, *Philippics* 2.35.

38 Cicero, *Philippics* 5.11.

39 Cicero, *Letters to Atticus* 14.12.1 (Shackleton Bailey 366). Cicero had previously defended Deiotarus when he was accused by his grandson Castor of attempting to assassinate Caesar in 45 BCE – Cicero, *In Defence of Deiotarus*. Deiotarus had Castor murdered in retaliation for the accusation.

40 Cicero, *Philippics* 2.95.

41 Cicero, *Philippics* 3.10.

42 Foubert (2016b) 474.

43 Goldberg (2015–16).

44 Cicero, *Philippics* 5.22, 13.18.

45 Cicero, *Philippics* 3.4.

46 Cicero, *Philippics* 2.69.

47 Cicero, *Philippics* 2.77–8; Plutarch, *Antony* 10.4–5.

48 Cicero, *Philippics* 2.77.

49 Plutarch, *Antony* 10.4–5.

50 Schultz (2022) 319–20.

51 Cornelius Nepos, *Atticus* 9.2.

52 Cornelius Nepos, *Atticus* 9.3–5. For discussion, see Welch (1996).

53 Hallett (2006) 157.

54 Suetonius, *Caesar* 83.2; Appian, *Civil War* 3.22, 3.94.

55 Ovid, *Tristia* 1.3.87–88, 1.6.5–16.

56 Ovid, *Tristia* 4.3.49–52, 53–56. For discussion, see Fabre-Serris (2022).

57 Ovid, *Tristia* 3.1, 5.14; Ovid, *Letters from Pontus* 3.7.11–12.

9 The Triumvir

1 See the Fasti Colotiani, *Inscr. Ital.* 13.1.18.

2 Livy, *Summaries* 119; Plutarch, *Antony* 20.1; Suetonius, *Augustus* 62.1.

3 Suetonius, *Augustus* 72.1.

4 See the Fasti Colotiani, *Inscr. Ital.* 13.1.18.

5 *RPC* I 512. Wood (1998) 41–2.

6 Ovid, *Arts of Love* 3.139–40.

7 Schultz (2023) summarizes the arguments for and against the identification of this woman as Fulvia.

8 Seneca the Younger, *On Mercy* 1.9.3–4.

9 Valerius Maximus, *Memorable Deeds and Sayings* 9.5.4.

10 Appian, *Civil War* 4.29.1.

11 Welch (2012) 179.

12 Suetonius, *Caesar* 50.2. For discussion, see Treggiari (2019) 121–2. On pearls, see Dalby (2000) 188.

13 *Laudatio Turiae* 2a.

14 National Archaeological Museum of Naples inv. 124666.

15 Webb (2023); Rollinger (2023).

16 Suetonius, *Augustus* 70.2; Pliny the Elder, *Natural History* 34.2.6. See Scott (1933) 20–21.

17 Seneca the Elder, *Suasoriae* 6, 7; Quintilian, *Institutes of Oratory* 3.8.46.

18 Plutarch, *Cicero* 47.8–9.

19 Ovid, *Arts of Love* 3.239–40; Ovid, *Amores* 1.14.16–18; Petronius, *Satyricon* 21.

20 Apuleius, *Metamorphoses* 8.13.

21 Apuleius, *Metamorphoses* 8.12.

22 Lange (2014) 79–80.

23 Diodorus Siculus, *Library of History* 24.12.1–3.

24 Plutarch, *Cicero* 49.2.

25 Syme (1939) 191.

26 Smith and Powell (2008).

27 Cluett (1998) 71–3.

28 Appian, *Civil War* 4.23.

29 Appian, *Civil War* 4.39.

30 Appian, *Civil War* 4.48.

31 Valerius Maximus, *Memorable Deeds and Sayings* 6.7.3.

32 Appian, *Civil War* 4.40.

33 Appian, *Civil War* 4.40; Valerius Maximus, *Memorable Deeds and Sayings* 6.7.2. This may be the woman whose husband commemorated her in the inscription known as the *Laudatio Turiae*, discussed previously.

34 Cassius Dio, *Roman History* 47.7.4–5.

35 Appian, *Civil War* 4.40.

36 Appian, *Civil War* 4.37.

37 Appian, *Civil War* 4.23.

38 Appian, *Civil War* 4.24.

39 *Laudatio Turiae* 11. For discussion, see Weigel (1992) 74–5.

40 Appian, *Civil War* 4.32–4. This episode is also recounted in Valerius Maximus, *Memorable Deeds and Sayings* 8.3.3 and Quintilian, *The Orator's Education* 1.1.6, both of whom praise Hortensia's public-speaking abilities. See also Plant (2004) 104–5.

41 Hemelrijk (1987) 220.

42 Cluett (1998) 73–4.

43 Cassius Dio, *Roman History* 48.4.1.

44 Cicero, *Letters to Atticus* 15.11.2 (Shackleton Bailey 311). See Treggiari (2019) 190–96.

45 Velleius Paterculus, *Compendium of Roman History* 2.74.2. On Lucius, see Roddaz (1988).

46 Beard (2007) 200–201.

47 Beard (2007) 280.

48 Cassius Dio, *Roman History* 48.4.1–6. For discussion, see Östenberg (2009) 120, 124–5.

10 Fulvia's War

1 Appian, *Civil War* 5.14. See Scott (1933) 22–3 for discussion.

2 Virgil, *Eclogues* 1 and 9; Propertius, *Elegies* 1.21, 1.22; Horace, *Epistles* 2.2.49–52; Horace, *Odes* 2.7.13–16.

3 Virgil, *Eclogue* 1.4, 11–12; 9.2–4.

4 Gabba (1971) 140.

5 Cassius Dio, *Roman History* 48.5.2.

6 Juvenal, *Satires* 6.231. See Sharrock (2020) for discussion.

7 Martial, *Epigrams* 11.20.

8 Suetonius, *Augustus* 85.2.

9 Pliny the Elder, *Natural History* 7.45.148.

10 Suetonius, *Augustus* 68.

11 Suetonius, *Augustus* 68.

12 Hayne (1978) 105.

13 Cokayne (2003) 134–52.

14 Roller (2017) 50–51.

15 Appian, *Civil War* 5.14.

16 Schultz (2022) 321–2.

17 Appian, *Civil War* 5.14. For discussion, see Schultz (2022) 321–2.

18 Plutarch, *Antony* 28.1, 30.1–4; Appian, *Civil War* 5.19.

19 Velleius Paterculus, *Roman History* 2.74.2–3.

20 Appian, *Civil War* 5.21.

21 Appian, *Civil War* 5.33.

22 Livy, *Summaries* 125–6.

23 Hallet (1977); Porter (2020).

24 *CIL* XI 6721.5; *CIL* XI 6721.14.

25 *CIL* XI 6721.14.

26 *CIL* XI 6721.11.

27 *CIL* XI 6721.9A. See also Ashmolean Latin Inscriptions Project ANFortnum V.241.

28 Cassius Dio, *Roman History* 48.10.3. For discussion, see Foubert (2016b) 474.

29 This image of a woman taking up a sword as a sign that things have gone horribly wrong with the world recurs in Tacitus' account of the civil wars of 68–69 CE, with the soon-to-be emperor Vitellius'

brother's wife Triaria, who is described as 'violent beyond her sex', *Histories* 2.63 and 3.77. See Pyy (2020) for discussion.

30 Metropolitan Museum of Art inv. 03.14.7.

31 Livia Drusilla was Octavian's future wife, and ultimately her son Tiberius would be adopted by him and declared his successor as emperor in 14 CE.

32 Barrett (2002) 16. However, when they were not received as well as they had hoped by Sextus Pompey, they returned to Rome and Livia Drusilla, now pregnant with her second child, convinced her husband to beg Antony and Octavian's pardon.

33 Suetonius, *Augustus* 14–15; Seneca the Younger, *On Mercy* 1.11.1; Cassius Dio, *Roman History* 48.14.3–5. For discussion, see Scott (1933) 27–8.

34 Lange (2014) 88–9.

35 Velleius Paterculus, *Compendium of Roman History* 2.74.4.

36 Propertius, *Elegies* 1.22.1–10.

37 Appian, *Civil War* 5.54.

38 Cassius Dio, *Roman History* 48.5.5.

39 Velleius Paterculus, *Compendium of Roman History* 2.76.2; Appian, *Civil War* 5.50. Watkins (2019) 115–16.

40 Appian, *Civil War* 5.52. Cluett (1998) 74–5.

41 Cassius Dio, *Roman History* 48.22.3.

42 Cassius Dio, *Roman History* 48.16.1. Lange (2015) 134.

43 The duration of this journey was calculated using ORBIS: https://orbis.stanford.edu/.

44 Callistratus, *Descriptions* 6.

45 Appian, *Civil Wars* 5.59; Cassius Dio, *Roman History* 48.28.3.

46 Pausanias, *Description of Greece* 2.10.3.

47 Pausanias, *Description of Greece* 2.10.2; Athenaeus, *Learned Banqueters* 7.288C.

48 Virgil, *Aeneid* 7.803–17.

49 Virgil, *Aeneid* 7.805.

50 Xinyue (2017) 170.

51 Sharrock (2015) 159.

52 Virgil, *Aeneid* 1.493.

53 Morello (2008).

54 Valerius Maximus, *Memorable Deeds and Sayings* 4.6. external 2. Mayor (2014) 340–51.

55 Plutarch, *Pompey* 32.8–9.

56 Mayor (2014) 350–51. The Roman fascination with Amazons and female warriors in this period is underlined by the Amazonomachy depicted on the so-called Mausoleum of the Julii at Glanum, in which the Amazons battle the Romans, and Gaius Julius, the dedicatee of the monument, takes spoils from the enemy. The cenotaph dates to the period 40–20 BCE, and was set up by the family of one of either Caesar's or Octavian's veterans.

57 British Library inv. Royal 20 CV f.119.

58 *Laudatio Tauriae* 9a.

59 Valerius Maximus, *Memorable Deeds and Sayings* 3.2.15. See also Plutarch, *Brutus* 13.4–11; Cassius Dio, *Roman History* 44.14.1.

60 Martial, *Epigrams* 1.42.

61 Treggiari (2019) 207–8.

62 Plutarch, *Bravery of Women* 1.1 (*Moralia* 242F).

63 Plutarch, *Bravery of Women* 14 (*Moralia* 250C–F); see also Livy, *From the Founding of the City* 2.13.6–11.

64 Plutarch, *Bravery of Women* 14 (*Moralia* 250F).

65 Livy, *From the Founding of the City* 2.13.11; Servius, *Commentary on Virgil's Aeneid* 8.646; Pliny the Elder, *Natural History* 34.13.28–9.

66 Caesar, *Civil War* 3.9.3; Historia Augusta 19: *The Two Maximini* 33.1–2; Historia Augusta 21: *Maximus and Balbius* 11.3, 16.5–6; Florus, *Epitome* 1.38.17–18. Non-Roman women: Frontinus, *Stratagems* 1.7.3; Florus, *Epitome* 1.31.10.

67 Servius, *Commentary on Virgil's Aeneid* 1.720; Lactantius, *Divine Institutes* 1.20.27.

68 Loman (2004) 42; Graf (1984) 245. For the death of Pyrrhus, see Plutarch, *Pyrrhus* 34.2–3.

11 Fulvia's Last Act

1 Museo Gregorio Profano inv. 9998.

2 Pepe (2018).

3 Cicero, *On Oratory* 2.11.44.

4 Cornelius Nepos, *Atticus* 17.1.

5 *CIL* VI 10230.

6 Lucan, *Civil War* 5.231–6. Lucan's claim is supported by an inscription that places Appius in Karystos at around the time of his death, Mason and Wallace (1972).

7 *Laudatio Murdiae* 4. See Lindsay (2004).

8 Skinner (2011) 56–7.

9 Cicero, *In Defence of Milo* 73; Plutarch, *Cicero* 29.3–4; Plutarch, *Caesar* 10.5; Plutarch, *Lucullus* 34.1.

10 Plutarch, *Pompey* 42.7.

11 Treggiari (2007) 128–30, 134–5.

12 Propertius, *Elegies* 4.7.13–14.

13 Propertius, *Elegies* 4.7.23–34.

14 Appian, *Civil War* 5.59, 5.62.

15 Valerius Maximus, *Memorable Deeds and Sayings* 4.6.2–3.

16 Appian, *Civil War* 5.66.

17 Appian, *Civil War* 5.56–9.

18 Plutarch, *Antony* 31.

19 Harders (2019) 123.

20 *CIL* X 5159.

21 Moore (2021) 379–80.

22 For a similar counterfactual exercise with a slightly different emphasis, see Ober (2001).

23 Welch (1995).

24 Here we might compare her to Servilia, who had five children – two sons and three daughters – and married them all advantageously, the marriages of the daughters Junia Prima, Junia Secunda, and Junia Tertia (to Publius Servius Isauricus, Lepidus, and Cassius respectively) supporting the political aspirations of the sons Marcus Junius Brutus and Marcus Junius Silanus (consul in 25 BCE).

25 Woodhull (2004).

26 Cowan (2018).

27 Horace, *Epistles* 1.18.58–64.

28 Lucan, *Civil War* 6.6–8.
29 Macrobius, *Saturnalia* 2.4.29.

12 Fulvia's Children

1   Juvenal, *Satires* 6.592–97.
2   Hallett (2006) 150.
3   Cassius Dio, *Roman History* 48.5.2–4; Plutarch, *Antony* 20.1; Suetonius, *Augustus* 62.1.
4   Cicero, *Letters to Atticus* 14.13A (Shackleton Bailey 367A) – Cicero enclosed a copy of the letter Antony wrote in a longer letter he wrote to Atticus.
5   Cassius Dio, *Roman History* 42.25.3.
6   Cicero, *Letters to Atticus* 14.13B.4–5 (Shackleton Bailey 367B) – Cicero also enclosed a copy of his reply to Antony in a longer letter he wrote to Atticus.
7   Wiseman (1970) 217.
8   Valerius Maximus, *Memorable Deeds and Sayings* 3.5.3.
9   Musée du Louvre inv. N 386/D 34/MR 889.
10 *CIL* VI 1282 = *ILS* 882 = *AE* 2000, 135.
11 Velleius Paterculus, *Compendium of Roman History* 2.86.2; Cassius Dio, *Roman History* 51.2.5.
12 Schultz (2022) 327.
13 Cassius Dio, *Roman History* 47.6.6.
14 British Museum inv. 1867,0101.606.
15 Cassius Dio, *Roman History* 51.6.1–2.
16 Plutarch, *Antony* 81.1; Suetonius, *Augustus* 17.5; Cassius Dio, *Roman History* 51.15.5.
17 Watson (1995) 202–4.
18 Harders (2009).
19 Syme (1986) 144.
20 Plutarch, *Antony* 87.1.
21 Cassius Dio, *Roman History* 54.35.5.
22 Cicero, *Philippics* 13.3; Suetonius, *Grammarians* 18.1–3.
23 Horace, *Odes* 4.2.33–60.
24 Pseudo-Acro, *Commentary on Horace's Odes* 4.2.33.

25 Servius, *Commentary on Virgil's Aeneid* 8.9.

26 Syme (1986) 398–9.

27 Cassius Dio, *Roman History* 54.26.2.

28 Velleius Paterculus, *Compendium of Roman History* 2.100.4; Pliny the Elder, *Natural History* 7.45.149; Seneca the Younger, *On the Shortness of Life* 4.5; Cassius Dio, *Roman History* 55.10.15.

29 Velleius Paterculus, *Compendium of Roman History* 2.100.2.

30 Seneca the Younger, *On the Shortness of Life* 4.5.

31 Macrobius, *Saturnalia* 2.5.9.

32 Velleius Paterculus, *Compendium of Roman History* 2.100.2.

33 Tacitus, *Annals* 4.44.4–5.

34 Tacitus, *Annals* 4.44.4–5.

35 *CIL* VI 11959.

Conclusion: Fulvia's Legacy

1 Moore (2020) 377.

2 Octavia, for one, would have been aware of Fulvia since she was a very young child, due to the close relationships and connections between Fulvia and Caesar, his family members such as his niece Julia and great-nephew Lucius Pinarius Scarpa, and his political allies Clodius, Curio and Antony.

3 Roller (2018) 220.

4 Suetonius, *Augustus* 69.1.

5 Suetonius, *Augustus* 69.2.

6 Flory (1993) 292–5.

7 Moore (2020) 380.

8 Virgil, *Eclogues* 4.7–10.

9 Moore (2021) 377–8.

10 Suetonius, *Caesar* 27.1. Epstein (1987) 85–6.

11 Seneca the Younger, *On Mercy* 1.9.6; the conspiracy is recorded at Cassius Dio, *Roman History* 55.14–21, along with a much longer version of the conversation between the couple. See Barrett (2002) 39, 131–3, 318–19.

12 Appian, *Civil War* 5.93–4; Cassius Dio, *Roman History* 48.54.3; Plutarch, *Antony* 35.1–4.

13 Cassius Dio, *Roman History* 53.30.4.

14 Propertius, *Elegies* 3.18.

15 Suetonius, *Virgil* 32; see Virgil, *Aeneid* 6.883.

16 Seneca the Younger, *Consolation to Marcia* 2.3–4.

17 Barrett (2002) 232–3.

18 Suetonius, *Augustus* 65.5.

19 Cohen (2008).

20 Seneca the Younger, *On Benefits* 6.32; Cassius Dio, *Roman History* 55.10.12.

21 Ovid, *Tristia* 2.207.

22 Velleius Paterculus, *Compendium of Roman History* 2.100.3–5; Cassius Dio, *Roman History* 55.10.12–14; Suetonius, *Tiberius* 50.1.

23 Suetonius, *Augustus* 19.2.

24 Suetonius, *Augustus* 65.4.

25 Suetonius, *Augustus* 19.1.

26 McHugh (2012).

27 Barrett (2005) 304.

28 Tacitus, *Annals* 1.69.1–3.

29 Tacitus, *Annals* 1.69.1.

30 Tacitus, *Annals* 1.69.3.

31 Brennan (2012) 357 Erker (2009) 146.

32 Tacitus, *Annals* 2.82.

33 Suetonius, *Caligula* 5.

34 Tacitus, *Annals* 3.1.

35 Tacitus, *Annals* 3.16; Suetonius, *Tiberius* 52.3; Suetonius, *Caligula* 2; Cassius Dio, *Roman History* 57.18.10.

36 This inscription is known as the *Senatus Consultum de Pisone*. See Cooley (2023).

37 Tacitus, *Annals* 3.12–16.

38 Tacitus, *Annals* 11.1, 12.59.1.

39 Cassius Dio, *Roman History* 55.7.6.

40 Tacitus, *Annals* 11.1. See also Barrett (2001) 101.

41 Cargill-Martin (2023) 242–7.

42 Tacitus, *Annals* 12.59.

43 Barrett (2001) 154. Frontinus, *The Aqueducts of Rome* 2.128.

44 Tacitus, *Annals* 13.5.

45 Kelly (2014) 58.

46 Kelly (2014) 63, 74.

47 Cyrino (2008); Harrisson (2008); compare Griffin (1985) 41 on Antony's secret return to Fulvia in 45 BCE as recounted by Cicero, *Philippics* 2.77.

48 Suetonius, *Augustus* 61.2; Cassius Dio, *Roman History* 47.17.6. See Cyrino (2008), Augustakis (2008), and Harrisson (2015) for discussion.

49 *Dante's Inferno* (2010): http://www.dantesinferno.com/ (accessed January 2024).

50 In keeping with the ancient Roman propaganda, Antony appears here as Cleopatra's minion, with the Queen of Egypt serving as the level's final boss. He literally lives inside her body, and she summons him to battle Dante on her behalf. Then, in the third circle, the circle of Gluttony, the player encounters Clodia Metelli.

51 The *lex Iulia de maritandis ordinibus* in 18 BCE sought to encourage and regulate marriage. The *lex Papia Poppaea* in 9 CE modified it to promote the production of children. The *lex Iulia de adulteriis coercendis* in 9 CE sought to repress all forms of sexual relations outside of marriage that the Romans considered unacceptable. See Evans Grubbs (2019) for discussion.

52 Hemelrijk (2004) 192–3.

53 Orosius, *History Against the Pagans* 6.17.

54 Suetonius, *Augustus* 27.3–4.

55 Plutarch, *Cicero* 49.2.

INDEX